POLITICS IN DENMARK

POLITICS IN DENMARK

BY

JOHN FITZMAURICE

ST. MARTIN'S PRESS, NEW YORK

© John Fitzmaurice, 1981

St. Martin's Press, Inc., 175 Fifth Avenue, New York, NY – 10010
Printed in Great Britain
First published in the United States of America in 1981

ISBN 0 – 312 – 62663 – 0

Library of Congress Cataloging in Publication Data

Fitzmaurice, John.
   Politics in Denmark.

   1. Denmark—Politics and government.   I. Title.
JN 7161.F58   1981   320.9489   81 – 1682
ISBN 0 – 312 – 62663 – 0   AACR2

For Catherine

ACKNOWLEDGEMENTS

My thanks go to many people and institutions without whose generous and imaginative help this book could most certainly not have been written. I should like in particular to thank the Library of the *Folketing*; the Danish Embassy in Brussels; and Mr Fumobsen, now of the Danish Foreign Ministry, for many interesting and stimulating ideas which have found their way into these pages.

I should like to thank a whole series of people active in public life in Denmark, too numerous to mention individually, who have provided information and comments which have been indispensable in writing this book. I should like to single out Mr B. Wigotski, formerly on the staff of the Social Democratic Party office; Mrs Eva Gredal, former Minister of Social Affairs; Mr Ivar Nørgaard, Minister of Trade; Mr Niels Anker Kofoed, former Minister of Agriculture (V); Mr Per Dich (SF), former MF, Mr Jens Maigaard (SF); Mr Ib Christensen (DR), MF, Leader of *Danmarks Retsforbundet*; and Mr Henrick Olsen (FRP).

Last but by no means least my thanks go to Mrs A. Gawenda for her patience and intelligence in dealing with the combination of difficult Danish names and my quite abominable handwriting.

Naturally, all the opinions expressed in this book and responsibility for any errors are mine alone.

CONTENTS

INTRODUCTION

Denmark is a small country in Northern Europe, which has attained remarkable political stability, self-assurance as a nation, and one of the highest living standards in Europe, in spite of the fact that geography—its strategic position at the mouth of the Baltic and its lack of natural reserves—and the fractiousness of its party system would presuppose none of these things. The interest in studying the politics of Denmark lies in exploring these apparent contradictions.

Denmark has been a member of the EEC since 1973. Traditionally she has, at least since 1945, kept closely in step with Britain in her broad foreign policy options. Thus unilateral EEC membership—a Gaullist blandishment—was rejected in the early 1960s. Denmark has shared many of Britain's reservations about the EEC, and has consistently preferred a pragmatic approach to 'federalism' and 'integration'. Of late, though, especially in view of the pressures building up for reform of the Common Agricultural Policy (which Denmark wishes broadly to preserve), clear divergences of interest have opened up between the two countries. This is an interesting development. The pressures of SALT III and the rocky path of détente, which appears to require a firming-up of NATO, will also face Denmark—one of the more sceptical NATO members—with difficult choices in the 1980s. The choice of Europe in 1973 was, it has to be said, largely a choice of the head, which in no way cancels the affair of the heart with Scandinavia. Danish governments since the early 1970s have striven to combine the EEC and Nordic dimensions of their foreign policy. This balancing act will continue to affect Danish policy towards the EEC over the coming decades.

Denmark has suffered from many of the economic and political problems with which Britain has wrestled since 1945. She has seen the difficulties which a mature, Social Democratic party, that has accomplished many of the basic reforms for which it had fought, faces in adapting to changing circumstances. There have been the economic problems facing countries with a strong dependence on trade in an inflationary period. She has faced the same problems of competitiveness, balance of payment deficits and exchange rate depreciation that have been characteristic of Britain.

There has been the narrowing of the range of ideological and economic options as governments wrestled with problems to which there appeared to be only a limited range of answers. The problem of rising public expenditure to finance the Welfare State has been particularly acute in Denmark, leading to a taxpayers' revolt, which found radical expression in the 13.9 per cent vote which the Progress

Party of Mogens Glistrup obtained in its first election in 1973. At this catalysmic election, five new parties entered parliament, while the Social Democrats, Liberals and Conservatives all lost heavily; indeed all the established parties, including those of the far-left, lost votes. The new-left and the right gained votes. The responsible centre, from which government coalitions are usually formed, became extremely narrow. There was considerable talk of ungovernability. Indeed it was difficult to form governments in the 1973−7 period; it was even more difficult for them to act. The system has, however, shown remarkable qualities of adaptation and recovery. By the time of the election of 1979 a new stability had emerged, which shows many signs of reversion to the pre-1973 party structure, although there are still ten parties in parliament.

The essence of Danish democracy lies in co-operation and negotiation. No party can aspire to a majority; it knows that after an election, however bitter, it will have to seek allies. There is also a tradition of making parliamentary seats 'work'. Parties seek influence on legislation; a party which remains cut off from influence, which remains outside the system over a prolonged period, will eventually wither. These traditions make for a process of permanent negotiation in the search for allies. Majority coalitions are the exception and are often not successful. Another consequence of this co-operative democracy is a considerable pragmatism and narrowing of sharp conflict.

These will be some of the themes which will be explored in the succeeding chapters. We shall look at the impact of geography, economic factors and historical experience in the shaping of the environment of Danish politics and forging the character of Danish democracy. We shall also look at the interaction between domestic forces and foreign policy issues, so vital in a small country dependent on its relations with the outside world for security and wellbeing. Finally, we shall look at the reality of Danish democracy today, under the strains of rapid change, and in particular the future of mature social democracy and Welfare State politics in the face of recession, inflation and a latent taxpayers' revolt. (These happen to be themes of equal interest to the British.) We shall also look at Denmark in international society, as part of the Nordic Community, active in the United Nations, and as a member of the European Economic Community and NATO. The importance of these international issues is illustrated by the almost unique amount of control exercised by the Danish parliament over the government's external policy. We shall look at some of the possible contradictions in Danish foreign policy and attempts to reconcile them.

Denmark is of interest to those nations to whom she is a close and reliable partner in common enterprises such as NATO and the EEC; and as a small, mature parliamentary democracy, grappling with problems and changes with which the countries of Western Europe and North America can closely identify.

ABBREVIATIONS USED IN THE TEXT

S	*Social Demokratiet*	Social Democrats
RV	*Radikale Venstre*	Radicals
KF or K	*Konservative Folkeparti*	Conservatives
DR	*Danmarks Retsforbundet*	Justice Party
SF	*Socialistisk Folkeparti*	Socialist Peoples' Party
DKP	*Danmarks Kommunistisk Parti*	Communists
V	*Venstre*	Liberal Agrarian Party
U	*De Unafhaengige*	Independent Party
LC	*Liberalt Centrum*	Liberal Centre
FRP	*Fremskridtspartiet*	Progress Party
KRF	*Kristeligt Folkeparti*	Christian Peoples' Party
CD	*Centrums Demokraterne*	Centre Democrats
VS	*Venstre Socialisterne*	Left Socialists
LO	*Landesorganisationen i Danmark*	Trade unions
DA	*Danmarks Arbejdsgiverforening*	Employers' organisation
EF	*Europaeisk Falleskab*	European Economic Community (EEC)
FB	*Folkebevaegelsen mod EF*	People's Movement against the EEC
DR	*Danmarks Radio*	
MF	*Medlem af Folketinget*	Member of parliament

These are the standard abbreviations in use in Denmark, and are used in the text—as in Danish—without the definite article.

I. A BRIEF HISTORY OF DENMARK

Denmark is now a small Northern European country, which underwent no industrial revolution in the nineteenth century and, with the exception of Tranquebar and some smaller West African and Indian Ocean enclaves, and of the Virgin Islands, which were sold to the United States in 1916, it had no colonies. In modern times, her influence in European and even regional affairs has been limited, and since her defeat at the hands of Prussia and Austria in 1864, it ought to have been impossible to harbour any illusions about her weakness. Indeed, weakness and 'small-power' status became, in 1914–18 and in the period of increasing tension in the late 1930s, a conscious policy. After 1945, this line was abandoned to the extent that Denmark became, after much soul-searching, a founder-member of NATO in 1949, and later joined several European organisations including, most importantly, the EEC in 1973. However, even today this 'small-power' status attitude plays a part in Danish policy calculations. Denmark constitutes a threat to no one, it is argued, and thus hopes to remain, if possible, aloof from any conflict.

It was not always so, as we shall see. Down to 1864, Denmark had considered herself—not entirely without cause—a power of some importance, at least in Northern European affairs[1].

From about AD500, the Nordic tribes began to be clearly distinguishable from the Germanic tribes. With its islands and the woods and marshes in Southern Jutland, Denmark was a relatively self-contained area within which two tribes came to be dominant: the Jutlanders in the west and the Danes in the east. These tribes unified into a nation in about 700, and in 800 the Nordic language was fully developed.

The people were farmers, and cattle raising was their main activity. Village and tribal leaders were more important than kings at this early stage, but quite rapidly kings obtained more power, especially as these societies developed military and naval strength. Usually, however, their power was rather limited.

The Viking period began with the breakdown of Charlemagne's empire into weak and competing states after AD 840. These small states, offered easy and rich prey to Viking raiders, having no sea power. At the same time, population growth in Scandinavia meant that the available agricultural land was inadequate to feed the population, making some explosion inevitable.

The Viking period lasted for over 200 years, and ended around

1100. In its early stages, the raiders merely attacked coastal settlements, then they moved inland, wintered abroad, and eventually
established settlements and empires as far afield as England,
Normandy, Greenland, and even in Italy and the Black Sea. They
established an empire in England, north of a line running from
London to the Welsh borders. From 1013 to 1042, the whole of
England was a Viking kingdom. The most effective Viking king was
Canute, who reigned from 1018 to 1035, and spent much of his time
in England. He was already a Christian, since Christianity had come
to Denmark from Northern France, introduced by Harald Blue
Tooth (940 – 85). Both in England and Denmark Canute played an
important role in introducing stability in Church and State organisations after the turbulence of the preceding period.

Under Svend Esrudson, the Danish Church was established into
eight bishoprics and placed on a sound financial footing. It also soon
obtained special legal status, and the archbishopric was established
in Lund in 1103.

The Viking period was now almost over. Harald was defeated at
Stamford Bridge in 1066. Armies were later raised to reconquer
England, but were unable to set out.

The following period, up to 1157, was one of weakness and
conflict, and royal power did not expand. Only under the Valdemar
dynasty (1157 – 1241) were the foundations of the Danish medieval
monarchy laid. Valdemar the Great and Bishop Absalon established
a close alliance in the interest of strengthening both Church and
state. The southern marches of the kingdom were brought under
control and military organisation was tightened; new towns
(Copenhagen and Vordingborg) were built to defend the coasts.
Most important, though, was the increasing royal power. The
Crown was recognised as having the right to legislate, which had
earlier been denied. This was the beginning of statute law, as
opposed to customary law.

Later kings (Valdemar Sejr) developed the institutions of the
medieval state: laws were codified, local courts established, and the
first legislative assemblies held. The administration of justice was
improved. The finances of the Crown were organised and improved.
The King had his *ombudsmaend* (officials), who acted as his
representatives in the country and as a chancery at the court. So far,
the organisation of the state remained based largely on concepts of
federal obligation; farmers had financial and military obligations to
the King. However, in the latter part of this period, the concept of
taxation was introduced.

Economic life was developing. Towns began to play a role in
public affairs. The first guilds and town charters date from about

1200. Cultural life, through the medium of both Latin and Danish, developed considerably in this period.

However, as in medieval England, developments were never consistent and depended largely on the character of individual kings and statesmen. Institutions were too new and fragile to have much independant life of their own. At the same time, all references to increases in royal power or the establishment of stronger state institutions must be tempered by the fact that medieval Danish kingship was by no means an absolute monarchy. The King's power was always limited in a number of ways. The first and most obvious was geography and the difficulty of communications between the islands. There was always a limitation imposed by the rudimentary central and local infrastructure of the state. The powers of the King were also limited by the existence of the Estates, by customary law and by the fact that the King's exclusive legislative power was always contested and at best tolerated. There was also always an elective element in the kingship, although at times this might be more formal than real.

After 1241, the country entered a period of conflict and weakness. The Estates came into conflict with the Crown; there was also a growing conflict between Church and state. As elsewhere in Europe, the temporal claims of the Church were reaching new heights; the so-called Vejle Constitution considerably increased its immunities. King Erik Maendved (1286–1319) sought to restore Denmark's Baltic conquests which had been lost after 1241, and became involved in long and costly campaigns in Northern Germany. The Crown was unable to finance these military adventures, and both Church and state took advantage of these weaknesses of the Crown to impose important restrictions on his successor. The King had to concede substantial revenues to the nobility and total tax immunity to the Church. Laws could not be amended without the consent of the major nobles and prelates of the realm. The new King Christoffer broke these pledges and provoked serious unrest, which led to his removal and a period with no king. Skaane (Southern Sweden) was also in revolt and joined Sweden.

Competing dukes eventually agreed in 1340 that Valdemar Atterdag should become King; he reigned from 1340 to 1375. At the start of his reign, he controlled only Holstein, Slesvig, and part of South Jutland, but in the period up to 1360, he regained control first of Jutland and then of the Islands. This reign was an important step forward in the ebb and flow of constitutional development in Denmark. The first pressing need was the re-establishment of law and order. New royal courts were established, and royal finances were re-established on a sound footing. The three provinces of

Southern Sweden—Skaane, Halland and Blekinge—were regained
and the attempts by the Hanseatic towns to increase their dominance
and control of the Baltic trade were repelled.

On Valdemar's death, the five-year-old Oluf became King. His
mother, Margrethe, acted as Regent, and although only twenty-two
years old, she was a most able and effective stateswoman. Forced
initially to make concessions to the nobility, she was soon able to
retract them and in close alliance with the Church, she greatly
developed the royal power and the military and naval strength of the
realm. When Oluf died in 1387, her power was such that she was
elected ruler of both Norway and Denmark. In Sweden, a conflict
broke out between King Albrecht and the nobility, which Margrethe
was able to exploit to advance Oluf's claims to the Swedish Crown.
The nobles recognised her as Queen of Sweden, and Albrecht's
German army was defeated, leaving him a prisoner.

For the first and last time Nordic unity was realised, and even if it
lasted only for a short time, the very fact that it ever took place, even
if this was more than 500 years ago, has cast a long shadow. This
period represents a certain ideal to which Scandinavia could one day
return. Margrethe was theoretically only the Regent of the three
kingdoms. She placed her sister's daughter's son, Erik of
Pomerania, on the throne and he was crowned in Kalmar in 1397.
This was the Kalmar Union.

Margrethe ruled until her death in 1412. She had greatly strengthened the power of the Crown, regaining control of many estates,
which had earlier escaped the royal authority. Denmark in fact
dominated the Union, and this fact was ultimately to lead to its
downfall. On Margrethe's death, Erik ruled in fact as well as in
name, but was at once involved in a series of wars with the Hanseatic
League. Revolt broke out in Sweden, and Erik was removed from
the Swedish throne. He was replaced as king of the three kingdoms
by the weak Kristoffer of Bavaria (1439–48, of Scandinavian
descent). The State Councils in each kingdom constituted the real
government, which effectively made the Union a personal one. In
1448, Swedish opponents of the Union gained the upper hand and
elected Karl Knutsson as their own King. Christian I became King of
Denmark and Norway, but was required to pledge that he would
only make laws and levy taxes with the consent of the Council. In
1497 the Union was renewed for a short period, but when King Hans
was defeated in Holstein, the Swedes led by Sten Sture revolted and
broke it again (1501). The last revival of the Union was in 1520, when
Christian II became King of Sweden as well as Denmark and
Norway, after internal strife in Sweden between Unionists and anti-
Unionists. However, this reconstitution of the Union was once again

to be short-lived, lasting only until 1523. The actual restoration was followed by the "Stockholm bloodbath", in which several hundred Swedish nobles and leaders were murdered for their support of the earlier revolts. Clearly this was a bad start. The Swedish leader Gustav Vasa, who escaped the bloodbath by being in prison, led a rising which was joined by German states. Christian was forced into exile, and Gustav Vasa became King of Sweden.

For the first period of his reign, Christian II had done much to strengthen the central power. He imposed royal courts even in matters hitherto subject to ecclesiastic jurisdiction; jury trials were abolished. He wanted to create a purely hereditary monarchy. He looked for allies in the towns, eliminating feudalistic restrictions on trade, such as taxation which accrued to the nobility. He was carrying on the work of Valdemar Atterdag, but he was also in tune with other modernising contemporary rulers such as the Emperor Charles V and Henry VIII of England.

For all that, the monarchy remained elective and subject to restrictions. He had to accept control by both the Estates and the State Council (prelates and noblemen). He had clear obligations in law to maintain order and justice. Gradually, a bureaucratic infrastructure was built up, and the army and navy were also improved. By the 1520s taxation was placed on a more regular basis. Denmark was moving towards a more centralised and powerful monarchy, but traditions of limited and elective monarchy remained very strong.

The next period saw a reaction. Frederick I (1523–33) was under the control of the Estates, to which he owed his throne. At this time, the Reformation, with its dramatic events, arrived in Denmark. The same corruption and decadence were evident in Denmark as contributory causes of the Reformation. As in England and elsewhere, economic reasons were also important; for the Crown and the nobility the Church lands representing in Denmark almost one-third of all land in the kingdom, were a rich prize. The Church's political power was also a cause of opposition to it.

In 1533 the clergy—led by Hans Tavsen—introduced the Lutheran Augsburg Confession. Rapidly, the Reformation became inextricably linked with complex political events and several dramatic reversals of alliances. An alliance of radical Lutherans, led by the Mayors of Lübeck, Copenhagen and Malmö and farmers on Fyn and in North Jutland, attempted to place the exiled King Christian II on the throne again. For Lübeck, the aim was to regain control of the Baltic and eliminate Dutch power from that sea. At the same time, Gustav Vasa of Sweden came to the aid of Christian II, and the revolt failed after considerable initial success.

The result was that the Reformation became definitive in

Denmark. Church influence was eliminated from state affairs, the Crown became the owner of half the land in the nation, and the influence of the nobility was much reduced. This was the last time that the peasants played an important political or military role, raising a revolt to try and replace the exiled King on his lost throne. Hereafter, they no longer represented a significant political force.

The following period was one of transition. Denmark was in decline and Sweden was on the way up. As often, this reality was not evident at the time. Frederick II (1559–88) sought to re-establish the Union by force, but the Nordic Seven-Year War (1563–70) gave no decisive result, which was already a bad sign for Denmark. The indecisive war weakened the Danish Crown, and the serious financial difficulties it caused were only overcome after many years of effort.

Christian IV (1588–1648) was one of Denmark's greatest kings. He was something of a Renaissance man, fascinated by technology, science, industry, shipbuilding and the arts. During his reign many of Copenhagen's most beautiful buildings were constructed. His domestic policy was dynamic and effective. There was much building generally, and the towns came into their own. He set up the East Indies Trading Company, and took other imaginative measures relating to new industries, an effective postal service and the University of Copenhagen. Although costly for the country, they represented important investments in the future.

However, he became involved in three wars, which was in every sense a costly error. Denmark's weakness became more and more evident. The Kalmar War (1611–13) was again indecisive. In 1625–9, he intervened in the Protestant cause in the Thirty Years War, and suffered a serious reverse to the point where imperial troops occupied Jutland. This intervention was already a serious error, which became compounded by his refusal to join in alliance with the rising star of Sweden, which might have permitted Denmark to recover its position. Christian IV preferred to conclude a peace treaty at Lübeck in 1629, which represented a defeat for Denmark. As a result of these defeats, the influence of the Crown within the country fell considerably, and at meetings of the Estates, called to meet the serious financial difficulties of the Crown resulting from the war, serious criticism of the privileges of the nobility began to appear. At the same time—and this was to store up problems for the future—the decision to increase the sound dues provoked a serious reaction from Sweden and the Netherlands, the major sea power at that time.

The next reign saw the culmination of the errors of the previous period. Frederick III had to accept serious limitations imposed on his freedom of action by the Council of State, dominated by the nobility. The King sought a war with Sweden, which was totally unwise; The Swedes were too quick for him and invaded Holstein with an army of 8,000 men. In January 1658, the sea between Jutland and Fyn and between Fyn and Seeland froze over: the Swedish army crossed the ice and occupied Copenhagen and Fyn. At the Peace of Roskilde, Denmark suffered even more extensive losses of territory than in 1864: Skaane, Halland and Blekinge in Southern Sweden and the Baltic island of Bornholm passed to the Swedes.

After the peace of Roskilde, the Swedish King Karl Gustav wanted to pursue the war against Brandenburg. To this end, he needed to secure Denmark and close the Baltic against Brandenburg's powerful Dutch allies. He first sought Danish co-operation in this, but when this was only very reluctantly forthcoming, he decided to eliminate all Danish power and invaded Jutland and Fyn, and again laid siege to Copenhagen. With Dutch aid, the siege was held off, but the Danish islands were occupied by Sweden until they were liberated by combined Danish and Brandenburg armies, which defeated the Swedish army at Nyborg in 1659. Denmark was spared total catastrophe, but in the subsequent peace of Copenhagen (1660) it became crystal-clear that this was only because it was in the interests of the great powers that it should be so. Moreover, the sea powers, including Denmark's Dutch allies, were not prepared to see both sides of the sound controlled by a single power. Denmark therefore recovered only Trondheim and Bornholm; her Swedish possessions were lost for good.

In 1660 Denmark was in a poor condition. The losses had almost halved the population and removed the most dynamic part of the realm. The wars had left the towns, agriculture and the whole economy devastated. The country's power was broken, and would not revive. The lesson of these events—that Denmark was no longer a mover in international relations—was not really learned. On at least three subsequent occasions, as had happened repeatedly in the first half of the seventeenth century, Danish leaders made the error of ignoring such realities, which led them to choose the wrong side in conflicts where other powers would decide the outcome.

Not surprisingly, the events of the years 1658–60 led to a major domestic upheaval and a constitutional crisis. Whereas the conduct of the nobility had been irresponsible, the towns-people—the 'bourgeois' class—and the farmers rallied to the patriotic cause, thus playing a major part in saving the country from total disaster. The nobility were held to have caused its weakness and failure, and at the Estates, which met in September 1660, an alliance of the "third Estate" led by Hans Nansen, Mayor of Copenhagan, and the clergy led by Bishop Svane mounted a fierce attack on the nobility. They argued for a hereditary monarchy, which would completely abolish feudal and noble privileges once and for all. In this they had the support of the King, who took advantage of the situation created by the decision of principle on 13 October to draw up a basic law introducing an absolute monarchy, which went further than the lower Estates had intended.

These decisions were enshrined in the *Konge Lov* (Royal Law) of 1665, which was to be the country's constitution until 1849. There were no limitations on royal power. Government was organised through a number of colleges (10–15 members) responsible for areas of policy co-ordinated by the *Gehejmkonseil* ('inner council'). Royal courts saw their authority extended and reinforced, and taxation was extended to all classes. Danish absolutism was harsher on paper than in reality, and the older constitutional notions never totally died.

Swedish power soon reached its high point and began to decline, especially since Charles XII considerably over-reached himself and underestimated the growing power of Prussia and Russia. Successive Danish kings from the 1670s saw an opportunity in this, to regain lost territories—which, it should be remembered, still harboured considerable pro-Danish sentiment—but were unable to exploit them fully. In 1676, when Sweden was at war with Brandenburg, Denmark declared war and landed an army in Skaane. However, due to the support of Louis XIV, Sweden was able to avoid ceding any land to Denmark at the Peace of Lund in 1679.

When the Great Nordic War broke out in 1700, Denmark once again saw her opportunity. Charles XII was over-stretched in the east in his war with Russia and Poland. In 1709, when he had been defeated in the Ukraine, Denmark and Poland entered the war, but were unable to make serious progress either in Skaane or in Germany. Charles managed to return to Sweden, raised a new army and invaded Norway in order to give himself something to bargain with in the peace talks, which he knew could not be far off. He was killed there in 1718. The war continued for several years, but gradually Sweden concluded separate peace treaties with all her enemies. Her power was broken, and she lost all her possessions on the European continent, and even the Viborg region of Finland. However, the peace terms with Denmark (Fredericksborg, 1720) were relatively favourable to Sweden since she ceded no territory. The close of the Nordic War was the end of an era. Both Sweden and Denmark, as well as Poland, were reduced to second-rank powers, and were never to recover. Prussia and Russia rose as the new competitors for domination in the region, setting the pattern for the modern period.

The immediately following period, covered by the reigns of Christian VI (1730–46) and Frederick VI (1746–66), was one of relative calm, a much-needed period of peace and consolidation, in which Denmark avoided international entanglements. This was the high noon of mercantalism. There was an active policy of trade promotion, government support for industry, and improvements in infrastructure and education. It was a period of economic protectionism and fierce competition. Although there was considerable easing of feudal restrictions, the abolition of serfdom was still considered premature: however, towards the end of the period, thinking was moving in that direction. The ground was being prepared for much greater economic and political liberalism.

In 1766, the mad King Christian VII came to the throne, and reigned in name only until 1808. Policy was in the hands of successive statesmen. From 1770 till 1777, the government was controlled by Struensee, the lover of the Queen. He was an energetic reformer, and in sixteen months issued more than 600 regulations covering a wide range of policy issues, including some timid agricultural reforms, freedom of expression and educational reform. His reforming zeal, and no less his German origins and his supposed usurpation of power, brought him many enemies which resulted finally in his execution in 1772. He was succeeded by a conservative regime, which lasted until 1784, when the Crown Prince and his ally A.D. Bernstorff took control of the government by forcing the King to sign an order appointing a new State Council containing a majority favourable to reform.

In Denmark, as elsewhere, the latter half of the eighteenth century was a period of intellectual ferment. Rationalism and the Enlightenment came to Denmark, their way having been prepared by the genius of Holberg, the country's foremost poet and playwright. These ideas were given a more pragmatic and mild expression in Denmark than elsewhere. They did not lead to a democratic revolution, but to an enlightened despotism acting in the interests of the people. The first and most urgent issue was agricultural reform. Since 1750 prices had been rising, and were to double before 1800. Opportunities in agriculture were considerable, but the peasants were unable to exploit them; they were forced to remain suffocated in feudal structures—obligations in cash, crops and labour—which were a heavy burden and prevented all initiative and mobility. On the one hand, they were bound to the land, and on the other they could even be moved by the lord from one farm to another. Thus a dynamic farmer could build up his farm, only to be moved to another poorer holding.

The reformers did not wait on events. A Royal Commission was set up in 1786 and reported the next year. The government immediately approved a series of measures, of which the most important was a Decree of 1787 fixing the legal status of peasants, and the 1788 Decree abolishing feudal obligations. These reforms led to a rapid increase in peasant farm ownership: productivity rose considerably and new land was ploughed. The only less positive result was the creation of a numerous class of landless farm workers, whose rights were, in practice, very limited.

In other areas too the reform policy was active. The slave trade was abolished; Jews were accorded civil rights; press freedom was granted in 1790; major educational reforms were introduced. Mercantilism was giving way to economic liberalism. Denmark remained neutral in both the American War of Independence and the first phase of the Revolutionary wars. This benefited her trade considerably, even if there were conflicts with the British over the rights of neutral shipping. The customs law of 1797 removed many trade restrictions and reduced the rates of duty on a wide range of products.

Up until this period, the national question had not assumed much importance. German had long been the dominant language at court and in the government, and Kings had often not understood Danish (earlier, Latin and French had been important in religious, political and intellectual life). Now, for the first time, reaction against German set in, and a new national spirit began to develop which was to be important in the next century. At the same time, a nationalist and independence movement began to surface in Norway.

By the turn of the century, the calm in foreign affairs was over. After A.P. Bernstorff's death, the wise neutrality policy was abandoned and Denmark once again embarked on a dangerous course of adventurism which was beyond her means. Denmark, Sweden and Russia concluded the armed neutrality of the North to oppose the pretensions of the British to search neutral ships on the high seas, so as to enforce the blockade of the continent. Denmark had initially been forced to admit this right after a Danish ship was captured while convoying merchant ships in the Channel, but she hoped by the combined strength of the neutrals to reverse this concession. Denmark was the most vulnerable member of this alliance, and her navy was defeated in the Battle of Copenhagen in 1801. Shortly afterwards, Tsar Paul was assassinated, which broke up the alliance. Denmark was forced to concede the right of search definitively.

Peace was short-lived. In 1805, the war spread into North Germany, and Denmark was threatened; she faced difficult choices. Events moved so quickly that there was a great danger of being outmanoeuvred by the shifting alliances. Denmark feared the sea power of England more than the land power of Napoleon, who could do no more than threaten Jutland. This meant that if neutrality could not be maintained any longer, then Denmark would have to ally herself with England, or at least avoid conflict with her.

Two series of events upset these calculations. After the peace of Tilsit (1807), Russia allied herself with Napoleon, and the two Emperors secretly agreed to force Denmark to close her ports to English shipping and force her to join their alliance. Should she refuse, her fleet would be seized. These intentions came to the knowledge of the English (but not of Denmark!), who immediately sent a large fleet and 30,000 troops to Copenhagen. The English offered Denmark an alliance, but this was refused due to misunderstanding, since the Danish government knew nothing of the Tilsit agreement. Now the Danish fleet was removed, whereas if the alliance had materialised it would have merely been held by the English until peace returned. Copenhagen was also bombarded.

The Danish government was now thrown into a war against England from 1807–14. Worse was to follow. In 1805, Sweden had joined in the alliance against France; an expedition of Danish and Spanish troops was to invade Sweden but failed when British ships prevented the crossing, and events in Spain turned the Spanish troops against France. After the Tilsit peace, Russia, now an ally of Napoleon, invaded Finland, which Sweden was forced to cede to her in 1809. Denmark and Russia were also allies, and their plan was to occupy and divide Sweden. This threat caused radical upheaval in Sweden. Absolutism was abolished, and Marshal Bernadotte ascended the throne. With astute political intuition, he rapidly changed sides and concluded an alliance with Russia in 1812 and accepted the loss of Finland. From the 'inside', he was able to prevent Denmark from joining the coalition against Napoleon, which she sought to do in 1813. By now it was in any case too late. The mistake had been made. So in 1814 Denmark was on the losing side and was forced to cede Norway in the Treaty of Kiel in 1814. After the Hundred Days, Denmark *was* included in the coalition, and Danish troops participated in the occupation of France, but now it was too late to reverse events or regain any losses.

Denmark was now weaker than ever. She had lost Norway, as well as her Swedish possessions. The German dukedoms now represented half her population. In an era of nationalism, these dukedoms, which were members of the German Confederation, were an anomaly, and would inevitably soon be threatened. The war and its aftermath also led to a serious economic crisis, in which the State Bank could not meet its obligations (1818). Agriculture faced a downturn, because prices fell as a result of the British Corn Laws of 1815. Trade also suffered, as did industry and commerce.

As if by delayed reaction, political life began to wake up in the 1830s. Demands were made for a democratic constitution. In 1831, Frederick VI was forced to agree to the calling of provincial Advisory Estates. These were not the medieval Estates, which had ceased to meet with the introduction of the absolute monarchy, but were provincial advisory assemblies in which the middle classes played a dominant role. Slesvig and Holstein were not given joint Assemblies. Already serious problems were arising in relation to the relations of each of the two dukedoms with each other and between them and the Kingdom. There was already the clear danger that the Holstein succession would go to the Augustenborg* line, whereas that of the Kingdom would go to a different line. At the same time, the King established a joint government for the two dukedoms. This was a dangerous and short-sighted measure, which went against developments on the ground. In fact, Danish sentiment was growing in Slesvig and German nationalism was growing in Holstein. In the former, a Slesvig Association was founded and major demonstrations were organised.

Even if the Estates were without real power, they were a forum and a training ground for politics. With the new King Christian VIII, the hopes of the liberals rose, but he was more concerned with practical reforms than with major constitutional change. The Liberal faction was well organised, with effective leaders such as Lehman, Plough, Monrad and Tscherning. However, it was only in alliance with the peasants' social agitation that the movement became a real power, through the *Bondevennesskabet* (Friends of the Peasants Association), led by Tscherning.

Frederick VII, who came to the throne in 1848, promised a constitution, and issued a proposal as early as January 1848, based on earlier preparatory work. However, since the proposal was that Slesvig-Holstein and the Kingdom should be equal partners, but therefore also that Slesvig remained in a common government with Holstein, it aroused strong opposition among the Liberals, who since 1842 were more and more involved in the Slesvig issue, becoming "National Liberals". Indeed the issue of Slesvig-Holstein was now to become closely intermeshed with the question of political reform.

The year 1848 saw revolutions all over Europe. The Revolutionary

---

*Descendants of the Duke of Augustenborg in Holstein. This problem arose because the Kingdom and the Dukedoms had different rules relating to succession in the female line.

movement was, in Germany as elsewhere, nationalist. The Slesvig-Holstein Estates, which met in Regensburg in March 1848, voted for a common Slesvig-Holstein constitution, and the inclusion of both dukedoms in the German Confederation. When this news came to Copenhagen, a Liberal meeting was immediately organised, and on 21 March a delegation demanded from the King a popular government and a common constitution for Denmark and Slesvig. He agreed, rejecting the German demands, and the 'March Government' was formed. The revolt continued in Holstein, and a provisional government was formed there. War was now inevitable to decide between the policy of 'Denmark to the Eider' or 'Slesvig-Holstein to the Kongeå'—the German view. (The Eider and Kongeå are rivers.)

The war began well for Denmark, but the intervention of Prussia in favour of Slesvig-Holstein placed her in a dangerous position. Diplomacy by England and Russia prevailed on Prussia to abandon the war and accept a compromise based on the idea of a government for Slesvig nominated by both Denmark and Prussia. This broke down since the rebels remained in control on the ground. The war continued in desultory fashion, without real Prussian involvement, until 1850. Denmark was able to reverse early Holstein successes, winning the battle of Fredericia (1849) and Isted (1850). Some Danish leaders sought a compromise, which would have entailed a division of Slesvig, but public opinion was totally opposed to that wise counsel. Two peace agreements broke down since the rebels prevented their operation. Finally, Denmark regained control of Slesvig, which was to be governed in the King's name by a special commission.

In the period 1851–3, negotiations continued with Prussia and Austria, the latter of which indirectly controlled Holstein. Denmark persisted in misreading both the balance of forces and the situation on the ground. She greatly over-estimated the importance of her apparent victory in 1849. She therefore attempted to impose solutions which were beyond her means. Now that Denmark had a liberal constitution and the forces of reaction were triumphant elsewhere, she could no longer count on Russian support. A convoluted formula was agreed whereby 1) Slesvig could not be more closely linked to the realm than Holstein, 2) a 'federal' constitution would be worked out for the three areas, and 3) no area could be placed under another (equality of treatment). This involved drawing up separate constitutions for Slesvig and Holstein, and a 'federal' constitution for the whole, which would limit the liberal 1843 constitution to 'internal' Danish issues. The drawing up of these texts caused major problems both for the Danish Parliament, which sought to defend the democratic elements in the 1849 constitution, and in Holstein, where the Danish proposals were rejected. The final text of the 'common constitution'(1855) was relatively liberal, but failed to function due to the complete opposition of the German-speaking members of the Common State Council, who eventually boycotted it. Prussia and Austria once again weighed in. In 1858, the Danish Government suspended the common constitution for Holstein. In Denmark there was now pressure from the National Liberals for 'Denmark to the Eider', and for the full application of the June constitution and the 'Nordic Alliance' card. National feeling was growing both in Denmark and Germany, which made compromise almost impossible. The proposal for a special constitution for Holstein provoked strong opposition from Prussia and Austria and led to the resignation of the majority of the Slesvig Estates. The Government then proposed a joint constitution for Slesvig and Denmark (1863).

Denmark's position was now dangerously isolated, which was to a great extent her own fault. She could expect no support from Russia or Sweden. Britain was only prepared to mediate in favour of a reasonable compromise. Prussia now had the decisive leadership of Bismarck, who had a clear objective—the unification of Germany and elimination of Austria from pan-German affairs. (In this 'game plan', Denmark was a mere pawn.) The sudden death of Frederick VII in 1863 also seemed like a good opportunity to strike.

The 1863 constitution was considered illegal by Prussia, and the Augustenborg family now claimed its inheritance in the duchies. Britain encouraged Denmark to compromise. She refused. War was inevitable. Prussian troops occupied Holstein in December 1863, and in February 1864 Danish troops abandoned the Danevirke, the southern frontier of Slesvig. The military situation was hopeless. In spite of a heroic Danish defence of Dybøl, the Prussian and Austrian troops soon advanced as far north as Limfjord. In April, there were complex negotiations in London. Each mediation attempt was rejected either by Denmark or by Prussia. Denmark was unwilling to accept a partition which would have given her a frontier similar to that agreed in 1920 after a referendum, and the war continued. By June, Zeeland was in danger and Denmark was forced to sue for peace, which was signed in Vienna. All of Slesvig and Holstein (with minor exceptions) was ceded to Prussia and Austria. After the Austro-Prussian war in 1866, the duchies went to Prussia, but a clause was included in the Peace of Prague (which ended that war) that Northern Slesvig could return to Denmark after a referendum. This clause was struck out by Prussia after her defeat of France in 1871. The situation was thereafter to remain unchanged until after the 1914-18 war. A constant battle had to be fought to prevent the abandonment of Danish positions, both through the pressures of growing Germanisation, especially after 1889, when severe new language laws were imposed, and through emigration; only by holding on could Danish claims be justified when the time was ripe.

Parallel with these developments, and closely linked to them, was the constitutional reform. As we have seen, the first draft of January 1848 was rejected, and in any case was soon overtaken by the events of March. The 'March Ministry' drew up proposals in the summer of 1848 for the election of a Constituent Assembly. Three-quarters of its members were to be elected by males over thirty, which was a massive extension of the suffrage and a total abandonment of the 'Estates' principle. The final quarter were to be nominated by the King. The Assembly adopted a liberal constitution, in spite of the general recession of the liberal tide.

Executive power was in the hands of the King and his ministers. The responsibility of the executive to Parliament was not specified, and this was later to cause major difficulties. There were to be two Houses of the *Rigsdag* with legislative and taxing powers and the right to declare war and raise troops. The Houses were to be co-equal, with members elected in single-member constituencies by males over thirty. The *Landsting* or Upper House would be more conservative in that only persons over forty and with certain property were eligible for election to it. The constitution also guaranteed basic rights and freedoms—speech, assembly, due process of law. It was a typical nineteenth century liberal constitution.

By the end of the war in 1864, conservative opinion was gaining ground, and sought to continue the more conservative trend of the 'common constitution', which had become redundant, into the arrangements that would now be required to pick up the pieces. The National Liberals took the apparently illogical line that the common institutions should remain in force until they replaced themselves, so as to prevent the Conservatives imposing 'absolutist' control over those policy areas which had been 'common' matters. The Government agreed with this view, but failed in the face of a Liberal/Conservative alliance. So it was that a new constitution was approved only by the *Rigsdag* (and not by the 'Joint State Council'). It was indeed more Conservative: the *Rigsdag's* Upper House now was to include twelve members nominated by the King and fifty-four indirectly elected by an electoral college, which in turn was elected by property owners.

The country was in a bad way. The loss of Slesvig-Holstein had a dramatic effect on trade and industry, and on the national stock of agricultural land. It was realised that a new national effort was needed to increase trade, improve the infrastructure and, above all, to 'win internally what had been lost externally' by bringing into use the moor and bog land in Jutland. It was also necessary in the face of falling grain prices, with the opening up of production in the United States and the British Empire, to change over radically from grain production to dairying.

The following thirty years were dominated by a constitutional crisis. The Liberals and Conservatives placed quite a different interpretation on the constitution. For the Liberals, it instituted a responsible government, responsible to the lower House of the *Rigsdag*. The landowners and the National Liberals combined to form a new party, *Højre* ('Right'), while the progressives formed the *Forenede Venstre* ('United Left'). *Venstre* had a majority in the popularly-elected *Folketing* (or Lower House), whereas *Højre* had a majority in the *Landsting*. The cabinet was from the Right, and sought to adopt the Finance Act by ordinance, where the two Houses were unable to agree. Behind this was the basic democratic issue of who governed. With the administration of Estrup (1875 – 94) the conflict became increasingly sharp, and from 1885 – 94 the government was carried on by provisional laws.

At first *Venstre* and its allies (the Social Democrats) sought to freeze out the *Højre* government by refusing to pass any bills in the *Folketing*. In 1894, a compromise was attempted between the *Højre* and the moderate elements of *Venstre*, but these attempts did not receive electoral approval. Finally, in 1901, the Right gave way in the face of the overwhelming *Venstre* majority, which led to the first *Venstre* government, led by Deuntzer. This was the '*System-skift*' (system change), by which the principle of parliamentary government was achieved.

By the time of the First World War, the party system had settled into the pattern it was to have for the next fifty years[2]. The Social Democratic Party had been founded by Louis Pio in 1871 and held its first congress in 1876, where it adopted its first (*Gimle*) programme, which was Marxist in inspiration. It supported *Venstre* in the constitutional battle, but thereafter rejected its economic policy. However, its 1913 programme was considerably more moderate. In 1905, the *Venstre* had split, the more radical elements such as smallholders, urban progressives and pacifists forming the *Radikale Venstre*. This party was to play a major part in Danish politics, forming its first government in 1905 under Zahle with Social Democratic support. This alliance was to dominate Danish politics for fifty years. In 1915, the Right was transformed into the Conservative People's Party, becoming more moderate and accepting democratic principles.

The First World War did not involve Denmark directly, as she was able to maintain her neutrality. A broad-based government was formed which, for the first time, included Social Democrat ministers. This government maintained a skilful balance between the powers. Clearly Denmark's sympathy lay with Britain and France, but reality dictated that any confrontation with Germany, the dominant power in the region, should be avoided. Germany forced Denmark to agree to the mining of the approaches to the Baltic in order to close it to the Royal Navy; Denmark obtained Britain's approval of this measure and remained neutral.

With the collapse of Germany in 1918, and with President Wilson's policy of self-determination having become one of the Allied war aims, Denmark could expect a favourable resolution of the Slesvig question, in spite of not having been among the Allied powers. The Danish Government showed great moderation, perhaps too great. The whole of Slesvig was divided into three zones. One of these—Flensborg—was in dispute, and possibly due to lax control of the registration of voters who had once been domiciled in the area but had subsequently left, it voted for Germany in the plebiscite of 1920. The area north of Flensborg as far as the Kongeå once more became Danish, which required some adjustment to the constitution. During the war, the old electoral system had been replaced by proportional representation, since the small parties and the Right feared that with a continuation of the old system they would lose all parliamentary representation. Denmark also ceased to possess any colonies with the sale of the Danish Virgin Islands to the United States in 1916.

The 1920s were easier for Denmark than for more industrialised countries, but the agricultural boom of the First World War rapidly came to an end. In 1920, there were dramatic incidents. The Government was dismissed by the King, in spite of having a parliamentary majority, on the border issue. The Social Democrats showed their increasing political muscle when Thorvald Stauning, their leader, threatened a general strike, since wage negotiations had also collapsed. In 1924, the Social Democrats became the largest party in Parliament, and formed their first minority government. This government was short-lived, but it had been demonstrated that the Social Democrats were capable of governing. In 1929, they obtained a majority in Parliament with the Radicals, an alliance which was to last throughout the 1930s. The Social-Liberal governments of the 1930s were successful in pursuing an economic and social policy which limited the impact of the depression.

These governments could not muster a majority in the upper House, which was controlled by the Liberals and Conservatives. In the so-called *Kanslergade forlig*, or agreement (the prime minister's office is in the street Kanslergade) with the Liberals in 1933 they created a majority for the introduction of the first Welfare State measures. Attempts to reform the constitution based on an agreement with the Conservatives, which would have eliminated the veto power of the Upper House, failed in a referendum held in 1939 since it obtained a majority of the votes cast, but failed to obtain the necessary 45 per cent of the electorate in its favour.

Denmark did not see the rise of extremist political movements, which elsewhere in Europe endangered democracy and provoked violence. The Communist Party was represented in Parliament from 1932, but never had more than three members; on the other hand, the Danish Nazi Party first obtained representation only in 1939, although it contested the elections of 1932 and 1935. It only obtained three seats, and obtained no more, even in the 1943 election during the occupation. The *Bondepartiet* (Farmers' Party), which became more and more Fascist and collaborationist in orientation, obtained 3.2 per cent of the vote and five seats in 1935, 3 per cent and four seats in 1939, and only 1.2 per cent of the vote and two seats in 1943. Even in 1939, 'anti-system parties' only obtained 7.2 per cent of the vote and ten seats out of 148.

If Danish domestic policy was relatively successful in the 1930s, it is difficult to make such a positive judgement about the foreign policy pursued during the same period. It is, of course, scarcely disputable that no effective policy was possible against Nazi Germany. However, the false optimism and refusal to face hard reality, so characteristic of the foreign policy of the late 1930s, left the country ill-prepared to face the Nazi occupation when it came.

Denmark attempted to remain outside the conflicts of the late 1930s. She did not re-arm, but placed her faith in the doctrine of collective security under the League of Nations and Scandinavian solidarity. If this policy was initially morally virtuous, it rapidly became naive to the point of madness. The foreign policy of Munch was based on the premise that Denmark was no threat to Germany, and that Germany would respect weakness. It ignored the fact that Germany was led by a fanatic; it ignored the danger posed by Nazi support among the German minority north of the 1920 border; and, above all, it ignored the fact that Britain could no longer afford any meaningful protection, and without that, neutrality would be untenable. Germany's strategic concerns were also different from what they had been in 1914. The non-aggression pact offered by Germany was equally worthless.

So it was that on 9 April 1940[3] Denmark was invaded and occupied almost without resistance, *en passant* as the Germans moved north to Norway, their real objective. The Government remained in office and Parliament continued to sit, which was unique in occupied Europe, although at that time it contained three Communists! Declarations by the Germans that there would be no interference in Danish internal affairs were taken at face value, but were soon shown to be of little worth in the face of continual demands in such diverse fields as press censorship, administration of justice and economic issues. Danish independence was in reality totally illusory. The attitude of the authorities has been the subject of much subsequent controversy, but few questioned its correctness at the time, and no doubt it was the only course to be followed in the initial period. It consisted in a pragmatic, supple policy of negotiation, of dragging out issues, of watering down the persistent German demands, and of keeping as much control in Danish hands as possible, even if that meant that the Danish Parliament had to make repressive and probably unconstitutional laws and Danish courts had to impose harsh sentences on resistors.

For three years, this process continued; German demands increased while the ostensible 'independence' of Denmark was maintained. The Government was forced to make serious concessions, to include more ministers who sought more sincere co-operation with Germany and exclude others who opposed such a development. The attitude of Erik Scavenius, the Foreign Minister and, after 1942, Prime Minister, has always remained equivocal on this point. Certainly 'normalcy' to the point of holding an election in March 1943 may have limited the suffering which the occupation imposed on the Danes, but it also helped the Germans, in that it enabled their exploitation of Danish agriculture to continue while requiring the minimum occupation force. It also left Denmark in danger of being considered an ally of Germany after the liberation, not least by the Soviet Union, since the Scavenius Government had, under pressure, adhered to the anti-Comintern Pact.

However, resistance was growing, and demonstrations in July-August 1943 provoked a crisis. The German Army and more political elements in Berlin felt that the liberal policy in Denmark was dangerous both militarily—because of the possibility of Allied landings—and politically. They were prepared for a showdown. Either the Government must meet extreme demands for the death penalty and other repressive measures, and become overtly collaborationist, or it could refuse and resign, leaving a vacuum for a German military administration to fill. The latter course was chosen and the breach came on 29 August 1943.

In September, a Freedom Council was formed to co-ordinate resistance. The Germans interned the Danish army and police. They moved against the 6,000 Danish Jews, but by an extraordinary act of national courage and solidarity all but about 550 escaped to Sweden. This German move was counter-productive in another way; it revived the torpid conscience of the Danish people and, more than any other act, set alight the flame of resistance and rekindled national honour. The Danish Resistance mounted effective sabotage, especially of the railway system, and organised a people's strike in Copenhagen in July 1944. Early in 1945, an underground army of 30,000 men was ready to rise if necessary, and a well-armed Danish brigade was standing ready in Sweden.

Gradually, German exactions became tougher, but they never reached the level of savagery found in Poland, Russia or even the Netherlands or Norway. Even as the sands ran out for the Third Reich, a relatively moderate policy was carried out in Denmark where, despite inter-agency rivalries, the German Foreign Ministry and Army retained considerable influence on occupation policies. The police were deported *en masse* and collaborationist militia groups were set up in their place. Death sentences were imposed on resistance fighters.

The Danes could not—except for some sabotage actions—develop a *maquis*. They excelled in a specially Danish form of resistance: passive resistance and obstruction, in which humour played a major part! The people's strike in Copenhagen in 1944 was a triumph for the Freedom Council. The Germans were forced to negotiate indirectly with the Council and to repeal a series of repressive measures in order to end the strike. The Freedom Council was not a government, even if it gained great moral authority and was in contact with the Allies, not least the Soviet Union, who accepted one of its representatives in Moscow. This was important, since it was possible that Denmark would be liberated by the Red Army; Denmark had been forced to sign the anti-Communist Pact, a fact which the Soviet Union could have used to brand Denmark as an ally of the axis.

In the end, liberation came almost without fighting, except for the island of Bornholm in the Baltic, which was bombed by the Russians. German forces in Northern Germany and Denmark surrendered to Field-Marshal Montgomery on 4 May 1945. The Resistance took control and linked up with British units moving north. In accordance with a pre-arranged plan, a new Liberation government assumed power, under the Social Democrat Vilhelm Buhl, with an equal number of ministers allocated to the political parties and to the Freedom Council.

When elections were held in September 1945, the Social Democrats lost ground in spite of a relatively left-wing programme which was in accordance with the spirit of the time, largely because the Communist party obtained an unprecedented 12.5 per cent of the vote and eighteen seats. The next largest party, the Liberals, with only 23.4 per cent of the vote, formed a homogeneous minority government, which fell in another election in 1947 over the Slesvig question, having attempted to re-open the border issue, which the Liberation government had decided, with considerable statesmanship, not to re-open.[4] The election of 1947 saw the return of a Social Democrat minority government and opened a long period during which the Social Democrats became the 'natural' party of government, or at the very least were pivotal in all political negotiations even when in opposition (except for the period 1968–71). Apart from 1950–3, 1968–71 and 1973–5, the Party has been continuously in power from 1947 until today. It has therefore been in opposition for less than eight out of the last thirty-two years. Until 1973, this was a period of relative political stability and economic progress. By the mid–1950s, Denmark had fully recovered from the economic effects of the war, and had chosen to integrate herself into the European and Atlantic system by joining the Council of Europe, EFTA and NATO.

The Party system settled down to a basic four-party pattern: Social Democrats, Radicals, Liberals, Conservatives with two poles: Social Democrats/Radicals or Liberals/Conservatives. Small parties have come and gone: *Dansk Samling* (right of centre), Independents (right of centre), Liberal Centre and Communists (1932–60 and 1973–9). Other parties showed a greater ability to survive—the Justice Party (1926–60 and from 1973) and the Socialist People's Party (from 1960)—but these parties have played a relatively small role in government. After 1947 the Social Democrats again took up the issue of constitutional reform. After difficult negotiations, two elections and a referendum, a new constitution was approved in 1953 which totally replaced the old one of 1849. The sections on human and social rights were expanded; the succession to the Crown in the female line was authorised; the principle of parliamentary government—the subject of dispute in the period 1870–1901—was formally enshrined in the constitution; the Upper Chamber (*Landsting*) was abolished; and the possibility of an abrogative referendum for some laws was introduced. This device has only been used once in 1963 against relatively radical land reform laws carried through Parliament by a Social Democrat-Radical coalition. Provision was also made for delegating sovereignty to international organisations. Denmark now had a modern constitution.

In 1957, the Social Democratic-Radical coalition, in power since 1953, lost its absolute majority in the *Folketing*. It only obtained

eighty-four seats against eighty-four for the three parties of the right
(Liberals, Conservatives and Justice). A deal was made with the
Justice Party, which entered a majority coalition with the Social
Democrats and Radicals which lasted for three and a half years, and
presided over a minor economic miracle and the formation of
EFTA. The Radicals and Social Democrats were prepared to
continue the coalition in 1960, but in that election the Justice Party,
at that time essentially a protest party, lost all its seats in Parliament.
The other two parties remained in power, either in coalition (until
1964) or forming the majority (until 1966).

The 1966 elections seem in retrospect to have been a watershed of
major importance. The Social Democrats lost votes, but this was
more than compensated for by the doubling of support for the
Socialist People's Party (SF). This party was led by the popular
Aksel Larsen, former General Secretary of the Communist Party,
who had left the Communists in 1956 after the uprising in Hungary
to form the new party. The SF, at least under his leadership, became
a non-Stalinist, non-Moscow-oriented party and a genuine mass-
democratic party. It assigned itself the role of a left-wing ginger
group, the conscience of the Social Democratic Party. This meant
that for the first time there was a Socialist majority in Parliament.
For reasons of foreign policy (EEC membership and NATO), a
coalition government between the two Socialist parties proved
impossible, although the possibility was explored. For fourteen
months they co-operated on domestic issues through a contact committee, which their opponents maliciously named the 'Red Cabinet'.

This interesting experience was brought to a premature end by a
swelling revolt inside the SF, which chafed under the restrictions
imposed by the alliance. When the pound sterling was devalued in
November 1967, Denmark was forced to follow suit. The internal
measures which followed from this decision, in particular a wage
freeze, split the SF. In a decisive vote in the *Folketing* in December
1967, the government was led to defeat when six SF deputies voted
with the 'bourgeois' opposition parties. These six deputies later
formed a new party (the Left Socialists) and four were re-elected in
the subsequent general election of 23 January 1968.

These developments provoked a polarisation in Danish politics.
The Radicals, who since 1909 had been close allies of the Social
Democrats, now entered the 'bourgeois' camp, and the three 'bour-
geois' parties went into the 1968 election with a prior agreement to
form a 'bourgeois' government if they obtained a majority together.
The Radical Party almost doubled its vote, and its leader, Hilmar
Baunsgaard, became Prime Minister. The 'triangular VKR'
majority government, which effectively negotiated Danish member-

ship of the EEC, stayed in office until 1971 when the S-SF obtained a majority; this in turn led to the formation of a new Social Democratic minority government which carried through Denmark's EEC membership.

Pressure from the SF and the accession of Anker Jørgensen to the premiership after the surprise resignation of Jens Otto Krag, which immediately followed the EEC referendum in October 1972, saw the Social Democrats leaning leftwards, and led to a split in the party. Erhard Jakobsen resigned in protest against this tendency and formed the Centre Democrats. Furthermore, the EEC referendum, the pressures of taxation and protests against liberalisation of the abortion and pornography laws were also bringing considerable pressure to bear on the domination of political life by the 'old parties'.

The 1973 election saw the lid blown off this cauldron; it was a catalysmic event. The five parties represented in the previous legislature all lost heavily—over fifty seats in the new Parliament were held by the five new parties. The Social Democrats were reduced to forty-six seats. The Liberals formed a minority (extreme minority!) government, based on only twenty-two seats. This government lasted for a very difficult year. The elections of 1975, 1977 and 1979 saw a gradual but perceptible return to more stable conditions. The 'old parties' recovered their confidence and their relative strength, and they did so with the minimum of concessions to the newcomers. The 'earthquake' movement stopped and even lost momentum. All the new (or new/old) parties have shown signs of durability, but they appear not to be expanding. The strength of the extreme left and of the Progress Party has stabilised. There would appear to be a return to old patterns in that the poles of the party system have again become the Social Democrats, with the tacit support by other parties to their right or left, or *Venstre* (the Liberals) supported by other smaller 'bourgeois' parties.

Whatever government is in power, its room for manoeuvre is limited; it will face the same economic problems: energy import costs, the balance of payments, inflation, wage pressure on competitiveness and the effect of inflation and the world recession on employment. Within the confines of the mixed economy and international delegations, there is a narrow range of available solutions.

In international affairs, Denmark has learned since 1945—reluctantly perhaps—the lessons of the 1930s and the occupation. These lessons were strongly reinforced by the onset of the cold war after 1947. With the failure of negotiations for a Nordic defence union, Denmark joined NATO in 1949. She joined the Council of Europe in 1950 and EFTA in 1958. From 1961, she was an applicant for membership of the EEC, which she eventually joined with Britain in 1973. Parallel to these European and Atlantic commitments, Denmark has attempted to maintain and deepen Nordic co-operation. The Nordic Council, which is a useful forum for discussions between legislators and governments, was set in in 1952; in a sense it formalised earlier initiatives. Nordic co-operation has always been pragmatic and has avoided sovereignty issues, which are sensitive in all Nordic states. This problem, as well as divergent interests and foreign policy goals and obligations (Swedish neutrality; Finnish obligations to the Soviet Union; Danish and Norwegian NATO membership, and since 1961, the Danish desire to enter the EEC), has meant that Nordic co-operation has not been able to take the form of any significant political or economic integration. If Danish foreign policy has moved in the direction of clear commitment to the European and Atlantic frameworks, ambiguities still remain. These movements of policy have, in most cases, been contested and reluctant, based on the absence of any viable alternative, rather than on any strong positive conviction or preference.

What conclusions can we draw from our brief excursion into Danish history? What influences appear as significant in terms of present attitudes and realities? The first relates to the reluctant, but inevitable realisation of Denmark's strategic and economic vulnerability. She is basically a projection of the North German plain, and the gateway to the Baltic and the North Sea, and has thus been astride first German and later Soviet naval corridors. This is her strategic importance and vulnerability. She may have attempted, at least since 1864, to have a policy of being a 'non-power', but it must be clear, as events of 1940 so brutally showed, that such a position is only tenable where a balance of power exists in the Baltic and Nordic region. Denmark has in any case not been able to ensure her own defence unaided, at least since 1660. She has been at the mercy of events, and her own weight has even been of slight importance in the overall balance. Indeed, more astute choices of camp could in several cases since 1660 have paid major dividends, simply because that camp was victorious. Only since 1945 has she based her policy on this brutal logic, but she has never done so with wholehearted emotional commitment.

Denmark is economically vulnerable, dependent on imported energy (even before the oil crisis), on raw materials and on dispersed export markets. Denmark has a very open economy, which must respond to movements in the world economy. It was the White Commonwealth grain production after 1870 which enforced a total transformation of Danish agriculture. Trade patterns after 1945 have led to light industrial exports overtaking agriculture as the most important source of foreign currency earnings; it was the fact that if Britain entered the EEC, Denmark's two major customers, Germany and Britain, would both be behind the protective wall of 'Community preference', imposed by the Common Agricultural Policy, that was the major determinant of Denmark's decision to apply to join the EEC in 1961. Political and economic pressures give Danish politicians little room for manoeuvre.

The second main conclusion relates to the strong thread of pragmatism running through Danish domestic policies. Pragmatism and tolerance have enabled smooth change without violence. Abolutism was mild, and it was abolished without violent revolution. In the 1900s, the old aristocratic parties ceded to the new mass parties which had waited patiently for the change. The democratic impulse was never far below the surface, even in the periods of strong kingship in the Middle Ages or during the Absolute Monarchy (1660 – 1849), and was able to resurface easily and smoothly when the tide once again ran in its favour. The reverse side of the coin, less satisfactory perhaps, is the fact that radical reform movements tend to be easily controlled, canalised and emasculated, without ever reaching their full flood.

REFERENCES

1. For a history of Denmark see P. Lauring, *A History of the Kingdom of Denmark*, Copenhagen: Høst, 1960 (in English). For a short account of more recent Danish political history see W. Glyn Jones, *Denmark*, London: Ernest Benn, 1970.
2. For an analysis of the party system as it developed, see Erik Damgaard, 'Stability and Change in the Danish Party System Over Half a Century', *Scandinavian Political Studies*, Vol. 9, 1974.
3. For accounts of Denmark during the Nazi occupation see *Besaestelsenstidens Hvem? Hvad? Hvor?*, Copenhagen: *Politiken*, 1965.
4. For an analysis of the Slesvig question after 1945 see A.J. Lindstrøm, *Landet Slesvig-Holstens Politiske Historie i Hovedtraek 1945 – 54*, Flensborg: Danmarks Centralbibliotek for Sydslesvig, 1975.

II. THE LAND AND PEOPLE :
ECONOMY AND SOCIETY

1. *The Geography*

Metropolitan Denmark consists of the Jutland peninsula, which is an extension of the North German plain forming a barrier between the Baltic and the North Sea, and of four large islands east of Jutland (Fyn, Sjaeland, Lolland and Falster), as well as a large number of small islands, including the island of Bornholm, which lies far out in the Baltic, mid-way between Sweden and the Polish coast. In the North Atlantic, Denmark has also governed the Faeroe Islands, Iceland and Greenland. Iceland became independent in 1944 during the Second World War, although she had enjoyed internal self-government since 1919. The Faeroes and Greenland remain part of the Kingdom, which is responsible for their external relations and defence.

Jutland is flat and marshy in the south, close to the German border, and is heavily indented in the east by fjords. The centre is more hilly, but in an example of Danish self-depreciating humour, the country's highest point—a mere 150 metres—lying in mid-Jutland, is called Himmelbjerget ('Heaven's Mountain'). Until the late nineteenth century, much of central and northern Jutland was marsh, sand dunes (on the west coast) and heathland. Reclamation has enabled almost all of this land to be cultivated. The eastern islands vary considerably: Fyn and Sjaeland are more hilly and rolling, whereas Lolland and, to a lesser extent, Falster are flat, which made them suitable for larger-scale intensive cultivation of crops such as sugar beet.

The population[1] of Denmark is currently 5,088,000 (mid-1977) and projections give 5,191,000 for 1985 and 5,248,000 for 1990. The density of the population is 118 per square kilometre, as against 229 per square kilometre for Britain and 98 for France. Other small countries in the EEC have a higher population density: Belgium has 322/sq.km. and the Netherlands 336. As for the other Scandinavian countries, these are of course much more thinly populated (Sweden 18/sq.km. and Norway 14/sq.km.).

The distribution of the population between different parts of the country is uneven.[2] Greater Copenhagen contains 1,756,000 people, which represents almost 34 percent of the total population. The density of the population in Jutland and the islands is much lower than for the country as a whole—83/sq.km. for the islands and less than 70/sq.km. for Jutland, which is lower than any region of the

United Kingdom, excepting Scotland.

Apart from Greater Copenhagen, the other important urban areas (all of them ports) are Aarhus (Jutland) - 111,266; Aalborg (Jutland) - 154,787; Esbjerg (Jutland) - 76,056; Odense (Fyn) - 103,850.[3] With the relatively low population density, the emptiness of Jutland, and the existence of so many islands and fjords, communications have always been a major preoccupation. In the nineteenth century, rail and steamship routes developed rapidly, but since 1945 domestic air routes have largely taken over, at least for passenger traffic between Copenhagen and Jutland. These air routes are well developed for such a compact country.

The population is almost totally homogeneous. There are few ethnic or linguistic minorities. The Danish spoken on the Baltic island of Bornholm appears closer to Swedish, but no difficulties have arisen in this respect. The North Atlantic territories are, of course, ethnically and linguistically separate. The population of Greenland is now some 50,000, of whom most are Eskimos. The population of the Faeroe islands is 42,000. These territories enjoy internal self-government, and their position has rarely been an important factor in Danish political life.

Minorities exist on both sides of the border—fixed, as we have seen, after a plebiscite in 1920. The border reflects majority sentiment relatively accurately, but has left a German-speaking university north of the border and a larger Danish minority to the south. Since 1945, when the border question was not re-opened, the emphasis has been on assuring special statutes for the languages and cultural and political associations for the minorities. This has been made easier by the establishment of a democratic and federal state in Germany since 1949. The German minority north of the border now numbers less than 10,000 and, since the late 1960s, has been unable to elect a member to the Danish *Folketing* without an alliance with another list, despite the special concessions made to minorities in the electoral law.[4]

2. *The Economy*

Until the latter part of the nineteenth century, Denmark was largely a grain-producing nation. Agriculture was not intensive. The towns grew slowly, as ports and commercial centres.[5]

The 1870s saw two radical shocks to the Danish economy: the opening up of major new sources of grain production in the United States and the British Empire, which led to a long-term decline in grain prices, and secondly, the loss of Slesvig-Holstein, which was important both as a market and as a producer. In reaction to these events, a modernisation and improvement drive set in. The *Hedeselskabet*, established by Dalgos, reclaimed large tracts of land in central Jutland and brought them under cultivation. Denmark ceased to export grain; her main export products became butter and cheese. Major improvements in dairy-farming techniques were introduced, especially the centrifuge.

The Co-operative movement began in 1882 with the creation of a butter factory at Hjeding. By the Second World War, there were over 1,400 such co-operatives, with an annual turnover of 900 million kroner. The movement spread to other branches of production with the setting-up of the co-operative bacon factory in Horsens in 1887. These developments were a logical result of the ending of feudalism and the development of a smallholding type of farming, which began from 1787 (see Chapter I).

The urban population was steadily growing, and with it trade and light industry. In 1769, the urban population represented only 19.6 per cent of the total; by 1801 the proportion of town-dwellers had only increased marginally to 20.8 per cent and by 1860 to 23.7 per cent. However, by 1901 the urban population had risen to almost 1 million, and 36.7 per cent of the total population.

The customs laws of 1863 and 1908 went a long way towards creating free trade and therefore did much to encourage industry. In the latter part of the nineteenth century, there was an important growth in local trade schools and associations. The harbours in Esbjerg and Copenhagen were improved. Denmark also joined the Gold Standard in 1873, which was (at that time) a considerable benefit to trade and industry.

After the First World War, Denmark remained relatively prosperous with economic growth at about 3 per cent per year. The trends of structural change discernible since the 1870s continued. Denmark remained primarily an agricultural economy, but the drift of capital and labour out of agriculture continued. Unemployment remained high, but lower than in more industrialised economies (even including Sweden), at 8 per cent of the labour force. This unemployment was structural rather than cyclical in origin. Falling agricultural prices led to the marginalisation of numerous small farm units, and a movement of population from rural to urban areas in search of employment. However, the small-scale industries in Denmark were at the same time in a phase of development, which involved the change-over to more capital-intensive processes of production, giving them a limited capacity to absorb labour.

The 1930s saw a struggle for pre-eminence between export-oriented agriculture and domestic market-oriented industry. The battle was won by industry. The autarky policies of the European dictatorships set up barriers to Danish agricultural exports; internally, the terms of trade moved against agriculture, since industries operated in a more protectionist and less competitive environment.[6] The Depression merely retarded these long-term trends, but did not reverse them. In the face of unemployment and real misery in both urban and rural areas, the authorities were forced to act. The foundations of the modern Welfare State were laid: easy credit, deficit-financed public works, subsidies, price floors for agriculture, welfare measures.

The Scandinavian economies emerged intact from the war, but patterns of trade and production had been greatly distorted. Capital stock had not been renewed. Rationing and controls remained essential until at least 1950. One consequence of the proto-Welfare State measures of the 1930s was that, contrary to expectation, overall demand was to remain high and rising in the reconversion period after 1945. In Denmark, this development was slower than in Sweden or Norway. However, full employment was realised by the early 1950s. The main characteristics of the economy after 1950 were continued economic growth until the early 1970s, when the rate of growth in real terms slowed down, but nevertheless never became negative; by this time there were persistent problems of inflation, balance of trade deficits, wage-induced cost inflation, and energy cost difficulties after 1973. The general restructuring of the economy, which had been in progress since the 1880s, continued, and accelerated in pace as the 1960s advanced. However, there are some signs that the movement of manpower into the industrial sector has recently lost momentum.

After 1945, there was a gradual return to a free market in all sectors of the economy, except agriculture, which retained an elaborate system of subsidies to control food prices, encourage exports and maintain farm incomes. The agricultural sector only represented some 20 per cent of GDP by 1954, and this fell even further to about 10 per cent in 1970. By 1977, agriculture and related activities still represented 7.1 per cent of total value added in the Danish economy, as against 4.5 per cent for the European Community as a whole, and 2.3 per cent for the United Kingdom. The fall in employment in agriculture has been equally dramatic, falling from 43 per cent in 1900 to 28.6 per cent in 1939, to 11.2 per cent in 1970 and 9 per cent in 1977. This drift from the land has been encouraged by the widening differential in earnings between agriculture and industry (7 per cent in 1960, 32 per cent in 1969). However, the rate of movement has, in the last few years, lost momentum.[7] Nevertheless, in Jutland and the islands such as Lolland, the share of value added in agriculture is about double the national average, and agricultural employment may reach 25 per cent of the total work force.[8]

Denmark's agriculture and fishing represents some 33.9 per cent of exports (1977). She has a surplus for export of many products— cheese (325 per cent self-sufficient), butter (305 per cent), pork (354 per cent), poultry and eggs (245 per cent), beef (328 per cent), wheat (148 per cent), rye (139 per cent) and sugar (153 per cent). In comparative terms, she has a significant production of cheese, butter, pork and sugar; in production of these commodities she ranks from fourth to sixth in the EEC. Her agriculture is modern and efficient, with continuing centralisation and consolidation of the number of farm units, with a resulting increase in average acreage from 40 acres in 1960 to 55 acres in 1972. In 1970, there were 140,000 farm units, falling at 7,000 per year.

Fishing is also an important economic activity. There are about 8,000 boats, and the total annual catch is above 130,000 gross registered tons, of which a considerable part is available for export. Fishing and allied activities provide employment for 13,000 people.

Industry and services have increasingly dominated the economy since 1945. Industry now represents 30.4 per cent of employment and 32.9 per cent of value added.[9] Denmark has no raw materials and almost no indigenous energy resources. Heavy industry has not developed; production of iron and steel and other non-ferrous metals is not significant in EEC terms, but it does represent a major part of the industrial base. The only basic industrial production in which Denmark has some relative importance in EEC terms is in cement, phosphates for agricultural use, and shipbuilding. The main centre of the iron and steel industry is the plant at Fredericksvaerk, near Copenhagen. The iron and steel industries provide 28 per cent of industrial employment. The shipbuilding industry is centred at Copenhagen, Aalborg and Nakskov (Lolland). Aalborg is also the centre of the cement and chemical industries. The main centres of the textile industry are Herning and Vejle, both in Central Jutland.

Denmark's industry is centred in the light industrial sectors: food processing, which is obviously linked to her high-quality agriculture and fishing; high-quality electronics such as hi-fi equipment; and furniture. Indeed, industrial products have overtaken agricultural products as the largest source of export revenue, rising to over 40 per cent of exports in 1977. However, it should be noted that Danish industries are often extremely vulnerable, and since the onset of the economic crisis of the early 1970s, numerous closures have occurred and a large number of jobs have been lost. This vulnerability arises from several different causes: wage inflation, vulnerability to competitiveness in an extremely open economy, and the fact that many industrial activities in Denmark are controlled by multinational companies, to which they are of marginal importance.

Trade is, and always has been, vital to Denmark. She forms part of the vast free-trade area which composes the European Community, and the remaining EFTA countries: Scandinavia, Portugal, Austria and Switzerland. Exports represented 21.9 per cent of her GDP in 1978 and imports 28.8 per cent. Only the Benelux countries and some smaller industrialised countries, such as Ireland and Austria, show a higher dependence on trade. Denmark has long had a tradition of free trade and as early as 1937—which was, after all, in a period of considerable protectionism elsewhere—her average rate of duty was only 7.5 per cent, while three-fifths of all goods were admitted duty-free.

Between 1970 and 1978, the value of Denmark's exports almost tripled from 3,290 to 9,305 EUA and imports rose from 4,388 to 11,598 EUA. Her balance of trade was negative over the whole period. In 1978, her trade deficit was 2,292 EUA, or 6.9 per cent of GDP. This represented its highest-ever level except for 1976 and 1977, and it has been growing fast since 1970 when it was over 919 EUA. By the end of 1980 there were signs of improvement, but the deficit was still running at 92m. EUA monthly. Exports have grown by 38 per cent since 1970 in volume, and imports by only 25 per cent; however inflation, especially in oil prices, has prevented this from having a favourable effect on the balance of payments. Like Britain, the 'invisible' side of the balance of payments is positive, attenuating somewhat the trade deficit. There was, in 1977, a net inflow of 547 EUA from services, reducing the deficit from 2,324 to 1,777 EUA.[10]

The distribution and direction of Danish trade has changed quite considerably over the last four decades. Immediately before the Second World War, agricultural products represented almost 17 per cent of total exports, which had fallen by 1978 to 33.9 per cent. In 1939, Britain took more than half of Denmark's exports, Germany about 35 per cent and the rest of Scandinavia about 8 per cent. At the end of the 1950s, when Denmark began to consider her options in the face of the establishment of the EEC, some two-thirds of her trade still went to two major partners, Britain and Germany, although Britain takes a much smaller percentage than before the war. Some diversification towards Scandinavia, the United States and the Third World has also been taking place. In 1978, 47.6 per cent of Danish exports went to the EEC (which, of course, includes both Germany and Britain), 5.7 per cent goes to the United States, 1.9 per cent to Japan and 1.9 per cent to the fifty-two African, Caribbean and Pacific states associated with the EEC under the Lomé Convention. Of the rest, some 30 per cent goes to Scandinavia. This, of course, represents a major change in trade patterns compared to the pre-war situation, in respect of both the structure and the flow of trade.

With almost no indigenous sources of energy, Denmark is almost totally dependent on imported energy. She produced a mere 503,000 tons of oil equivalent in 1977, almost all in the form of North Sea oil. However, the Danish sector of the North Sea seemed to contain almost no oil deposits. Some gas is expected to be extracted in the 1980s. As an advanced Western society, her energy consumption *per capita* is high, being 3,871 tons oil equivalent per head. This is well above the EEC average of 3,536 tons.[11]

Her energy dependence has remained almost total. It was 96.8 per cent in 1963 and 99.6 per cent in 1973. Even the vigorous energy conservation and diversification measures of the last few years have done little to reduce this dependence which, in 1978, was still 98.9 per cent. Furthermore, oil represented 82.6 per cent of her total energy consumption in 1977 (coal was 16.7 per cent). Naturally, the cost of these oil imports has represented a serious and increasing burden on her economy. Indeed, almost 15 per cent of her total imports in 1978 was made up of petroleum products. However, recent forecasts expect North Sea oil and gas to cover almost one-third of home needs by the late 1980s, giving a major balance of payments saving.

Until the oil crisis of the 1970s economic growth had, with the exception of short-lived recession periods in the late 1950s, been almost continuous. GDP grew by 4.7 per cent between 1961 and 1970, and by 3.6 per cent between 1970 and 1973. Taking the period 1967–77, the rate of growth slowed to 3.4 per cent in real terms. By the end of the 1970s, there was almost zero growth of GDP in real terms. Unemployment too has risen sharply in recent years. In 1973 it was a mere 0.7 per cent of the workforce (EEC average 2.5 per cent); by 1977 it had risen to 6.7 per cent, as against an EEC average of 5.6 per cent, reaching 7.5 per cent by the end of 1980.[12]

The retail price index continued to rise[13]. Taking 1975 as 100, the index stood at 123 in 1978. The rise in food prices has been less sharp, but for other items such as clothes, rents and household utensils, the rise has been much above average. After a fall in 1979, the index again showed an annual rise by the end of 1980.

In 1978, gross hourly earnings in agriculture were 38.75 Dkr. as against 40.18 Kroner in industry. The highest rates were found in electronics, distilling, plastics and the iron and steel industry. In the two years 1976–8, the industrial wages index rose (1975 = 100) from 107.1 to 128.5 (United Kingdom figures 106.1 to 121.7). The hourly cost of labour in industry was 7.10 EUA (European Unit of Account = US$1.42273, as of 8 June 1980). Only Britain (3.10 EUA) and France (5.9 EUA) showed lower rates in the EEC. In agriculture (1975 = 100), the hourly wages index stood at 112.8 in 1978 and 130.4 in 1979, showing a considerably faster rise than the general wage index for the same period. The average wage rate per hour in agriculture was 26.80 DKr. in 1977, but this covered considerable variations according to the type of activity and farm. In stock farming, rates were on average 27.31 DKr. per hour, and on larger farms (over ten workers) as high as 32.80 DKr. per hour.

The general standard of living in Denmark has, since 1945, been among the highest in the world, in regard both to levels of income and the 'social wage', since Denmark's GDP per head is among the ten highest in the world and her Welfare State is well developed. Consumption of more expensive foods per head of population (sugar, meat, milk, butter, fats) is above the EEC average, as is consumption of energy. In 1977 there were 270 private cars per 1,000 of population, which was below the EEC average of 292 per thousand, but above the United Kingdom figure of 254 per thousand. She had 338 television sets per thousand of the population, the highest figure in the EEC, exceeded in the OECD area only by Sweden (352), Canada (411) and the United States. She had 493 telephones per thousand (EEC average 353), the highest in the EEC. She had more doctors per 100,000 of the population than the EEC average, but fewer chemists and hospital beds, although more of each of the latter than for Britain.[14]

Social Welfare expenditure is high and has been growing steadily since the mid-1950s. The foundations of the Welfare State were laid in the 1930s and have been substantially developed since then, as we shall see in Chapter 6. A central feature of Danish social democracy has been its commitment to an expanding Welfare State within a mixed economy. The expansion of the state sector has come about through 'Welfarism' rather than through 'collectivisation' of production. The share of GDP going to government consumption has continued to increase; it was 13 per cent in 1954, 20 per cent in 1970, 22 per cent in 1973, and by 1977 it had reached 24 per cent. By 1971 the total size of the public sector reached 49.4 per cent of GNP in Denmark, made up of 29 per cent for real use of the nation's output and 20.4 per cent in transfer payments[15]. The main elements in public expenditure were social welfare, education and defence.

The Danish Welfare State is based less and less on the principle of insurance; to an increasing extent it is directly financed out of central and, to a much smaller extent, local taxation. Of the revenue of the State from taxation and social security contributions, only 1.2 per cent (1977) were from contributions. In 1973, the share of the cost of social welfare borne by local government was 22 per cent, but by 1976 its share had risen to 32 per cent. The share borne by central government fell from 64 to 56 per cent; however since the corresponding figures for 1974 and 1975 were 65 and 64 per cent, this fall may be fortuitous. In any event, the total borne by central and local government was never less than 86 per cent, and by 1976 stood at 88 per cent. The share borne by employers fell from 8 to 6 per cent in the same period. The main payments were: medical costs 30 per cent (1976); pensions 32 per cent; family allowances, unemployment benefit 10 per cent (up from 6 per cent in 1974).

3. *Current Economic Problems*[16]

In conclusion, it is worth quickly recapitulating and highlighting the major current economic problems and the approaches adopted by successive governments in attempting to deal with them. As elsewhere in the industrialised world, 1973 was a watershed year, with the dramatic increase in oil prices and the recession which was to result. Denmark, as we have seen, was particularly badly hit due to its almost total dependence on imported energy, mostly oil from the Middle East. Unemployment rose dramatically from 0.7 per cent of the workforce in 1973 (30,000 in early 1974), to over 3 per cent in early 1975 (110,000), and the rise continued. The minority Liberal government which came to power in early 1974 was forced to propose drastic cuts in public expenditure and a total wage freeze, in addition to its earlier tax reductions and cuts. These proposals did not find a parliamentary majority, and an election was held in January 1975. This resulted in the return of a Social Democractic minority government. The new government placed more emphasis on measures to preserve employment, on an effective incomes policy in co-operation with the trade unions, and measures such as expenditure cuts and monetary expansion targets to deal with the serious and increasing balance of payments deficit (up from 3 milliard to 11 milliard Kroner in the course of 1976).

Despite important rises in both production and productivity during 1976, which made possible an increase of some 30,000-40,000 in total employment, world trade did not expand as much as had been forecast, with the result that unemployment remained almost constant and was soon again on an upward trend.

The fragmentation of the political spectrum, the arrival of new and radical political forces, both of the right and the left, in the parliamentary arena after 1973 made a consistent economic policy difficult to maintain in the face of external difficulties and increasing trade union pressures. In 1975, 1977 and 1978, government intervention was necessary in order to prevent total collapse of the centralised wage bargaining negotiations for the next period. Political conflict has centred on the approach to incomes policy, the need for public expenditure cuts and reductions in personal taxation, as well as the extent of measures to preserve employment. The Liberals (in office 1973–4 and in coalition with the Social Democrats 1978–9), and the 'bourgeois' parties even more, favoured cuts and tax reductions, as well as a severe wages policy. The Social Democrats favoured smaller cuts and more extensive measures to safeguard employment and to save energy.

After their return to power in 1975, the Social Democrats sought to develop a longer-term coherent strategy, based on long-term agreements, with a coherent parliamentary majority behind them. This was the aim in the so-called 'September Agreement' (1975), 'August Agreement' (1976) and the formation of the Social Democrat-Liberal coalition of August 1978. The September Agreement of 1975 based on a firm 'majority grouping' was hailed as a pact for a legislature. However, the world economy did not recover, and the relatively optimistic assumptions on which the Agreement was based were not realised, thus imposing new and more drastic measures. The 1976 August Agreement involved a 6 per cent norm in wage rises, and heavier expenditure cuts. It passed by a majority of only three in the *Folketing*. Soon labour disputes broke out in protest against the norm, which the LO (the central trade union organisation) did little to control. The government responded with a price and wage freeze until the renewal of collective agreements in March 1977, and firm penal measures against unofficial strikes became necessary in the aftermath of the tanker drivers' strike in December. With a difficult period of collective bargaining due, with the accumulated external debt now equal to 14 per cent of GDP, and inflation already above 10 per cent and rising sharply, new measures were needed. The government could find no coherent majority for its proposed package of housing, economic and defence policy measures, and so in January 1977 it went to the country. After the impressive gains it made in that election, it was able to create a majority for a very similar package. The collective agreements proposed by the official mediator were rejected by the Employers' Organisation, and had to be enforced by law. A complementary package, involving an increase in VAT to 18 per cent, a job creation programme and other tax and duty increases, was approved.

By mid-1978, inflation was under control and fell back to under 9 per cent. But annual increases in earnings were running at 10–11 per cent, as against the norm of 6 per cent, which was a danger for the future. Unemployment was now above 8 per cent. The external deficit had not fallen as far as official forecasts had anticipated, only falling from a high point of 2,954m. EUA in 1977 to 2,198m. EUA in 1978, rising again in 1979. New measures were needed. The political situation too was different; the 'bourgeois' block, which had supported the August and September Agreements and the March 1977 measures, was moving towards a revival of the idea of a 'bourgeois' coalition of the four parties, which had narrowly failed to gain power in 1975. In addition to forming a coherent majority for its economic policy, the Jørgensen government sought to 'detach' one or more than one party from this 'bourgeois' block. This was the genesis of the *Venstre*-Social Democrat government formed in August 1978. The economic policy of the coalition was to be in essence 'more of the same': VAT was increased to a record 20.25 per cent, a freeze on prices and profits and limitations on wage claims up to the March 1979 renewal of collective agreements, and more expenditure cuts. Despite fierce LO opposition, this coalition lasted until October 1979. On several occasions it was forced to take difficult economic measures, including a virtual wage freeze in the spring of 1979, when collective agreements came up for renewal—a familiar scenario. Immediately after the election of October 1979, the government imposed new measures to control prices, wages and the money supply, and devalued the Krone by 4.7 per cent within the European Monetary System (EMS).

4. *Social Change*

The 1960s and 1970s have seen important social, economic and cultural changes, which have had considerable influence on the climate of politics and on the political agenda in Denmark. The period has seen the oil crisis; the environmental and anti-nuclear movements; the new-left and student movements of the 1960s; entry to the EEC; and the social and cultural permissive society and reaction to it. All these issues have provoked political debate, and have placed new issues on the agenda or forced new approaches to existing problems.

From the mid-1960s, the consensus of pragmatic welfarism which had been the basis of successive governments of the centre-left and centre-right since the 1940s came increasingly under attack. Its assumptions of continued economic growth, state responsibility for welfare and underlying materialism were vigorously assaulted from every ideological compass-point.

The influence of the radical left (until 1960 virtually confined to the DKP), to the left of the Social Democrats, had always been limited, especially in the depths of the cold war. The DKP, unlike other Communist parties in Western Europe, had an almost entirely working-class membership—and by then an ageing one. Its parliamentary and political influence was limited. Its rigid and Stalinist bureaucracy offered no attraction to the increasing number of students and the anti-nuclear weapons demonstrators (they protested against *all* nuclear weapons, not only American weapons!) of the late 1950s.

With the founding of the *Socialistisk Folkeparti* (SF),[17] which had entered the *Folketing* in 1960, and the splinter *Venstre-socialisterne* (VS) in 1968, the situation changed. These parties were independent of Moscow; they sought to be genuine mass parties, capable of influencing the political environment. They could exercise pressure on the Social Democrats in a way denied to the DKP. These parties attracted support from students, teachers, journalists, anti-nuclear campaigners and former left-wing Social Democrats. The influence exerted by these parties in Parliament and among the trade unions was, except for short periods, very limited, perhaps less than their 9–12 per cent of the popular vote should have entitled them to. However, from the mid-1960s the influence of the radical Left was much more significant than a mere analysis of their parliamentary impact would lead one to suppose. A clear distinction must be made between 'institutional power', which was limited, and 'cultural power', which was significant. 'Cultural power' is the power to influence the way people think about society, the way they perceive and analyse events, and the style and content of political and social debate. It is exercised through the press, the electronic media, literature, the arts, the universities.[18]

The 'radical generation' of the 1960s was particularly active in these spheres and, as time went on, its increasingly critical analysis of the existing society and its institutions, assumptions and power structure came to be more and more felt. These new modes of thought assumed a dominant 'agenda-setting' position. More conservative thought was temporarily placed to a large extent on the defensive.

However, by the late 1960s it had become clear that the radical message was not widely acceptable; in particular, the proposed alliance of workers and radical students was rejected by the workers. Existing structures—and this, one must suppose, can hardly have represented anything but a self-fulfilling prophesy to the radical Left—proved extremely resistant to the march of new ideas. They would neither disappear nor be easily by-passed as irrelevances, as some more utopian new-Left theorists appeared to imagine. A new approach developed, which was in a sense two-tracked —'going to the people' in order to create a new consciousness, and 'the long march through the institutions', which meant accepting political involvement in domestic political issues—through the most receptive of the existing structures, trade unions—and in mass movements or in some political parties, mostly the SF, the VS, the Social Democrats but also the Communists, who began to find a second wind with an influx of new, younger intellectual militants. By integrating themselves in the mainstream, the influence of their radical thought grew in the vehicles of 'cultural power' mentioned above.

The 'People's Movement against the EEC', which was set up in 1972 and led to the referendum campaign against Danish membership, was one manifestation of this development. Although the People's Movement was a 'one-issue' movement directed against the EEC, and in fact included the ultra-liberal Justice Party and dissident Conservatives, its leadership, driving force and prevailing ideology were largely new-left in inspiration: opposition to Western capitalist materialism, opposition to the idea that 'big is good', the battle of the 'people' against the political establishment. Indeed, this fact was clearly perceived by the other side, and many 'yes' partisans were just as eager to defeat the new-left as to support EEC membership. Even though the People's Movement lost the referendum by 2–1, it had done much to cement relationships between parties and organisations of the new-left on the one hand and individuals who had hitherto remained outside on the other; it had also spread new-left ideas to new groups and set the precedent of 'hybrid bodies', i.e. movements composed both of parties, organisations and individuals campaigning for a single issue. Its lessons were of great value to the later Women's Movement, tenant groups, and the movement against nuclear power.[19]

From this amalgam—this melting pot of ideas—came both a delayed reaction against the new direction, and more systematic developments of the new ideas which had burst into people's consciousness. The environmental movement, which gained its first real impact with the dramatic conclusions of the Club of Rome, received a powerful reinforcement with the oil crisis of 1973. Better husbandry of scarce raw materials, the search for new 'clean' and 'renewable' sources of energy, less destructive methods of production and less wasteful patterns of consumption were no longer mere idealistic objectives, but became hard, economic necessity.

In 1975, Ivar Nørgaard, the Minister of External Economic Relations, launched a wide-ranging debate on zero-growth through three articles in *Politiken*. These original articles and the ensuing public debate raised both the economic issue and the question of non-material growth and the quality of life. That a Social Democratic minister should have taken up an issue which was bound to be devisive for his own party, and which was an implicit questioning of many 'Welfarist' values, is perhaps indicative of the penetration of many new-left ideas. Two years later, in 1977, a former Radical minister, Kresten Helveg Petersen, and two academics published a book entitled *Oprør fra Midten* (Revolt from the Centre).[21] This book, in a sense, carried on where the zero-growth debate left off. It inspired an even greater public debate through press comment, articles and debates involving its authors and others, and led to a periodical magazine propagating their ideas being founded. The first part of the book is a critique of present Danish society and of the two main Western ideologies: capitalist liberalism and Marxism: both were stated to be endangering individual freedom and creativity, and, more seriously, to be growth-oriented and resource-wasting. They challenge the rationality of large size, and, in the second part of their work, attempt to sketch out an outline of Danish society based on the economic ideas expressed by Schumacher in 'Small is Beautiful'. This would require decentralisation, the creation of local democratic units, and small self-managing units of production in an ecologically balanced society. The existing state structure, political parties, and organisations such as trade unions would require radical transformation. The book presents these concepts as practical politics which *individuals*, and not new parties or organisations, can realise through accepting fully the logic of the ideas and working through existing structures for their gradual implementation, sector by sector. The debate is far from being finished. Certainly, initial response has been mixed, and many effective technical objections have been raised to the analysis. No one can tell what impact such a debate will have. There can be no doubt that many of the ideas expressed in the book, and, above all, the book's methodology are very much in the new-left tradition.

At the same time, the new-left has not remained unchallenged. As early as 1970, the Christian People's Party (KRF) was founded. It was a reaction against the increasingly 'amoral' tendency of public life; Denmark was becoming increasingly de-Christianised and atheistic; and moral values and standards were declining in an increasingly materialistic society (on this point at least there was a congruence with the analysis of the new-left). More specifically, it was a bitter reaction against the failure of the VKR coalition (1968 – 71) to 'roll back' these tendencies; on the contrary it was precisely this government which had brought in legislation liberalising abortion and freeing pornography from all censorship and control. From 1971, the Party participated in *Folketing* elections, injecting these new 'moral' issues into political debate.

The Danish Radio and Television (*Danmarks Radio*), founded in 1935, is a state monopoly. Since 1959, programming and control has been in the hands of a *Radiorådet* (Radio Council), in which twenty-two of its twenty-seven members are nominated by Parliament by proportional representation. Unlike Norway and Sweden, where the Radio Councils contain only some parliamentary appointees, the Danish *Radioråd* members (even the five coming from listeners' and viewers' associations) are mostly political figures. The *Radiorådet* is therefore a political body, in which ideological controversy can easily develop. Already, the KRF was concerned about left-wing influence in Danmarks Radio; however, when Erhard Jakobsen, the right-wing Social Democratic Mayor of Gladsaxe, left his party and founded the new *Centrums-Demokraterne* (CD) in 1973, he seized on this issue with his customary talent for the dramatic and spectacular. It became a major election issue for CD in all ensuing elections, and Erhard Jakobsen had more impact on it than KRF had been able to achieve. The Progress Party of Mogens Glistrup also took up the issue of the left-wing dominance in the arts, the media and the universities. Most of its voters tended to have culturally right-wing views, and indeed the party had a faintly anti-intellectual strain in its propaganda, with its attacks on 'all-knowing bureaucrats and intellectuals', on 'paper pushers' and 'desk popes'. Kresten Poulsgaard, a FRP MF, has been an outspoken opponent of left-wing and advanced culture. However, the main thrust of the Progress Party's attack has been against the waste of public funds in supporting activities of no interest—and indeed possibly repugnant —to the man in the street and the taxpayer.

The arrival of the Progress Party on the scene in 1972 also brought into question the Welfare State and its ever-increasing scope. The standard of tax revolt was linked with demands for dramatic reductions in the activity of the state, which would have reduced it to a 'night watchman' role. The extreme views of the Progress Party did not themselves command much support outside its ranks, but wide sections of public opinion and several parties (DR, KF, *Venstre*) were susceptible to some of its analysis. The party's very existence was a source of pressure. In parliamentary and political terms, it has been fairly successfully contained, but it is now a permanent feature of the political landscape. Its deterrent effect should not be underestimated, nor should the impact of its thinking on public opinion.

The interest which these issues have aroused, and the extent to which political parties have adopted them as central planks in their platforms, whereas they have been marginal in other Western democracies, shows that there has been something of a '*kulturkampf*' in Denmark in the 1960s and 1970s, in which both sides have made some gains, but which appears now to have reached something of a stalemate. It is clear that the 1980s will repeat the patterns of neither the 1950s, nor the 1960s and '70s.

REFERENCES

1. Population figures are taken from *Basic Statistics of the Community* (hereafter *Eurostat*), Statistic Office of the European Community (1979), table 1.
2. *Eurostat*, table 146, p. 183.
3. See *Denmark*, Copenhagen: Foreign Ministry, 1974 edition.
4. A.T. Lindström, *Landet Slesvig-Holstens Politiske Historie i Hovedtraek 1945–54*, Flensborg: Centralbibliotek for Sysdslesvig, 1975, pp. 150–1 and 165–7.
5. For an economic history of Denmark, see Svend Aage Hansen, *Økonomisk Vaekst i Danmark*, vols. I and II. Copenhagen: Akademisk Forlag, 1974.
6. Hansen, *op.cit.*, vol. II, pp. 51ff.
7. See C.G. Uhr, 'Economic Development in Denmark, Norway and Sweden' in K. Cerny (ed.), *Scandinavia at the Polls*, American Enterprise Institute for Public Policy Research (hereafter 'AEI'), Washington, 1977 (pp. 224–36).
8. *Eurostat*, table 146.
9. *Eurostat*, tables 18 and 65–81.
10. *Eurostat*, tables 93, 94, 97.
11. Energy figures taken from *Eurostat*, tables 47, 50, 51, 52.
12. Economic growth: *Eurostat*, table 17; unemployment: *Eurostat*, table 10.
13. For statistics on inflation and wages, see *Eurostat*, tables 111, 114–19.
14. *Eurostat*, tables 127–32.
15. For social expenditure, see *Eurostat*, tables 120–1, 124–6 and 127–32.
16. *Keesings Contemporary Archives*, 1976–9, *passim*.
17. On the new-left, see U. Schmiederer, *Die Socialistische Volkspartei Dänemarks: Eine Partei der neuer Linken*, Frankfurt: Verlag Neue Kritik, 1969.
18. D. Tarschys, 'The Changing Basis of Radical Socialism in Scandinavia' in K. Cerny (ed.), *Scandinavia at the Polls*, *op.cit.*, pp. 150–2.
19. J. Fitzmaurice, 'Scandinavian Referenda and the EEC' in *European Report*, Spring 1973.

III. THE STRUCTURE OF GOVERNMENT

1. *The Constitution*

Denmark's first democratic constitution was adopted in 1849 and amended in 1866, 1915 and 1920. After the Second World War, a totally new constitution was drawn up and, after approval in a referendum, came into force in 1953. The 1953 constitution[1] confirms that Denmark is a democratic constitutional monarchy. The monarch is the head of state, in whose name all acts of state are carried out, as in Britain. The Crown is removed from politics by the formal constitutional requirement that all official Acts should be countersigned by a minister, who thereby assumes responsibility for the Act.

Executive power is in the hands of the government, headed by a Prime Minister, who is the head of government. The government is responsible for proposing measures to Parliament, administering the laws, carrying out foreign policy and administering the budget. The government is responsible to the unicameral *Folketing* (parliament) of 179 members, elected by direct universal suffrage, by all citizens of more than eighteen years of age by proportional representation.

In addition to controlling the executive, the *Folketing* has legislative power, the sole right to vote supply, and the power to ratify treaties, declare war and cede parts of the realm. Danish sovereignty may be transferred to international bodies, but only to a limited degree, and where five-sixths of the members of the *Folketing* concur.

To replace the checks imposed by the second chamber, abolished by the 1953 constitution, a system of abrogative referenda was instituted. All bills, except those implementing treaty obligations and money bills, can be subjected to a referendum if one-third of the members of the *Folketing* so petition.

The constitution ensures the independence of the judiciary and creates the office of *ombudsmand* to investigate citizens' complaints against the administration. It guarantees basic rights and fundamental freedoms such as freedom of speech and assembly, and the right to due process of law, but also guarantees certain 'declaratory' social rights such as the rights to work and to social assistance.

The Constitution also guarantees the rights of local communities to a form of local administration. Greenland and the Faeroe Islands both have a special status; they have internal self-government under elected assemblies and executives. Their international relations are still in the hands of Denmark.

The procedure for constitutional amendment is very complicated and severe, and indeed no amendment has been undertaken since 1953. The amendments to the earlier 1849 constitution were largely formal; indeed they were made inevitable by external events such as the Slesvig war or the reunification with North Slesvig in 1920. An amendment must be adopted twice by Parliament with a general election intervening and then must be approved by a majority of those voting and by 40 per cent of the total electorate in a referendum, as against 45 per cent in the 1849 constitution. The only exception to this is a change in the minimum voting age, which merely requires approval by Parliament once and approval by a simple majority in a referendum.

2. *The Executive*

Denmark has been a hereditary constitutional monarchy since 1849. The King has been head of the executive, but has not exercised executive power directly. Until the early twentieth century, he did have considerable influence, and intervened directly in matters of state, but since then his influence has gradually declined to the point where all executive power is vested in the government.

Since 1953 the succession to the monarchy has been able to pass through the female as well as the male line. This change was made necessary by the fact that King Frederick IX had only daughters. In theory, the King is both head of state and head of the executive. Various official acts of state such as the appointment of the Prime Minister and other ministers, of senior officials, judges, ambassadors, the signing of bills, the act of clemency, the dissolution of Parliament, are acts which must bear the signature of the King or Queen. However, at the same time the 1953 constitution makes the monarch 'irresponsible' in the technical sense; he is discharged from any legal or political responsibility by the requirement of a countersignature from a member of the government, who thus assumes legal and political responsibility for the act in question. This requirement is carried to the point that in order to ensure the regularity of the appointment of a new Prime Minister, his nomination is countersigned by the incoming Prime Minister, who also signs the resignation of his predecessor.

3. *The Formation of Governments*

The only possible area of royal discretion lies in the appointment of a new government after an election or a political crisis.[2] Here the monarch has a wider field of choice than in Britain, where usually one party or another has a majority. Even in those cases where there is a change in the leadership of a party in power, there is usually no royal discretion in Britain, since both the main parties now elect their leaders. In Denmark, it is not infrequent that there is no obvious government coalition in view. Even if it is evident that one party is going to play the leading role in the government, it may not be totally clear which personality should lead the government.

Unlike Belgium, the Netherlands or Sweden, where political personalities are chosen by the Crown to conduct consultations with political leaders with a view to forming a government, the Danish monarch has the task of conducting the negotiations personally. Normally, the monarch convokes the leaders of all the parties represented in parliament to a round table meeting. Each leader will designate the person whom he considers should form the government. This indication is by no means equivalent to offering support for a particular coalition formula or a minority government. If a person is indicated by parties holding more than a majority of seats in Parliament, then it shows that at least there is no majority *against* that person. For example, the three parties of the left will usually indicate support for a Social Democrat, but this does not mean that they will give any support to a government led by a Social Democrat, only that for them this choice is the lesser evil.

If a clear majority indicates a particular personality, then the monarch will ask that person to attempt to form a government. This is no guarantee that he will be able to do so, for the 'indication' procedure is merely a 'negative clearing' process. However, it fulfils the constitutional and customary norms of Danish parliamentary democracy that a government does not need to have a positive majority in its favour, but needs merely not to have a majority against it. This permits many minority administrations to live on the 'tolerance' of a majority, which does not consider it opportune to bring it down.

The monarch may find that in the course of discussion, support emerges for a particular formula: a majority coalition composed of certain parties; or a minority government supported by other parties. Where, as in 1968, parties having a clear majority have publicly expressed their intention, before the election, of forming a coalition, where an outgoing government has the political support to continue, the situation will be clear. However, there are other cases where the monarch may charge a personality to explore a particular avenue, arising from the consultation procedure. In difficult cases, several rounds of talks may be necessary to arrive at a nomination. It is, however, rare for the person nominated by the monarch to fail to form a government, which of course often happens in other countries.

It is worth looking in detail at some cases in recent Danish history which illustrate the difficulties which may arise and the manner in which the monarch may become involved in political issues, even if only marginally.

The 1957 case shows no procedural particularities,[3] but it shows how contacts between various parties outside the formal consultations can considerably modify the situation. The election had led to serious losses for the Social Democrats and the *status quo* for the Radicals. The former S-R coalition would not have a majority. Even if the Communists were to indicate in favour of the outgoing Prime Minister, H.C. Hansen, there would be no more than just ninety votes—a crucial figure—in his favour. At that time, at the height of the Cold War, such a solution was politically difficult.

It was to be expected that the momentum of their election gains would carry the Liberals and Conservatives to power. The ultra-liberal Justice Party, which had gained three seats which gave it a total of nine, was expected to indicate a 'bourgeois' coalition. But there was an unwillingness on the part of the Social Democrats and Radicals to renounce power immediately, since the election had not provided a clear alternative. The first consultation round was inconclusive, insofar as the Justice Party remained non-committal in its attitude towards a 'bourgeois' coalition. This meant that no one obtained the magic designation of parties representing ninety votes in parliament.

The Conservatives and Liberals expected that their election gains and the logic of the situation would lead to their being asked to form a government. However, the Social Democrats and Radicals were not idle. They could, of course, have remained in power had they chosen to do so and await a parliamentary vote, but they had initially renounced this by resigning. This meant that the only clear way of outmanoeuvring the 'bourgeois' bloc was to obtain a majority coalition. Their minds began to turn to the Justice Party. Hitherto, this party had not been considered respectable, and almost as far beyond the political pale as the Communists; both Radicals and Social Democrats considered an alliance with it as 'against nature'. However, Finance Minister Kampman had for some time been in close touch with some leading figures in the Justice Party, and was able to convince his Prime Minister and Bertel Dahlgaard, the Radical leader (an outspoken critic of the Justice Party), that a 'triangular' coalition was possible.

The Justice Party was in fact inexperienced in the process of political bargaining. A protest party of course always takes a considerable risk in entering government, and in retrospect it is clear that the Justice Party was used by the two larger parties, who saw in it the means of achieving the purely negative end of preventing a 'bourgeois' coalition. They offered the Justice Party three cabinet posts and made only one major political concession to its programme—namely in agreeing to enact a special tax on incremental land values; this was to lead to a violent campaign against it from the right and from the Landowners' Association. The Justice Party served as a lightning conductor for all the unpopular measures taken by the government, eventually losing all its seats in the 1960 election, and this in spite of the fact that the general performance of the government both in economic and political terms had been regarded as above average.

The events which followed the 1975 election[4] also illustrate the complexities of the consultation procedure which surrounds the formation of a government. Here the Queen seemed to be seeking to avoid direct involvement in an extremely complicated situation, but even 'non-decisions' were 'decisions' which influenced the course of events.

The 1974–5 one-party *Venstre* (Liberal) government of Poul Hartling had lived dangerously. It concluded four major pacts on economic policy (February, May, June and September) in which a total of six parties participated. The Social Democrats joined in only two pacts (the first and third) and not the two most controversial in May and September. The core support parties were the KRF, the CD and the KF, each of which joined in three pacts. The most controversial (tax cutting) pacts both received the support of *Venstre*, the KRF and the KF. These two received support from either the FRP (in May) or the DR (in September).

The ten-point package presented on 3 December 1974 was to be considered as a '*helhedsløsning*' (a 'global policy package'); it was therefore barely negotiable, which fed suspicion that *Venstre* was seeking a pretext for an election. In the *Folketing* debate of 5 December, only eighty-one votes appeared to support the package and the four left-wing parties rejected it. Hartling avoided a vote, which would have forced the government to resign and thereby become a caretaker administration, giving himself an important advantage in post-election manoeuvring.

The ensuing election gave a rather confused result. The 'old parties' made a partial come-back after the seismic election of 1973. *Venstre's* share of the vote rose from 12.3 to 23.3 per cent, and it now held forty-two seats, more than at almost any time since 1945. But the group of small parties which had been the core of his support (KRF, KF, CD, sometimes RV, DR) lost heavily. Their combined share of the vote fell more than *Venstre's* gains, from 35.1 to 21.9 per cent. Altogether, they and *Venstre* would now only hold seventy-

eight seats as against eighty-four seats in the outgoing *Folketing*.
Even with the Progress Party, their position was not unassailable
(now 102), since it was impossible that *all* the parties *and* the FRP
would be able to agree on all issues. The Social Democrats made
useful gains (up to fifty-three seats) and the combined strength of the
three far-left parties rose to twenty.

Hartling had won a pyrrhic victory. He remained in office and
first attempted a coalition with the Social Democrats, which failed.
He then sought a coalition with his now embittered former partners
(V, RV, KRF), but this also failed. On 23 January, the *Folketing* was
obliged by the constitution to meet. This forced a clarification to
Hartling's disadvantage: despite his conciliatory speech, a Social
Democrat motion calling for his resignation was carried by eighty-
six votes to eighty-five with five abstentions (CD and Lemborn
[KF]). Now a device borrowed from the Benelux countries and
Sweden was tried. Karl Skytte was appointed as an '*informateur*'.
He sought to build up a S-V coalition (ninety-five votes), but failed
on 7 February 1975 since the Social Democrats remained anta-
gonistic to Hartling's proposed wage freeze. By now Hartling
himself was an obstacle to agreement.

He now sought a minority 'bougeois' coalition (V, KF, KRF, CD)
with sixty-five votes, which would have had the external support of
Glistrup's FRP. The list of ministers was ready when Glistrup with-
drew support since he was accorded no guarantees on policies. At the
eleventh hour, Hartling was persuaded to withdraw (and here the
Queen may have played a part), since his proposed coalition would
not have met the criteria of the Resolution adopted earlier calling for
a broad-based government, and would almost certainly have fallen
immediately. The Queen now had only one viable alternative which
she duly took: a minority Social Democratic government under
Anker Jørgensen, which would seek support both to its right and
left.

This government crisis was novel in that the Constitutional provisions on resignation (or not) played a role, as did the *Folketing*,
and the Crown attempted to avoid involvement to a greater extent
than usual, but appeared clearly at various points to favour either a
broad-based solution or a viable minority government—the actual
outcome.

The formation of the 1978 Social Democrat-*Venstre* coalition was
different.[5] There had been no election, nor had the government
resigned, nor was it threatened with imminent defeat in the
Folketing. The Prime Minister merely decided to enlarge his government. The Queen was not involved in consultations. The discussions
continued sporadically between various parties from the Spring

1978. First of all the parties of the September pact (1975), the core of support for the Jørgensen government, were canvassed. Then *Venstre* and the *Radikale Venstre* were sounded out. *Venstre* had the counter-proposal of a four-party government including the Conservatives. These initiatives were mere sparring. By August, *Venstre* and *Social Demokratiet* had dropped their proposed allies and entered into direct bilateral discussions—reviving, as we have seen, ideas already floated in the 1975 crisis.

These discussions between negotiating teams from the two parties began on 9 August, and were held at Marienborg, the Prime Minister's country residence. *Venstre*, under new leadership since the departure of Hartling to become the United Nations High Commissioner for Refugees, was very flexible. The Social Democrats had more difficulties, anticipating later LO (labour movement) and party left-wing opposition. Their delegation shifted to include ministers who were required to make concessions: Jens Kampman (Taxation), Poul Hove (Housing) and Kjeld Olesen (Public Works and Transport). All these significantly later either resigned or were excluded from the subsequent S-V government, but in fact only Kampman was associated with the left. Leading left-wing members of the outgoing cabinet—Ritt Bjerregaard (Education), Svend Auken (Labour) and Ivar Nørgaard (Trade)—retained their portfolios. The case of Auken was especially delicate in view of his responsibilities for incomes policy and relations with the trade unions. There were considerable comings and goings between the negotiating team, the parliamentary group (Rigsgaard Knudsen, its chairman, resigned from the negotiating team), and the party executive. There were also poisonous disputes between the party leadership and the LO chairman, Thomas Nielsen, as to how far the LO had or had not been kept informed and by implication approved the coalition.

The government formed after the 1966 election was not a coalition, even though discussions were held with SF on the possibilities of forming one. The Social Democrat government merely remained in office. Despite its losses, it was sure not to be censured because it reached agreement and established a formal contact committee (along the lines of the pact between labour and the Liberals in Britain) with the SF.

This illustrates in action a basic principle of Danish parliamentarism, namely that a sitting government enjoys an important tactical advantage. A government may remain in office if it is clear that there is no majority *against* it; it does not have to seek a positive majority. This enabled governments led by the Social Democrats to remain in office without resignation, and without negotiation, in

1964 and 1977. The situation in 1971 was similar by extension. The outgoing VKR government would have fallen if it had remained; a Social Democratic government supported by the SF would not fall, and thus it was the obvious alternative. This 'negative majority' principle kept the government in office at least until after the EEC referendum in 1972, since the 'bourgeois' parties were unwilling to bring it down before that issue was settled. Similarly, the 1950–3 V-K majority government remained in office without a clear majority for three years because the Social Democrats and Radicals did not wish to jeopardise the constitutional reforms then in progress.

4. *The Government*

The government will vary in size, consisting usually of between seventeen and twenty-one members[6]. Coalition governments will often be larger due to the need to accommodate the coalition parties and their various wings. Thus the 1978–9 S-V coalition had twenty-one members (fourteen Social Democrats and seven *Venstre*). The homogeneous *Venstre* government of 1974–5, at the other extreme, had only twelve members, some of whom held several portfolios. There have been several changes in government structures in recent years, and new portfolios have emerged. The responsibility for Nordic affairs has moved from the Prime Minister's office to the External Economic Affairs Ministry, and thence to the Foreign Ministry; EEC affairs have been separated from the Foreign Ministry and given to the External Economic Affairs Ministry. An Environmental Ministry has been created. Public Works and Transport have sometimes been separate and sometimes amalgamated. The Ministry of Taxation was created in 1975, separate from the Finance Ministry.

It is usual when a coalition government is formed for the coalition parties to agree on the number of posts and their allocation to each party. The choice of individuals to fill a party's allocation will fall to that party alone. Often the choice will be self-evident, and be in part dictated by the need to ensure the representation in the government of representatives of the different wings of a party. For example, when the S-V government was formed in 1978, it was generally accepted that the left-wing Social Democrat Svend Auken should keep the key post of Labour Minister. For the *Venstre* ministers, the principle of competence and previous experience were paramount in the choice of Andersen (Finance), Kofoed (Agriculture) and Natalie Lind (Justice). However, in 1957 when the 'triangle' coalition was formed, the Social Democrats and Radicals insisted that the Justice

Party include one of its most experienced figures, Oluf Pedersen (Fisheries).

There are no 'ministers of state' or deputy ministers in Denmark, although sometimes a Minister without Portfolio is explicitly designated to assist another minister, as in the case of Lise Østergaard, who in 1978 was given responsibility for development policy under the Foreign Minister; constitutionally, she became a member of the Cabinet. In some international bodies such as the EEC Council of Ministers, the *Departamentschef* (Permanent Secretary) of a minister may act in the latter's place as if he were a deputy minister. There is also no post of Deputy Prime Minister; however, when there is a coalition government, leaders of the coalition parties function as a sort of inner Cabinet.

Formally, government decisions are taken by a *Kongelige Beslutning* (Royal decision) in the *Statsråd* (State Council), composed of the ministers and the monarch, but increasingly decisions in almost all matters are in reality taken by the Cabinet, and subsequently ratified, as a pure formality, in the *Statsråd* without debate. The Cabinet meets at least once a week, on Tuesdays (more frequently when necessary), to consider major policy issues, approve bills or budgetary appropriations before presentation to parliament, foreign policy initiatives and ministerial interventions in the *Folketing*. Decision-making is mainly informal and by consensus. Cabinet discussion can have a special importance in coalition governments where some parties do not have ministers with direct responsibility for certain policy areas.

There are Cabinet committees composed of four or five ministers, who prepare issues for Cabinet decisions.[7] These exist for taxation, energy policy, economic policy and EEC policy. The EEC Committee is paralleled by a civil service committee representing the same ministers.

Ministers prepare bills or other policy action with their officials, co-ordinate with other ministers, and examine proposals in the appropriate ministerial committee before the Cabinet takes a decision. Social Democrat ministers have kept the special subject committees of their parliamentary group informed and taken note of their views, as well as consulting interested parties. Other political parties are usually not consulted at this stage, unless of course the issue concerned has formed part of a *'forlig'* (package deal)—something in which Danish politics specialises heavily. Before a bill goes to the *Statsråd* for formal approval, the minister will usually inform his parliamentary group. With the Social Democrats, this is routine; bills are approved by the Cabinet on Tuesday, are presented to regular group meetings on Tuesday afternoon, and then go to the

Statsråd on Wednesday.

Where a '*forlig*' is being negotiated, the Social Democrats at least prepare their position when in power in discussions between the Government and group (the term 'group' is used to denote the 'parliamentary party'). The competent ministers and the S-group chairman participates fully in the inter-party talks. When *Venstre* were in power in 1973 – 5, they followed a similar procedure.

Each May, ministers forward proposed legislation for the next *Folketing* session in October. These proposals are collected by the Prime Minister's office. This inventory is then the basis for discussion on the Government's programme to be announced by the Prime Minister at the opening session.

Not only are ministers politically responsible for the policies of their departments and in particular for the Acts which they countersign; they are also legally responsible. The 1849 constitution established a procedure similar in many ways to the impeachment of public officials which formerly existed in Britain and is still applied in the United States. Article 16(2)[8] of the constitution lays down that the monarch or the *Folketing* may prosecute ministers for breaches of responsibility. Such prosecutions take place before a special court with this unique function, namely the *Rigsret* (State Court) composed of fifteen *Højesterets* (high court) judges and fifteen members elected by the *Folketing*. The exact nature of the offences which could be prosecuted, the penalties which could be imposed and the relationship between the *Rigsret* and the ordinary courts and prosecuting authorities was left vague. In the early years, a number of cases were brought, mostly involving expenditure of funds, without the consent of the *Folketing*, but since 1910 no case has been brought before the *Rigsret*. Between 1855 and 1939 no less than fourteen bills were introduced to regulate the legal responsibility of ministers, but none were passed. In 1939, a bill did pass almost all stages but was never promulgated. The period of Nazi occupation could have given rise to *Rigsret* cases against several ministers after 1945, but it was tacitly agreed that this should not be done. It was in 1959 that a case next arose. The Opposition sought to raise a case against Mr Kjaerbøl, Minister for Greenland, in relation to a ship which had sunk off Greenland. It was shown that 'dereliction of duty', a traditional form of charge, was too imprecise. The case was not brought, but the Opposition tabled a Bill, which was taken over by the Government and became law in 1964 (Law No.117 of 15 April 1964), concerning the responsibility of ministers. This law establishes penalties of fines and up to two years' imprisonment for offences under it. But it does nothing to clarify an issue which has been much discussed in doctrinal debate: is the competence of the *Rigsret* exclusive? In other words, if the *Rigsret* is not asked to try a case, does this prevent the ordinary courts from doing so? The Højesteret seemed, in its judgement in a 1946 case, to maintain that the competence of the *Rigsret* was virtually exclusive, but doubt has remained.

5. *The Folketing*

Since 1955 the Danish Parliament has been unicameral. The *Riksdag* of pre-1953 days consisted of the *Folketing* (popularly elected chamber) and the more conservative *Landsting*. The present single chamber, the *Folketing*, is central to Danish political life and occupies a strong formal position under the constitution. Governments are responsible to it; it is the legislative; it votes supply; and it has important powers in the field of foreign policy. Everywhere in the developed world, modern parliaments, with their nineteenth-century liberal origins and structures, are finding it difficult to maintain control and influence over the ever-growing ramifications of government in a modern interventionist Welfare State. Power is in danger of slipping increasingly into the hands of the civil service, pressure groups and private companies which are large enough to influence the economy. This has been no less true of Denmark. However, the nature of Danish politics is such that the considerable amount of wheeling and dealing required to make the system work in an eleven-party *Folketing* takes place within the forum of Parliament, if not in plenary session, then in the corridors, in party meetings and in negotiations between the parliamentary leaders of various parties, but not outside the ambit of the *Folketing*.

Under the constitution (and the electoral law of 1953), the *Folketing* has a maximum complement of 179 members of whom two are elected in the Faroes and two in Greenland. Under the current electoral law, and indeed since 1953, the *Folketing* has in fact had 179 members, of which 175 are elected in metropolitan Denmark.

The *Folketing* is elected by direct universal suffrage of all Danish citizens over the age of eighteen. The move towards votes at eighteen has been very cautious, and was only achieved finally in 1978. Changes in the voting age must be submitted to a referendum. Sometimes it has taken several attempts to obtain popular consent to a reduction in the voting age: it was fixed at twenty-three in 1953 and reduced to twenty-one in 1961. The 1969 referendum to reduce the age to eighteen failed (78.3 per cent voted 'No') and in 1971 a less radical reduction to twenty only passed with 55 per cent in favour on an 87 per cent poll held in conjunction with a *Folketing* election. Women have been entitled to vote since 1915. In 1971, 17 per cent of elected MFs (Members of the *Folketing*) were women. By 1977, this hardly changed with 23 per cent, but in 1979 it rose to 31 per cent.

The electoral system is a fairly pure form of proportional representation, which only gives a marginal advantage to the larger parties. The 175 seats allotted to metropolitan Denmark are divided up with 135 being elected in the electoral districts and forty being supplementary seats used to correct the non-proportionality of the election in the districts.

The country is divided into three electoral areas: 1. Greater Copenhagen, 2. the Islands, and 3. Jutland. There are seventeen constituencies (three Greater Copenhagen constituencies and fourteen following *Amt* (county) boundaries. Within these seventeen constituencies there are 103 nomination districts. The latter relate only to the procedure of choosing the individuals to fill seats allotted to a party. In the allocation of the 135 + 40 seats to the parties only the seventeen constituencies count. Each MF represents, on average, 28,000 votes as against 87,000 in the United Kingdom.

Individuals and party lists may put up for election. An individual faces serious handicaps, since he can only put up in one of the seventeen constituencies, which would require their vote to be concentrated, but over a relatively wider area than a British single-member constituency. As a result, no individual has even been close to being elected since 1945, and in the last three elections there has not been a single individual candidate, even though only twenty-five signatures are needed for nomination.

Parties may present lists. A party which was represented in the previous legislature may present lists with no further formality, but new parties must present to the Ministry of the Interior a list of signatures corresponding to 1/175 of the votes cast at the previous *Folketing* election, which now represents about 17,200 electors. Parties must indicate which of the three permitted types of list they intend to use. Each type gives a different degree of influence to the voters in deciding the order in which seats allotted to a party fall to its candidates. 1, each candidate is nominated in only one of the nomination districts in his constituency; in this case he obtains his personal votes and only those party (impersonal votes) cast in that nomination district, 2, each candidate is nominated simultaneously in several or all of the nomination districts in the constituency. In this case he receives his own personal votes plus an equal share of the party's impersonal votes in the whole constituency; thus the order of election is decided solely by the personal votes. Or 3, the party tables a single list which determines the order of transfer of the impersonal votes, thus giving the party the maximum control over the order of election. Most parties now use type 2, but DKP and VS use type 3.

There are no rules about campaign expenditure, nor any significant government subsidies for campaigns. Local authorities may make rules for the preservation of order, which may control the putting up of posters and stickers. The Social Democratic party spent 1,849,147 DKr. on the 1973 election and 2,743,408 DKr. in 1975. The Radio Council establishes clear rules for broadcasting. No candidate may appear in any programme (even old films!) during the campaign. Otherwise, the TV and radio offer each party authorised to participate in the election an equal number of broadcasts which the party may produce itself with finance from the Radio Council, or else use Radio Council facilities. These broadcasts increasingly take the form of 'phone-ins'. One or two panel discussions are organised during the campaign in which all the parties participate on an equal-time basis.

There are no rules about the day on which an election should be held, but usually it is a Tuesday. Voting takes place between 0900 and 2100 hours. Each voter may cast a vote either for a party list or cast a personal vote for a candidate on a list. Results are usually very quickly centralised at the Ministry of the Interior, which now uses computers to establish the distribution of seats. Normally, a clear result is known by midnight. At that time, a TV panel discussion with all the party leaders is held for a first reaction to the results.

Turnout in Denmark is very high, varying between 80 and 90 per cent. The lowest turnout in comparatively recent years was 79.2 per cent in 1939. The highest was 89.5 per cent in 1943. In peace time it was 89.3 per cent in 1968 (the most polarised election in recent years). There is no evidence that turnout is falling. The winter election of 1977 saw a turnout of 88.7 per cent.

The distribution of seats to each electoral area and constituency is carried out by using a special formula fixed in Paragraph 17 of the Electoral Law (population and electorate and area in square km. × 20 ÷ 175 for the total of 175 seats and the sum of the three constituencies divided by 135 for the constituency seats). For the 1977 election, these operations gave the following results:

	Constituency seats	Supplementary seats
Greater Copenhagen	19	+ 5
Islands	54	+ 16
Jutland	62	+ 19

Compared with the position in 1971, Copenhagen had lost two seats and the Islands had gained two. The position of Jutland was unchanged.

The allocation of seats to the parties uses the d'Hondt divisor method but instead of applying the d'Hondt divisor 1,2,3,4. . ., the electoral law uses 1.4, 3, 5, 7, which is a modification of the Saint-Laguë method. The total vote for each party (or individual candidate) in each constituency is divided by the successive divisors until the total number of seats falling to that constituency has been allocated. The largest quotient gives the first seat, and so on. An example is illustrated in the table on page 56.

These figures show that the system gives some advantage to larger parties. With 41.56 per cent of the vote, the Social Democrats have half the seats. In an eight-seat constituency, the Social Democrats obtained four seats for 41.83 per cent of the vote. In the largest constituency with fifteen seats, the results were only slightly more proportional. The Social Democrats obtained six seats (40 per cent) for 34 per cent of the vote.

When all the constituency results have been computed, the Interior Ministry goes on to calculate the distribution of the forty supplementary seats. Since 1964, the qualifications for participating in the distribution of the supplementary seats have been, first, winning at least 2 per cent of the votes cast, or secondly, winning at least one constituency seat, or thirdly, obtaining in two of the three electoral areas at least a number of votes equivalent to the average number of votes needed to elect one MF in that area. Before 1964 the 2 per cent requirement was stiffer, being fixed at 60,000 votes in the whole country. Under these more difficult rules, the Independents failed to qualify in 1953 or 1957 in spite of obtaining 2.3 and 2.7 per cent respectively. The Justice Party, eliminated in 1960 with 52,330 (2.2 per cent), would have survived under the new rules. No party has qualified under either the second or the third qualification only. No doubt if VS had failed to qualify in 1968 with just 2 per cent of the votes cast, excluding blank or void votes), it could not have qualified under the second qualification.

For the parties which qualify, the number of constituency seats won is compared with the proportional number of seats. For 1977, this calculation was as shown in the table on page 57.

The large parties have obtained the lion's share of the constituency seats; indeed, without the supplementary seats, S would have been only three seats short of an absolute majority. The small parties with a concentrated vote, usually in Copenhagen, were able to obtain constituency seats (DKP, SF, CD). With a larger number of parties, almost all the parties with 2 per cent of the vote obtained a fairly large proportion of their entitlement in constituency seats. This was not as true, with fewer parties, for example in 1971. The seats are then distributed over the parties and electoral areas using the Saint-Laguë (modified divisors) and finally over the seventeen different

ALLOCATION OF PARLIAMENTARY SEATS TO PARTIES
(*see pages 54–5*)

Copenhagen South	Total	S	R	KF	DR	SF	DKP	KRF	V	VS
	120,034	49,895 **1**	11,419 **6**	19,625 **4**	1,733	22,931 **3**	4,192	995	4,161	5,083
1. Quotient/divisor 1.4		35,632 **2**	8,156	14,018	1,238	16,379	2,994	711	2,972	3,631
		16,632 **5**	3,806	6,542		7,644				
		9,979								
		7,128								
Total seats:	6	3	1	1	0	1	0	0	0	0

	Proportional	Seats won in constituencies	Supplementary seats
S	65	65	0
RV	6	0	6
KF	15	11	4
DR	6	1	5
SF	7	2	5
DKP	7	3	4
CD	11	5	6
KRF	6	2	4
V	21	20	1
VS	5	0	5
FRP	26	26	0

constituencies by the same divisor method.

The last stage is the calculation of the particular candidates which are elected. Taking together personal votes and the number of votes cast for the party in the particular nomination district, or the proportion of party votes calculated according to each candidate's proportion of personal votes, gives the total number of votes for each candidate. Thereafter, seats (constituency seats first, then supplementary seats) are distributed in order of total votes obtained by each candidate, until all seats falling to each party have been allocated.

(a) Organisation of the Folketing[10]

The *Folketing* is elected for a four-year term but may be dissolved earlier by the Crown on the advice of the Prime Minister. Since 1971 elections have taken place on average every two years. Earlier a 'full term' ran to about 3½ years. Under the constitution, the *Folketing* meets as of right twelve days after its election and holds an annual session starting in October.

The *Folketing* is sole judge of the validity of elections and of the qualifications of its members. These are verified by its Elections Committee, which meets immediately after the election. It also reports to the *Folketing* on casual vacancies (those caused by death or resignation) which are filled by the next unelected candidate on the list of the party to which the outgoing MF belonged.

The *Folketing* elects its President each session. He will normally be an 'elder statesman' from a large party or the Radical Party which qualifies as one of the 'old parties'. He is somewhere between the politically active Speaker of the U.S. House of Representatives and the apolitical Speaker of the British House of Commons. He is the

Folketing's presiding officer and runs its administration. He is supported by four Vice-Presidents; informally, one vice-president comes from each of the four largest parties. Together the President and Vice-Presidents constitute the Praesidium which runs the *Folketing's* internal housekeeping and takes decisions on procedure and the organisation of debates. The last two Presidents have been Karl Skytte (RV) and K.B. Andersen (S).

Before 1971, the *Folketing* had a system of committees broadly similar to the traditional British system—a very small number of permanent committees and *ad hoc* legislative committees. In 1971, there was a radical change in committee organisation to the 'continental' model, with permanent committees for the various policy matters dealing both with legislation and other matters. There are currently twenty-four of these. Two deal exclusively with parliament's internal affairs (Election Committee and Rules Committee); four with foreign affairs and security matters (Market Relations; Foreign Affairs; External Relations; Defence); and the remainder with economic, social and financial matters. Most correspond to the competence of a ministry, which they 'shadow'.

The situation of three of the committees—those for Market Relations, Finance and Foreign Affairs—is special. The last is established directly by the constitution and the other two are set up by law, but all three exercise special functions, as we shall see.

Committees mostly have seventeen full members, and in addition two substitute members per party. The committees are elected by proportional representation. A group of ten members thus elects one committee member. Since many parties could not elect committee members alone, alliances can be formed. These are often mere arithmetic coalitions without political meaning. However, some alliances do have political significance as, for example, between anti-Market parties to gain seats in the Market committee; an alliance of the far-left parties; and, most recently, between the Social Democrats and *Venstre* as coalition partners giving them majorities in all committees (with one independent). Chairmanships are usually distributed between the parties and have even been held by far-left parties such as SF (e.g. Maigaard was Chairman of the Environmental Committee). The Chairman of the Finance Committee and the Market Committee are normally either from the government party or are Social Democrats.

Each party with members in the *Folketing* constitutes a parliamentary group with an executive of variable size from ten (S) to two for the smaller parties such as the VS. The key officers are the chairman and the '*politisk ordfører*' (spokesman). They represent the group in debates but also in the continuous negotiations between the parties to set up alliances and package deals on legislation. The executives will consult their respective groups on all key issues such as its voting position on issues, formation of alliances, appointment of spokesmen for various questions, and nomination of members to serve on committees. In most parties the group, often through one or more of its officers, has direct representation in the party's national executive, but it is rare for the group and party chairmanships to be held by the same person. Power is usually diffused. In the Social Democratic Party, it is the Party's national chairman who is its leader, whereas in the 'bourgeois' parties the party chairman is often a less important figure than the group chairman. The ranking order may also vary from time to time, depending on personality.

The parliamentary parties, and even less the individual members, have little in the way of staff or research facilities. The *Folketing's* budget provides a fixed sum for the expenses of the parliamentary groups, but no support for individual members. A large group such as the Social Democrats may have up to a dozen staff, notably secretaries to handle correspondence and filing, and may appoint one or two specialist advisors. The committees and the Praesidium as well as the full sessions are serviced by the permanent staff of the *Folketing*, and the *Folketing's* library provides a limited, neutral source of information and research for members and parliamentary groups. In this respect, the position of members is more like that of the British parliament than like many other continental assemblies which often provide considerable back-up for members.

(b) The Work of the Folketing[11]

The *Folketing* is at the centre of Danish politics; it is a cockpit, a theatre, a place of permanent negotiation between the parties. Like all parliaments, it has procedures and rules; it has customs governing behaviour, which give certain formality to its proceedings, but in spite of this its work and its style, like Danish society in general, are extremely informal.

The different types of activity of the *Folketing* (legislative, budgetary and control functions) and the various procedures provided for in the rules are in fact often closely interrelated, but we shall consider them separately for analytical purposes, then showing how the procedures are linked.

In one sense, the central task of the *Folketing* is to control the executive. Under the constitution, a government must resign if the *Folketing* passes a motion of censure against the Prime Minister.

Other ministers may be the object of a censure motion and must likewise resign. However, in practice, collective cabinet responsibility means that a motion of censure against one minister is considered by the government as an attack on the government as a whole. It is this central fact of 'parliamentary responsibility' which dominates political life. Other procedures of control over the executive gain their 'bite' from this central fact.

Formal censure motions are, however, rare. Since 1945 only three have been carried. Naturally, governments do make certain questions issues of confidence. The refusal of the *Folketing* to accept the wage freeze proposed by the government in 1967 following the devaluation of the Krone led to the government's immediate resignation. The debate on Hartling's economic package in December 1974 showed that only eighty-one votes were available to support the package; accordingly he dissolved the *Folketing* without a formal vote.

As we have seen, governments do not require formal investiture by a majority. This is tactically very important. Few Danish governments have had a formal majority (1957 – 64 and 1968 – 71); in a few other cases formal alliances or coalitions virtually guaranteed their survival (S-SF 1966 – 8) and S-V (1978 – 9), the September and August pacts of 1975 and 1976. At other times, a government lives on a 'toleration', no majority being willing to bring it down. This was the case of the V-K minority coalition in 1950 – 3; the S minority government of 1971 – 2 (because of the EEC referendum); and in 1974 when there was no obvious alternative to the Hartling Liberal government. The Social Democratic minority government, in office from 1975 (except for the SV coalition 1978 – 9), has been in a similar situation.

Sometimes motions stopping short of expressing no confidence are tabled—and passed—seeking to bind the government to a particular course of action; in 1975, a resolution was proposed by the opposition calling for a broad-based government; in 1973 a motion was passed which bound the government to consult the Market Relations Committee more strictly. This motion was an alternative to a censure motion and was passed by a SR-SF combination. This type of motion can be used to control the government's future conduct.

The twenty-four standing committees of the *Folketing* can also play an important role in controlling the government. These committees build upon expertise in their field; they consult on a regular basis with ministers and officials; they can call for papers and table written questions to ministers, and they receive comments from many interest groups. The committees can meet in private, and some (especially the Finance Committee, the MRC and the External Relations Committee) may, at the request of their chairman or the appropriate minister, receive information in confidence which forbids committee members even to disclose this information to parliamentary colleagues. The committees can on this basis—in addition to their legislative work—perform a permanent expert monitoring function. Matters may be disposed of formally or informally in the committee, and knowledge gained in it may serve as a basis for other action.

Parliamentary questions are now resorted to increasingly often as a device for controlling government action, as a means of soliciting information on the record, of urging action on some matter, and indeed of scoring political points. As such, they are largely (as in Britain) an opposition backbencher's tool. There is an oral question period in the *Folketing* on Wednesdays, during which ministers reply to questions orally and the author of the question is entitled to a short supplementary question, otherwise members may receive a written answer. (See Rule 20 of the Standing Orders.) This development has been fairly recent. In the 1953–4 session, only sixty questions were asked, all receiving an oral answer. By 1963–4, this had grown to 199, of which 149 were answered orally. In the 1977–8 session, 1,231 questions were tabled and only 342 were answered orally. These questions were tabled by 123 different members. Twenty-six members asked only one question. Two members each asked fifty-one questions. The most-questioned ministers were Justice (131), Taxation (88), Foreign Affairs (92) and Public Works (102). The Minister of Ecclesiastical Affairs received the fewest (4) questions. Otherwise the smallest number was received by the Minister of Fisheries (18). The Minister of Finance answered all his forty-six questions received in writing, otherwise most ministers answered over two-thirds of their questions in writing. The distribution of questions by party shows that questions are used by the opposition: FRP 477; VS 126; KF 119; SF 102; DKP 94. All these parties were in opposition in 1977–8, and all except for KF did not join alliances with the government. *Venstre* asked sixty-eight; DR sixty-four (in opposition). The Social Democrats—the largest group in parliament (even eliminating the twenty or so Social Democratic MF's who were ministers)—asked a mere eighteen questions.

A heavier form of parliamentary artillery is the 'interpellation'. This is a device for initiating a short debate. A question is tabled which the minister answers. Thereafter, the parties express their views—often with two rounds of debate—and one or more resolutions may be tabled at the end of the debate with amendments.

This device is in reality not a back-bencher's weapon. The

Folketing must accept the question by vote, which will mean that negotiation will have taken place between the parties and in the praesidium. Once the question is accepted, it is placed on the agenda within a time limit of ten days. A spokesman for the questioner introduces the question. The minister replies (sometimes several ministers), often at length. For example, in the debate on an interpellation on EEC policy held on 12 January 1978, both the Fisheries Minister and the Foreign Minister spoke. Thereafter a spokesman for each party may speak for up to twenty minutes. The Minister then speaks again, and a second round (five minutes per speaker) follows. The minister then concludes the debate. Sometimes the debate takes a whole day. Resolutions, counter-resolutions and amendments may be tabled at any time during the debate. Since 1978, such motions can only be tabled during debates on interpellations or on government statements.

The art of drawing up such motions is one of the finer points of Danish parliamentary procedure. They may take two forms: 'taking note of . . ., this House moves on to the next item on its agenda', or 'taking note of . . ., this House continues its debate on. . . .'. Since the second type of motion is voted on at once and first at the end of the debate, a tactical game can be played with such motions. The aim of the opposition will be to bring the *Folketing* to criticise government policy or tie the government to a specific line. In extreme form, an opposition motion can qualify as a censure motion. The government will often seek to avoid this and to avoid any commitment by tabling 'lightning conductor' motions (voted on first), which simply state 'this House takes note of the Minister's statement and moves on to the next point on its agenda'.

It is usual for certain types of questions to be a regular feature of each session, in order to permit a general debate on a subject. There is usually an EEC debate, each session being on the basis of a question as general as 'What information can the Minister give on current EEC issues?' tabled in the name of several parties. A general foreign policy debate will also be held each session on a neutral question such as the one debated on 25 November 1977: 'What information can the Foreign Minister give on the current foreign policy situation?'

In the 1977–8 session, such interpellations were debated on diverse subjects such as building land policy, foreign affairs, treatment of mentally handicapped persons, taxation, economic democracy, small businesses and North Sea gas. In many of these debates there was a shower of conflicting motions, the record being eight.

The rules also provide for ministerial statements. The most important one is provided for in the constitution. The Prime Minister must present a statement on the state of the kingdom at the start of each session. This is in fact the basis for a general political debate (Paragraph 38 of the constitution). Motions can be tabled and these are often very specific and do not represent a vote of no-confidence, but merely draw attention to some issue. In 1977, a single motion on natural gas was presented by DKP (defeated 104–18).

In September 1978, following the formation of the SV coalition, there were six motions: five opposition motions from SF, VS (explicitly critical of the coalition) DR, FRP, CD respectively, and one pro-coalition motion from Kjeld Olesen (S), which was in fact a motion of confidence ('takes note of the Prime Minister's statement and expresses the hope that the government will create the basis for broad co-operation on economic problems'). This motion was carried by 118 votes to 47 (FRP, SF, DKP, VS, DR).

Ministers may make statements on other matters. If at least seventeen members so request, a debate may be held on the statement, which may be oral or in writing. It is not usual for these debates to be concluded with motions.

(c) The Legislative Function

The legislative function of the *Folketing* is of course very important, but is closely linked to its other functions, namely its representational and control functions.

As in most other advanced industrial welfare states, legislative activity has been increasing rapidly and legislative initiative has become more and more concentrated in the hands of the government, to the point where one commentator has been able to speak of a 'bill-reviewing' rather than a 'law-making' function for the *Folketing*. There is still considerable legislative activity by individual MF's or, more usually, opposition parties. Most of such proposals have little or no chance of being passed or even of achieving serious consideration. The aim of presenting bills under these conditions is almost entirely political: to fulfil electoral promises; to show a party's voters and affected interest groups that it is taking action; and to embarrass other parties and especially the government by forcing them to take up a position on the issue and to demonstrate thereby that certain parties are not willing to vote for the proposals in question.

In recent years, the bulk of such 'propagandist' legislation has come from those parties excluded from the political bargaining process: FRP, the three parties of the far left (SF, DKP, VS) and, to a much smaller extent, KRF on moral and cultural issues. After 1973, the FRP put forward bills to implement some of its radical

proposals for cuts in public expenditure and taxation and to eliminate bureaucratic controls. The main aim of this was to keep up
pressure on the centre-right parties. After 1975, when the minority
Social Democratic government returned, until 1978, when the SV
government was formed, the far-left, often with the Justice Party,
argued that an 'alternative majority' existed composed of S, SF,
DKP, VS and DR, which would obviate the need for the Social
Democrats to co-operate with 'bourgeois' parties, and would have
reversed the logic which led Anker Jørgensen towards the SV
government. To this end they put forward proposals in the housing,
energy, taxation and employment field, which had a dual aim: first,
to put into the shop window measures which such a combination
could achieve, and secondly, since their co-operation was refused, to
demonstrate that the Social Democrats rejected these measures for
which there could be a majority. Indeed, governments play this game
too. When the Social Democrats first introduced proposals for
economic democracy in 1973, they were well aware that there was no
Folketing majority to pass them. When Paul Hartling presented his
ten-point economic package in December 1974, he was seeking a
pretext for an election.

As the previous discussion makes clear legislative activity—at
least on the small proportion of controversial measures introduced
each year,—is closely related to the wider political situation. Timing
is important, as is the willingness of non-government parties to
provoke an election and of the government to accept one. A minority
government can often force measures through because of the opposition's reluctance to face an election. At other times, however, the
prudence will be on the government side and the machine will seize
up. Indeed, it was the onset of just such a situation which, among
other reasons, justified the search for a broader-based government
in the early summer of 1978.

One other important inhibition which even a majority government
faces is the existence of constitutional measures justified to protect
minorities. A minority of members can request the postponement of
the third reading of a bill for three days for reflection. More
seriously, where two-fifths of the members so request, an expropriation bill must be deferred until after an election has been held
and then re-passed. The greatest check was introduced in 1953 with
the abolition of the *Landsting*. Under Article 42 of the constitution,
any bill passed by the *Folketing*, except appropriation bills and
measures giving effect to international obligations, can be subject to
a referendum if one-third of the members of the *Folketing* so
require. Once this request has been made, the Prime Minister either
allows the bill to lapse or procedes to call a referendum. This, of

course, gives a Prime Minister a discretion which in reality could only apply to a bill not proposed by the government and passed against its will. The referendum must take place within eighteen weekdays.

Danmarks Radio (DR) will make rules to ensure fairness (allocation of broadcasting time). The tendency to allow all *parties* rather than 'yes' and 'no' supporters equal time on the air may in fact be unfair as it undoubtedly was in the 1972 referendum on the EEC where only one parliamentary party (SF) was opposed to market entry. Five parties, all large, favoured entry, and four divided and small parties (three not represented in the Folketing) opposed it. Such a procedure also fails to take account of potential internal divisions in parties as occurred in 1972. Voters vote for the bill or against it. For it to be rejected, there must be a majority of the votes cast against it, representing at least 30 per cent of the total electorate. Looking at Danish election turnout, it might be thought that this 'double' requirement is not important, since with a turnout of 85 – 90 per cent a 50 per cent negative vote would always be well over 30 per cent of the vote. This was true for the EEC referendum where turnout was even higher than in some elections, standing at 90.19 per cent, but it was less true in the other referenda held since 1953 (except those on the voting age) on four land reform bills,[12] where the turnout was only 73 per cent despite fierce controversy. It is certainly possible to imagine issues on which turnout could fall below 60 per cent; after all, turnout in the European elections was only 47 per cent. Indeed, the lesson from the 1963 referendum on the four land reform bills, which were rejected by the electorate, was that controversial legislation passed by a narrow *Folketing* majority (in this case S-R who had a mere eighty-seven votes together) is undesirable. Given the present balance of forces in parliament, only the Social Democrats, if they are in opposition, suffice to request a referendum; however, unlike in 1963, the two larger 'bourgeois' parties, V and KF, do not represent quite one-third of the seats in the *Folketing*. Certainly neither the parties of the far-left nor the anti-EEC forces have ever been able to command anything approaching one-third of the seats. It can be said that this provision underpins and reinforces the tendency, already manifest in Danish politics, to seek broad-based compromises.

The total amount of government legislative activity has not grown as fast as one might suppose. The government introduced 177 bills in 1953 – 4. In 1977 – 8 it introduced 165. The record years have been 1976 – 7 with 276; 1974 – 5 with 264 and 1968 – 9 with 230 bills. The total number of bills introduced by other members has considerably increased. There were seventeen such proposals in the 1953 – 4 session; the number had risen to thirty-eight in 1970–1 and then again to seventy in 1973–4 and 127 in 1974–5; 102 in 1975–6; 138 in 1976–7 but fell slightly to 99 in 1977–8. The main increase came after 1972–3, after the cataclysmic election of 1973, which brought in five new parties, most notably the Progress Party.

Each year the government must, according to the constitution, inform parliament of the 'state of the kingdom' and of the measures it intends to propose. This is the programme speech. The majority of the bills from the government are relatively uncontroversial and pass without any significant debate; indeed they often pass unanimously. In 1977–8, 146 of the 165 government proposals were passed. This was probably lower than it might have been because of the formation of the S-V government, which led to some bills being abandoned. In 1953–4, out of 157 bills 144 were passed. The best result in terms of proportion of bills passed has been achieved by majority coalitions: the SR-DR coalition, for example, passed 137 bills out of 145 in 1959–60. The VKR government, which had a very large majority, passed 228 bills out of 236 which were tabled.

Bills tabled by other members of parliament have little chance of passing. In 1977/8, only five out of ninety-nine such bills passed; in the record session of 1976/7, when 138 bills were tabled by private members, only four of them were passed. Only broad cross-party initiatives have any chance of success. For example, in 1977/8, of the five private members' bills passed, no less than four had this character. The FRP was most active with twenty-seven bills and the parties of the far left were also active with twenty-six bills, of which the Communists accounted for fourteen. The smaller 'bourgeois' parties such as CD and KRF tabled eleven bills.

As we have seen, the parliamentary session runs from October to October each year. In 1962, an agreement was made between the government and the *Folketing* to try and bring some order into the timing of legislation. It was agreed that measures requiring enactment in a given session would be tabled before 15 March; this rule was strengthened in 1973 to fix 1 February as the latest date, unless circumstances made the tabling of legislation after that date necessary. These agreements have not been altogether successful, but they have had some impact. There are four main periods of concentrated activity: October and November, January, May and, to a lesser extent, late August.

The legislative procedure begins with the presentation of a bill. This may occur in writing or orally. In the overwhelming number of cases, the written method is now chosen: the statement is printed in the *Folketingstidende* ('Hansard') and the bill is distributed to members. At this stage, there is no debate and no vote. The next stage is the first reading, which corresponds to the second reading in the British parliament. At this stage, the minister responsible (if it is a government bill) or the spokesman for the proposal will already probably have received some informal response to the bill. They can present its main aims and deal with early criticism. Spokesmen for the parties may then speak on the bill. They may state positions of principle, set conditions for their approval, suggest amendments and—as frequently happens—ask for clarification of certain points.

The bill is then sent to the committee, which examines it in detail. A very few bills are dealt with without a committee stage: in the 1977–8 session, 254 of the total of 264 bills tabled went to the committee. Of the remaining ten, six were passed on without committee examination and four did not even obtain a first reading. The committees have several different types of procedures at their disposal in seeking to obtain information on matters before them; these, it should be emphasised, are naturally not confined to the legislative work of the committees. In the committee stage, the committee may hold closed hearings of ministers (427 such sessions were held in 1977–8 in all committees; when the MRC [121 such meetings] is excluded, the number falls to 306). The committees also receive deputations from organisations to hear their views and receive written submissions. In the 1977–8 session, there were 272 deputations (the taxation committee with fifty-one and the legal committee with twenty-nine led the field) and 1,276 written submissions. The taxation committee received 178 submissions; the public works committee 149, the social affairs committee received 125 submissions from organisations and individuals.

Committees may also ask written questions to ministers. These can take two forms; written questions for written answers by departments and questions for discussion with ministers during committee proceedings. The first kind totalled 4,290 in the 1977–8 session. There were 674 questions of the second type. The twenty-four committees together held 761 sessions in the 1977–78 session, averaging some thirty meetings per committee. The record was held by the legal committee with sixty-five meetings, followed by the public works committee with fifty-nine, the taxation committee with fifty-eight and the finance committee with fifty-nine—in other words, an average of almost two meetings per session week. The defence committee, energy committee and the external relations (development questions) committee each held under ten meetings in all.

These rather dry figures cover intense activity and interaction between the committees, the government and interests. It should be remembered too that Danish governments can expect to be able to exert even less control over committees than their British counterparts.

The committee reports to the *Folketing*, and each report may include several minority reports. It will ask for disposal of a measure and explain its background. It may suggest acceptance or rejection and may propose amendments. The *Folketing* then proceeds to the second reading, in which the bill is examined line by line, and amendments may be tabled. At this stage, the *Folketing* will vote on the bill as a whole as it stands amended. In some cases, it may be referred back for a second committee stage. There were thirty-seven such cases in 1977/8. Finally, after the interval stipulated by the constitution and the rules of procedure, the bill is presented for a third reading. Here too amendments may be presented, and spokesmen for the parties may intervene. It is not unusual, though, even where considerable opposition remains, for there to be no debate at all on third reading. Of the 165 government bills in the 1977 session, 146 reached third reading and were passed. Of these, twenty-six were passed unanimously and the other five were passed with only abstentions being recorded. Additionally, on some bills there was opposition by only one party or by fewer than thirty members (seventeen bills). This seems to represent a change from the pre-1973 period when an even larger number of government bills passed without serious opposition, except for the DKP and later the SF voting against the appropriations bills to record their opposition to military expenditure and to 'oppositional behaviour' by the Justice Party before 1957 and by the Independent Party (right wing) after 1960–6. Of the five private member bills adopted, only one was unopposed.

Unlike in Britain, it is not possible to speak of an 'opposition', although in certain periods a party or group of parties could more or less clearly be identified in that role and their voting record on legislation tabled in that period confirmed that identification. This was true of the three 'bourgeois' parties in the period 1966–8 and 1971–3 and the Social Democrats in 1968–71. However, since 1973, it has been impossible to identify an 'opposition'; there have been 'oppositions' which have often but not always voted against government bills. The Progress Party has been the most consistent opposition party both in the 1973–4 period, when Poul Hartling was in power, and since. The three parties on the 'outside left'—SF, DKP and VS—have also been an opposition group to which SF has belonged less consistently than the others. Especially from mid-1978 until the collapse of the S-V government, the Justice Party also often joined the left-wing parties as a 'workers' opposition' and on other occasions joined the FRP in opposition to taxation and state expenditure. In the 1977/8 session, the Progress Party alone voted against several government bills; on two bills it was joined only by the VS; on two others it was joined only by the VS and the DKP. The bill giving women equal rights in employment was opposed on its third reading by FRP, DR and KRF, whereas VS abstained and SF and DKP supported the bill. An important Rents Act was passed by a bare ninety votes: S-SF-RV-DKP-VS-DR. The FRP voted against. A bill on energy saving in new buildings was opposed only by the FRP. The finance bill was opposed by the FRP, the DKP and the VS, with the SF merely abstaining. On a motion tabled during the debate demanding free collective bargaining, only the three left-wing parties plus the DR supported the motion.

An interesting example of these mechanics at work was provided by the bill imposing a tax on packaging materials. This taxation measure was part of the second *August forlig* in 1977. The bill was tabled on 23 November 1977 and received a first reading on 29 November. The committee reported on 9 December. The majority report (S, V, KF, RV) approved the bill with minor amendments, but there were no less than five minority reports: FRP, CD, SF (with amendments), DKP and KRF. During the third reading (16 December), a motion was tabled condemning the bill as a bureaucratic interference in economic life. This motion received thirty-one votes (FRP, KRF, DR). The final vote was ninety-one (S, V, KF, RV) to fifty-five (FRP, CD, DR, DKP, VS, KRF) and seven abstentions (SF).

The *Folketing* can also pass '*Folketings beslutninger*' (decisions), which require a less onerous procedure than laws. These decisions may affect internal organisation, representation of the *Folketing* on outside bodies (e.g. the Radio Council) for bind the government to present legislation or ratify treaties. They may come from the government, from committees and from individual members. There is a similar pattern to that which we observed with bills; since 1953/4 the government has tabled fewer than ten such proposals for a decision per session (ten in 1976/7 is the maximum; none were tabled in 1971/2). The committees likewise table relatively few (fewer than ten, and four in 1977/8). There has been a steady inflation of such proposals for decisions from individuals—reaching ninety-three in the 1977/8 session, of which a mere three were approved. Eighty-six were sent to the committee and four were approved without committee examination. Two were withdrawn and six were defeated at the first reading. These proposals are only subject to two readings.

(d) Financial powers

According to paragraph 43 of the constitution, the sole power of appropriating public money and imposing taxation lies with the *Folketing*. This, like every other function of government, has become considerably more complicated since the nineteenth century, and even since the 1953 constitution, which in any case is essentially no more than a reiteration of the rules established in 1849. The essence if not the letter of these provisions is respected by a number of devices. Each June, the Budget Minister communicates to his colleagues the 'framework' allocation for their ministries and receives statements of proposed expenditure. He draws up a single appropriation bill, which in principle includes all the expenditure of the state. The bill takes a standard form each year. It is headed by general recapitulative tables; each ministry has one paragraph, and a general entry permits the incorporation of additional revenue arising for example from new taxation.

The financial year now runs from 1 January to 31 December; before 1978 it ran from 1 April to 31 March. The appropriation law must be tabled at least four months before the start of the financial year. This means by 1 September. The *Folketing* examines the bill like any other bill, except that in the finance committee each member examines a section of the budget. The committee may and does make amendments to the bill. The minister likewise will probably propose amendments in the course of the procedure. For example, in the 1977/8 session, the government's initial proposal was for expenditure of 76.8 milliard DKr. and revenue of 63.5 milliard DKr. After three readings and two committee examinations, the final version of the bill, which was approved by 128 votes to thirty-six (FRP/DKP/VS) with the SF abstaining, was globally not very different, with overall expenditure fixed at 76.9 milliard Kroner and revenue fixed at 63.9 milliard Kroner. During the third reading (as the rules of procedure then still permitted), motions were tabled. One from the left-wing parties sought a return to free collective bargaining, and it obtained only their votes plus those of the Justice Party. FRP tabled a general no-confidence motion on economic policy.

Under the constitution, no taxation may be imposed without there being an appropriation for it; in practice, however, this is merely a device to reinforce parliamentary control. The fixing of taxation occurs in other taxation laws and is quite independent of the Appropriation Act.

Since 1967 rolling forecasts have been introduced, and since 1973 a system of four-year budget forecasts has been brought in so as to give more coherence and longer-term control over expenditure.

Where urgent expenditure over-runs become necessary during the year, it is not possible to respect the constitutional requirement for the money to be appropriated by the *Folketing*. These amounts are only subsequently and retrospectively approved in a supplementary Appropriations Act. This would not allow any real parliamentary control. So it was that as early as 1894 the custom developed of ministers presenting such requests to the finance committee of the *Folketing*, which examines and votes on the request. A favourable vote allows the money to be spent and is a political guarantee that the supplementary appropriation will go through on the nod. It is customary for debates on these supplementary appropriations to be used for a general debate on economic policy, and critical motions may be introduced. During the 1977/8 session, two such bills were introduced covering the financial year 1976/7.

(e) Control of Expenditure

Through its right to audit the state accounts each year, the *Folketing* also, in accordance with Article 47 of the constitution, controls the execution of the Budget. It appoints five auditors, usually but not necessarily members, who examine the accounts of the departments and report; it must then decide whether to approve the accounts. The five auditors must in practice base their work on the internal audit carried out by the various government departments and organisations subject to audit. Their duties are laid down in Law No.95 of 4 April 1928. In addition to ensuring that the expenditure actually carried out corresponds to the appropriations written into the finance law or otherwise accepted by the finance committee and subsequently voted in a supplementary Appropriations Act, the auditors are required to satisfy themselves that the government departments are following principles of sound financial and economic management. The *Folketing* in fact without exception approves the accounts, but sometimes takes note of the comments made by the auditors in their report. Logically, if the *Folketing* were to refuse to pass the accounts of a particular ministry, then at the very least the minister would have to resign and might indeed be prosecuted before the *Rigsret*.

6. The Judiciary

In Denmark, the judicial power is almost entirely apolitical. It certainly has no tradition of making political judgements or resolving political problems judicially as is the case of the Federal Courts in general and the Supreme Court in particular in the United States or the *Bundesverfassungsgericht* in Germany. The Danish courts adopt an even greater attitude of 'judicial restraint' than the British courts, especially in recent years in the field of industrial relations.[13]

Part VI of the constitution deals with judicial organisation. Article 59 sets up the *Rigsret* and Article 61 outlaws any form of extraordinary courts. Articles 62 and 64 enshrine the independence of the judiciary. Judges can only be removed by a special tribunal (*saerlige klageret*) composed of three judges (one from the *Højesteret*, one from the high court and one from the local courts). They can be retired at the age of sixty-five. Most of these articles of the constitution provide for their detailed implementation by statute.

The basic principles of Danish law have been developing gradually since the Middle Ages. It was codified in Christian V's Danish law of 1683, since when there has been no new formal codification. Law has been modified by statute. The rules of court procedure are laid down in the *Retsplejeloven* 1916 as subsequently amended especially in 1969 (Administration of Justice Act).

The highest court in the country is the *Højesteret* (supreme court), composed of fifteen judges. It usually hears cases in two chambers of from five to seven members. It hears appeals in all civil, criminal and administrative cases.

The next layer of courts is the two *landsretter* (high courts) the *Østrelandsret* (Eastern high court) with thirty-six judges, which sits in Copenhagen, and the *Vestrelandsret* (Western high court) with twenty judges, which meets in Viborg in Jutland. These courts hear serious civil and criminal cases as courts of the first instance, with appeal lying to the *Højesteret* on the principle of Danish law that there should always be a basic right of appeal to at least one higher court.

The lowest tier of courts is made up of the eighty-four *Underretter* (lower courts) mostly with only one judge, except in cities. For example, the Copenhagen court has twenty-nine judges and the Aarhus city court eight judges. These *Underretter* deal with civil cases where the value of the suit is less than 10,000 DKr. and criminal cases where the penalty provided for by law is less than eight years' imprisonment.

The constitution itself establishes some rules on court procedure. It lays down that no person may be held in custody for more than twenty-four hours without being brought before a court, and the judge must then decide within three days either to release the accused person or remand him in custody. No one accused of a crime carrying only the penalty of a fine or a suspended sentence may be remanded in custody. The constitution also provides that non-lawyers should participate in the judicial process. This occurs in two different ways. On the one hand, there are special tribunals on which experts sit, such as the *Sø- og Handelsret* (maritime and commercial court) which hear maritime cases; the *Underretter*, sitting with lay expert assessors, which hear cases under the Rent Acts; and the *Landskatterretter* (tax tribunals) which hear taxation cases. On the other hand, in criminal cases the *Landsretter* sit with a twelve-member jury which judges the guilt or innocence of the accused. In criminal cases the *Underretter* mostly sit with two lay assessors as well as the judge. These assessors, like jurors, are members of the public.

The right to appeal to the *Højesteret* when an appeal has already gone to the appropriate *Landsret* is not absolute, and can only be granted by the Minister of Justice on the grounds that the case raises important legal issues or questions of public policy. Most court cases are based on oral and public pleas, except in appeals before the *Højesteret* which are largely dealt with through written pleas.

Legal aid is available in civil cases as well as in criminal cases where the defendant faces a prison sentence. The legal profession is not divided as in Britain. In order to qualify, an *advokat* (lawyer) must have a law degree and three years' training, usually under a qualified member of the profession. Before being permitted to plead before the *Højesteret,* a qualified lawyer must have five years' experience in pleading before the lower courts, and must pass a test admitting him to the bar of the *Højesteret.*

The most difficult political issue in relation to the judiciary, apart from a more recent debate about penal 'liberalism', has been the right of the courts to judge the constitutionality of laws passed by the *Folketing.*[14] The 1849 and 1953 constitutions are silent on this matter. Certainly there has been strong political opposition, especially from the Social Democrats and Radicals, to such a judicial power; this was directly expressed by the Social Democratic spokesman Mr Hedtoft in the *Folketing* debates on the 1953 constitution. On the other hand, the constitution does give the courts the general power 'to control the acts of the administration'. This has been taken to give a clear right to strike down secondary legislation (ministerial orders) as illegal if they do not conform to enabling legislation.

The courts have in practice sought to avoid conflict with the *Folketing* and government. When forced to declare their position, they have not denied that they have the competence—which they deduce as a logical consequence both of a written constitution entrenched above the ordinary laws and the concept of the rule of law —to consider the constitutionality of laws; indeed, they have declared quite explicitly that they do have that competence. In 1921, when passing judgement on a series of laws introducing an agricultural reform, which had been attacked by its opponents as a form of 'expropriation', the *Højesteret* held that it could decide the issue, but avoided declaring any of the laws unconstitutional. In 1942, the *Højesteret* affirmed the same principle, but avoided declaring even laws adopted in circumstances of doubtful constitutionality under the Occupation to be unconstitutional. The same issue arose over the continuance in force of taxation after the resignation of the government in 1943. This question, decided after the Occupation, turned on the constitutionality of retrospective tax legislation. As recently as 1972, the court decided a case seeking to attack the constitutionality of the law of accession to the EEC in the same ambiguous manner. The principle of the right to test constitutionality was upheld, but the law was also considered constitutional. This jurisprudence shows that the Danish courts have sought to play a low-profile role, preferring to avoid conflict and seeking interprestations which would make laws constitutional. That having been said, it cannot be excluded that the *Højesteret* will at some time declare a law to be unconstitutional, but it is not likely.

7. *The Ombudsmand*

The *ombudsmand* institution was introduced by the 1953 constitution. It was taken from Sweden where such an institution had been in existence since the early nineteenth century. In the constitutional commission, pressure for the *ombudsmand* came from the *Radikale Venstre*, and was opposed—at least initially—by the Conservatives and Social Democrats. The constitutional provisions were filled out by a law passed in 1954, and subsequently amended in 1961 to include within the competence of the *ombudsmand* the oversight of local government.[15]

The *ombudsmand* is clearly an arm of the *Folketing*, which elects him after each election. He is not a member of the *Folketing*. There have been two *ombudsmaend*, both of them distinguished lawyers. The *ombudsmand's* competence covers all matters of administration (including local government), except decisions of judges and courts and questions relating to Church doctrine, although the purely administrative decisions taken by the Ministry of Ecclesiastical Affairs and other Church authorities do come within his competence.

He has in a sense a dual role: curative and preventive. It is his function not only to condemn illegal, arbitrary and unjust acts of the administration, but also to prevent such acts recurring. He receives complaints and may investigate them with two provisos: first, if there is no longer any appeal possible within the administration, and secondly if the complaint is made within a time limit of one year. He may, however, take up cases on his own initiative. He may subpoena *any* records and files as well as any persons, and conduct on-the-spot investigations, an important power for example in complaints against the treatment of prisoners.

The *ombudsmand* may reject a complaint on the basis of his findings. Where he finds grounds for it, he may report to the local council or the minister involved or to the *Folketing*. He may make criticism or recommendations in respect of administrative procedures. In serious cases, he may direct the appropriate authorities to institute disciplinary or criminal proceedings against officials who have acted in breach of law or regulations. Each year he submits a report to the *Folketing*.

The two *ombudsmaend* from 1955, to the time of writing— S. Hurwitz (1955–71) and Lars Nordskov Nielsen (1971–)—have been men of strong independence who have got the institution off to a good start. No one can doubt the *ombudsmand*'s independence or willingness to act; however, it must be remembered that he cannot be a magic cure for ill-considered or partly executed policies, over which he has no control.

Over the period 1955–71, the *ombudsmand* received 18,055 complaints, of which 72 per cent were rejected as quite unfounded. From 1962 to 1971, 1,438 complaints were received against local authorities. Looking at the annual report for 1977, 1,887 new cases were opened as against 1,856 in 1976 (1975: 1,889 cases; 1974: 1,687; 1973: 1,461). Of these cases, 249 concerned local government. Eighty-five cases were opened on the *ombudsmand*'s own initiative (thirty-three in local government). Out of these 1,887 cases, no less than 1,039 were immediately rejected as being either out of time, still in the course of examination in the administration, or manifestly without foundation. However, even here 545 such cases were referred elsewhere. As at June 1978, a total of 183 cases remained open, including twenty-three from earlier years. The oldest case was from 1974. In the year from June 1977, 779 cases were dealt with and 565 showed no grounds for criticism; as to the rest, ninety-two cases required only recommendations and 122 criticism as well as recommendations.

The large proportion of the cases dealt with in this period concerned the Ministry of Justice, the prisons department and the prosecutor's department (272 cases), but in only twenty-four of these cases were there grounds for criticism. This was more than enough.

8. *Local Government*

Local government plays an important role in Denmark, and, as in Britain, it has seen important changes in the last two decades. In the late 1960s, it underwent a process of centralisation and modernisation, as area boundaries and procedures, often the product of laws enacted in the last century, were updated. The same process of increasing central government control, especially financial control, has been evident in Denmark as in Britain. The creation of larger units, especially in the country, has led to the increasing politicisation of local government and the increasing disappearance of local parties and lists of candidates in favour of national party lists.

The constitution, in Article 82, guarantees the right of local self-government. Thus the central government may regulate and limit the powers of local government, but may not abolish local authorities altogether.[17] The Ministry of the Interior is responsible for central government surveillance of local government and the drafting of legislation in this field. The central government is represented by an official in each *Amt* (county), who is responsible for exercising certain powers of control on behalf of the central government. Before 1970, he was chairman of the *Amtsråd* (county council).

The Danish system of local government was one of the most outdated in Western Europe. In theory, it consisted of a basic two-tier structure, but there was a distinction between urban primary tier units (*Købstader*) and rural boroughs (*Kommuner*) in rural areas. There was a serious discrepancy between the size of the twenty-five second-tier *Amter*.

The period 1969–77 saw major reforms in both the structure and organisation of local government.[18] Before 1970, there were, outside Copenhagen, eighty-nine boroughs, almost 1400 *Kommuner* and twenty-five *Amter*. The reform which came into force in 1970 reduced the number of *Amter* to fourteen, which involved a very considerable consolidation in some areas. For example, the whole of Jutland north of Limfjord now came under one single *Amt* where previously there were three. The number of *Kommuner* has been reduced to 277, and the urban borough has been abolished as a type of local authority. There are now two basic authorities: the *Amt* and the *Kommune*. The *Kommuner* can be divided into two categories: those with a *Magistrat* (executive) and those with a *Borgmester* (mayor) and committee structure only. The basic size of the *Primaer Kommuner* is 5,000 inhabitants.[19]

The system of local government in Copenhagen is a refinement of the *Magistrat* system. The supreme authority is the *Borgerrepresentation* (Assembly) elected by the people for a fixed term of four years. The *Borgerrepresentation* has fifty-five members, elected by a variant of the proportional representation system used for *Folketing* elections. Here the d'Hondt system (divisors 1,2,3,4 . . . .) is used, and there are no supplementary seats. However, lists can form alliances which enables the total vote of the alliance to participate in the division; subsequently the seats of the alliance are divided up among the component parties and lists. A list merely requires the signatures of between twenty-five and fifty electors to be presented. In Copenhagen, as elsewhere, purely local lists can be presented, but unless they formed an alliance, they would have little chance of success. At the last election in March 1978,[20] the state of the parties was S 20, SF 3, VS 5, DKP 5, the Christiania list (inhabitants and supporters of a 'new-left' collective in an old military barracks in Copenhagen) 1, which almost gave the Social Democrats an absolute majority and the left a total of forty out of the fifty-five seats. The KF obtained eight seats, V 1, CD 1, RV 1, FRP 3 and DR 1. Except for the KRF, all the national parties are represented, and the only local list is the Christiania list with one seat.

The *Borgerrepresentation* elects its chairman, who is currently a Social Democrat and a woman (Gerda Louw Hansen), and two vice-chairmen (presently one Conservative and one SF). It also elects the seven-member *Magistrat* from among its members by the d'Hondt system. This means that the Magistrat will not be like a cabinet, but will represent all the major political groups in the *Borgerrepresentation*. Currently there are three Social Democrats, 2 KF, 1 VS and 1 DKP. The *Overborgmester*, who is the chairman of the *Magistrat*, distributes the portfolios among his colleagues. The *Magistrat* acts collectively and takes decisions by majority vote. Within the limits of day-to-day administration, each *Borgmester* runs his own department. The *Magistrat* prepares proposals for the *Borgerrepresentation* and carries out policy. It must present a Budget each year before September, which is then examined and voted on by the *Borgerrepresentation*. Like the *Folketingets Finansudvalg* (finance committee), the finance committee of the *Borgerrepresentation* can authorise excess expenditure of up to 25,000 DKr. in the course of the financial year.

To ensure wider co-ordination, especially of physical planning and transport, on a wider regional basis in Copenhagen's metropolitan area, a *Hovedstadsråd* (capital regional council) was formed. This body consists of thirty-seven representatives chosen again by proportional representation from the councils of *Københavns Amt* (Copenhagen's *Borgerrepresentation)*, *Roskilde Amt*, *Fredericksborg Kommune* and *Fredericksborg Amt*. The *Hovedstadsråd* was set up in 1974.

Outside Copenhagen, the major cities of Odense, Aarhus and Aalborg also have the *Magistrat* system of local government. They also have larger councils than other *Primaer Kommuner*, with from thirteen to thirty-one members. Other *Primaer Kommuner* have from five to twenty-five members. The *Amtsråd* will have from thirteen to twenty-one members, depending on size and population. The councils are elected for four years by proportional representation, using the d'Hondt method, with the possibility, as in Copenhagen, of lists forming alliances.

The elections for the *Amts Kommuner* have become entirely politicised, representing useful intermediate tests of public opinion between elections. The level of turnout is about 70 per cent, which of course is lower than for *Folketing* elections, but is quite respectable and representative. Some parties have been less successful in local government than in central government. This is certainly the case for the Justice Party, which has only one councillor outside Copenhagen (in Aarhus) and the KRF, which has very few councillors; it has only one at the *Amtsråd* level (Bornholm) and about a dozen at the *Primaer Kommune* level, mostly in mid-Jutland and Lolland.

The elections for the *Primaer Kommuner* councils were much less political. Groups of citizens would form lists: green list, red list or list 'A', list 'G', etc. It is a public duty to serve on a local council if elected, hence lists could be composed of anybody! Now these elections too are becoming more and more political. At the last election in 1978, there were only a few rural *Kommuner* which were still entirely non-political (e.g. Blaabjerg in Jutland), and some small towns and rural *Kommuner* retained sizeable non-political representation side by side with political representation. In Brovst (North Jutland), for example, eight out of seventeen councillors were independents. In the country as a whole, there were perhaps less than 200 independents. In the large towns with the *Magistrat* system, elections were entirely political and the parties of the left were dominant. In the Aarhus Council (1978, there were thirteen Social Democrats, three SF, two DKP and one VS out of twenty-seven members, and in the *Magistrat* three Social Democrats, one *Venstre* and one KF. Aalborg Council has one independent, and on the *Magistrat* there are three S, one KF and one *Venstre*. In the South Jutland *Kommuner* such as Aabenrå, Sønderborg and Haderslev, the German minority party, the Slesvigs Parti, has obtained one councillor, even though it has not gained representation in the *Folketing* after 1964.

The *Magistrat* and *Borgerrepresentation* in Copenhagen form an all-purpose authority, covering all sectors of local government activity. Outside the capital, powers are divided between the two tiers.[21] The pre-1970 *Amter* had little real power. They dealt mainly with roads of a regional importance and exercised some co-ordinating functions over aspects of education and physical planning (land use, roads, transport, etc.). In any case, they were strongly controlled by the *Amtmand*, the representative of the central government. Since the reforms, the *Amter* have become more rational and viable; more functions of a substantive character have been devolved upon them by the central government, especially in the field of education, physical planning and social policy. They now have major functions in respect of secondary education, regional transport and hospitals, whereas the *Primaer Kommuner* are responsible for the provision of utility services such as gas, electricity and water, for local social provision, libraries, primary education and the local road network. The finance of local government is made up from charges, local taxation and state grants which are now block grants not earmarked for specific spending. In 1978, the total local authority budget was 87 milliard DKr., of which 40 milliard was revenue raised locally.

The reform of local government in the early 1970s was, in retrospect, typical of the technocratic modernising conservatism of the 1970s; indeed it was—as in Britain—carried out by a Conservative ministry (the VKR government) and its aims were very similar to those of the 1972 reform in Britain: the creation of two strong tiers of local government, with distinct functions. However, the reform took a long time to implement; in fact as late as 1977 the financial aspects of the reforms were not complete. In practice, several of the parties considered the reform less than satisfactory. The Conservatives, the Justice Party and the Progress Party consider that the *Amt* level should be abolished; *Venstre* also sees dangers in the creation of larger *Primaer Kommuner*. The Communists criticise confusion and overlapping between the three levels of government: the State, the *Amt* and the *Primaer Kommuner*.

REFERENCES

1. For an English translation of the constitution, see *Denmark*, Copenhagen: Ministry of Foreign Affairs, 1973.
2. For a discussion of government formation procedures, see Kenneth E. Miller, *Government and Politics in Denmark*, Boston: Houghton, Mifflin, 1968, chapter 2.
3. Tage Kaarsted, *Regeringskrisen 1957: Trekantregerings til blivelsen*, Aarhus: Aarhus Universitetsforlag, 1964.
4. H. Westergaard Andersen, *Dansk Politik igår og idag*, Copenhagen: Fremad, 1976, pp. 271-9.
5. *Keesings Contemporary Archives*, 1978.
6. Miller, *op.cit.*, chapter 2.
7. Information supplied to the author by Mrs. Eva Gredal (former Minister of Social Affairs).

8. For a discussion of the legal responsibility of ministers, see A. Ross, *Forfatningsret*, Copenhagen: Nyt Nordisk Forlag, 1966, pp. 439–60.
9. For an explanation of the electoral system, see *Folketingetsvalget*, 1971, pp. 36–46 and 57–8. For election results, see *Folketingetsvalget*, 1973, 1975, 1977, 1979.
10. See *Folketingetsåret 1977/78, Folketing*.
11. For figures on the work of the *Folketing*, see *Folketingetsåret 1977/78*, pp. 1–17.
12. H. Westergaard Andersen, *op.cit.*, pp. 249–53.
13. See A. Ross, *op.cit.*, pp. 183–5.
14. See cases u. 1921, 148 and 153 for statement of general doctrine.
15. For a comparative account, see W. Gellhorn, *Ombudsmand and Others: Citizen's protector in nine countries*, Cambridge, Mass.: Harvard University Press, 1966.
16. See 'Ombudsmands Beretning 1977', summarised in *Folketingetsåret 1977/78*, pp. 60–1.
17. Miller K.E., *Government and Politics in Denmark*, Boston, Mass.: Houghton, Mifflin, 1968, p. 187.
18. Miller, *op.cit.*, p. 198–202, and H. Westergaard Andersen, *Dansk Politik i går og i Dag*, Copenhagen: Fremad, 1976, p. 254.
19. Ministry of Foreign Affairs, Copenhagen, 1973.
20. For election results, see *Hoffkalender*, Copenhagen, 1978.
21. See P. Meyer, *Offentlig Forvaltning*, Copenhagen: G.E.C. Gads Forlag, 1979.

IV. NORTH ATLANTIC DENMARK: ICELAND, THE FAEROES AND GREENLAND

Denmark was never a major colonial power. She lost her small trading stations on the Gold Coast and in the Bay of Bengal in the nineteenth century. With the early abolition of slavery (1799), the sugar plantations in the Danish Virgin Islands were no longer economically viable. The Islands were sold to the United States in 1917 for $20 million, after the sale had been approved by a referendum in Denmark. Thereafter, Denmark only retained her three North Atlantic Dependencies: Iceland, the Faeroes and Greenland. All three had been obtained or retained in a somewhat accidental manner and remained marginal to Danish affairs.

1. *Iceland*

Iceland was discovered and settled by Norwegian Vikings in the sixty years after 874. They established some forty self-governing communities, linked together under an Assembly called the Alting, set up in 930, which was to meet annually. By the year 1000 Christianity had been introduced. For a long period in the early Middle Ages Iceland was independent; however, in 1152 the Icelandic Church was brought under the control of the Norwegian bishopric, which greatly eased the later establishment of political control. The mid-thirteenth century saw bloody civil war between the various noblemen on the island and the collapse of all central authority; this enabled Norway to impose its authority in 1260. When Denmark and Norway were united in 1389, Iceland automatically became part of that Union.

After 1814, when Norway was detached from Denmark, Iceland remained a Danish dependency. With the establishment of a democratic constitution in Denmark, her position also evolved. The Constitution of 1874 re-established the Alting which had earlier been abolished; it was to have thirty-six members, of whom thirty were elected and six appointed by the Crown. It exercised legislative power, but executive power remained vested in a Minister for Iceland, who was a member of the Danish Cabinet, and in a Governor with his seat in Reykjavik. This was less than the full Home Rule status desired by Iceland. The latter was attained in 1918, when Iceland entered a Personal Union with the Danish Crown. Under this arrangement Denmark retained control of defence and foreign affairs, but in all other respects Iceland was independent and executive authority was vested in the three-member Cabinet, responsible to the Alting.

When Denmark was occupied by Germany on 9 April 1940, Britain moved immediately to occupy Iceland, which it did on 10 April, to prevent German intervention. The Icelandic Government entered a protest and obtained an assurance that the occupation would only last for the duration of hostilities, and that compensation would be paid for any damage. At the same time, it established a Regency and assumed full external sovereignty. It also declared its intention of ending the Union when it expired in 1943.

In the summer of 1941, before the United States had entered the War, discussions took place about the U.S. taking over the British role in Iceland. On British insistence, the Icelandic Government was induced to request the U.S. Government to intervene. Major airbases, of vital significance in the Battle of the Atlantic, were set up.

In 1943 the Union Agreement expired and was unilaterally ended by Iceland despite Denmark's incapacity to negotiate, a fact which caused some resentment in Denmark. After a referendum approved a new Republican Constitution, Iceland became an independent Republic on 17 June 1944 and in due course a founder-member of NATO and of the Nordic Council.

2. *The Faeroes*

The Faeroes consist of forty-eight inhabited and three uninhabited islands with an area of 540 square miles and a population of 42,000, lying in the North Atlantic off the North of Scotland, between Iceland and Norway. The capital, Thorshavn, has a population of 8,200. The main economic activity is fishing (95 per cent of exports) and sheep-farming. The original inhabitants, Irish recluses, were expelled by Viking invaders from Norway around the year 1000. With the Union of Denmark and Norway the islands fell under Danish influence and remained so after the 1814 settlement.

The Faeroes were represented in the 1849 Constituent Assembly by five members appointed by the Crown and were subsequently represented in the *Rigsdag*. The 1953 constitution assures them two members. Despite the basic principle of the unity of the kingdom, of which the Faeroes—unlike Iceland before 1918 and Slesvig and Holstein before 1864—formed part, the islands were at an early date given greater autonomy than would have been signified by an ordinary *Amtsråd*. The local Assembly, the *Lagting*, obtained wide powers over matters of local concern and the right to be consulted on pending Bills and delegated legislation concerning the Faeroes only. These special powers and the existence of a separate body of

Faeroese legislation, set the stage for even greater autonomy.[1]

During the Second World War, the islands were cut off from Denmark and occupied by the British. The separation created a considerable movement in favour of Home Rule, at the least, if not full independence. A referendum held in September 1946 was somewhat inconclusive. Although 48.7 per cent voted for independence as against 47.2 per cent for Home Rule, with 3.9 per cent spoilt papers, only 64.8 per cent of the electorate voted. The Danish Government rejected the attempt by the *Lagting* to procede unilaterally, but was inclined to regard the result as a vote for independence. Their reflections were overtaken by the *Lagting* election of 8 November 1946, in which the pro-independence *Folkeflokken* (People's Party) was heavily defeated. Under these circumstances, the Government decided to procede with its initial intention of setting up a Home Rule system, which became law in 1948.[2]

The *Hjemstyreloven* (Home Rule Act) of 1948 created what we might call a 'devolved' system of government, not unlike that proposed in the now defunct Scotland Act. The unity of the kingdom is maintained and the arrangements are in no way federal; nor is the arrangement entrenched or protected against subsequent amendment by the normal legislative procedure.

An elected parliamentary assembly with thirty-two members, the *Lagting*, was set up to exercise legislative power over devolved matters. Executive power is in the hands of the *Landsstyret* composed of the *Lagmand* (Prime Minister) and three other members, responsible to the *Lagting*. An *ad hoc* Arbitration Court is to adjudicate disputes over competence between the central government in Copenhagen and the *Landsstyret*. Each government nominates two members and the President of the *Højsteret* three members, who only intervene if the four government nominees fail to agree. This procedure has never been invoked. Since it does not in any case apply to claims raised by private bodies or individuals, it may be supposed that the courts may also decide such questions if called upon to do so.

Matters set out in two Lists, A and B, in a schedule to the Act may be devolved.[3] Matters indicated in List A may be claimed by the *Landsstyret* or may be turned over by the *Folketing*. List A includes the structure of the devolved administration and local government, public utilities, agriculture, and indirect taxation. Education and social affairs are included, but have not been fully devolved. List B matters may be devolved only after agreement between the two Governments. List B matters include police, judicial organisation, radio, air transport and trade policy. Not all these matters have in fact been devolved. Other matters such as defence, a foreign policy and criminal law remain the responsibility of the Danish central government. However, since the Faeroes had assumed responsibility for trade policy and constituted, in the words of the *Hjemstyreloven*, 'a self-governing entity within the kingdom', the islands did not become part of the EEC in 1973. On matters remaining within the province of the central Government, the *Hjemstyret* has the right to be consulted before Bills, Treaties or Regulations are approved. The central government is represented in the Faeroe islands by a *Rigsombudsmand* (high commissioner) and subordinate officials and political responsibility is exercised by the Prime Minister.

The 1978 *Lagting* elections saw considerable gains for the moderate *Sambandsflokken* (Union Party). Despite these gains, the outgoing Social Democratic *Lagmand* was able to retain power, at the head of a coalition of the *Tjodveldisflokken* (Republicans), *Folkeflokken* (People's Party) and Social Democrats, controlling twenty of the thirty-two *Lagting* seats.[4]

3. *Greenland*

Greenland is the largest island in the world, covering 840,000 square miles, but is for the most part covered with ice and has a maximum average temperature in July of 49.5° F. There are nineteen towns and 117 villages and other settlements, for a total population (1970) of 47,000 of whom 7,200 lived in the capital, Godthåb, and no less than 43,000 in West Greenland. Of the total 7,200 are Danes. The population has grown slowly until recent times; in 1805 it was 6,046 and in 1925 13,600, to reach 23,642 in 1950.

The economy is based on seal hunting (5,000 employed), fishing (3,000 directly and a further 7,000 indirectly employed). There has been some limited mining for zinc, lead, coal and, most important, cryolite. There is an important uranium potential. From 1776 until 1951 trade with Greenland was the monopoly of the *Kongelige Grønlandsk Handel* and from 1921 the area was closed to all but Danish vessels.

Greenland was discovered in 984 by Eric the Red, and the first colonies were established in 986, but they disappeared in the fifteenth century. There were sporadic landings over the next two centuries, but it was only in 1721 that Danish trading activities began and in 1729 that political control was asserted.

Greenland was the object of considerable interest on the part of other powers. William Seward, President Lincoln's Secretary of War, was interested in acquiring it for the United States. In 1933, the International Court rejected a Norwegian claim to East Greenland, thus confirming Danish sovereignty over the whole territory. With the occupation of Denmark in 1940, the United States acted to prevent any other power, in particular Germany, intervening in Greenland. The local authorities, acting independently of the shackled government in Copenhagen, co-operated with Henrik Kaufmann, the Danish ambassador in Washington, to negotiate an Agreement with the United States to permit American forces to occupy Greenland and establish bases there. This Agreement of 1941 was confirmed by the *Folketing* in 1945 and became a permanent formal Agreement in April 1951, regulating the right of the U.S. to maintain three bases.

Until 1953, Greenland was a colony. Under the new constitution, it became an integral part of the kingdom. Before that time, its inhabitants had enjoyed no political rights and it had been subject to investigation by the United Nations Committee on Colonialism.[5] Since 1825 the administration of the Colony had been the responsibility of a Ministry for Greenland, a Governor and a Greenland Commission, with economic and trading matters being controlled by the monopolistic KGH. Since 1953 Greenland has been represented in the *Folketing* with two members, who in the early years, like the Faeroese representatives, played almost no role in Danish domestic politics. Since the late 1960s, Greenland members have tended to affiliate to party groups in the *Folketing*, and the so-called North Atlantic seats have on several occasions been important in deciding the balance of power in that assembly. Mostly, at least one of the Greenland members has aligned himself with the left (Michael Gram, Moses Olesen with S and Lars Emil Johansen with SF).

The local administration was, as with the Faeroes before 1948, endowed with wider powers than a normal local authority. Under the last administrative reform (in October 1979)[6] before Home Rule, there was an elected sixteen-member *Landsråd,* which together with the *Landshovding* (Governor) administered Greenland at the local level. The *Landsråd* had the right to be consulted on measures affecting Greenland being considered in Copenhagen. Since 1964 there had also been an advisory Greenland Council. In 1973 a Commission was set up to examine the possibility of Home Rule. It reported favourably in March and June 1978. A bill was rapidly passed on the basis of the Commission's report and became law in November 1978. After Home Rule was approved with a 70.1 per cent 'Yes' vote against a 25.8 per cent 'No' vote on a 63.3 per cent turnout in a referendum held in January 1979, and elections to the new *Landsting* had been held on 4 April, the Home Rule Administration took office on 1 May 1979.

The home rule system for Greenland is very similar to that set up in the Faeroes, with some amendments to take account of special conditions and the fact that, unlike the Faeroes, Greenland does form part of the EEC although having special interests and seeking a special status. The *Landsting* has twenty-one members and is elected for four years. Electoral law is the responsibility of the *Landsting* itself.[7] This body has legislative and appropriation powers in respect of devolved matters. Executive power is in the hands of the five-member *Landsstyre*, which acts like a cabinet, presenting proposals to the *Landsting* and running the administration. Devolved matters are set out in the schedule to the Act. These cover : the structure and organisation of the *Hjemstyre* and of local government; taxation, trade, industry, agriculture and fisheries; social policy, public health and labour law; planning and environment; internal transport; education and culture; church affairs. This list, already extensive, may be supplemented by further devolution approved by the *Folketing*. The matters specified may be claimed by the Home Rule administration, which must then take financial responsibility for them. Where additional items are devolved, the central government bears financial responsibility for them. The *Hjemstyre* is financed by taxation which it levies and by a block-grant negotiated on a three-year basis. There are procedures for consultation with the *Hjemstyre*, not only on draft bills and regulations, but also on international negotiations, especially inside the EEC, which concern Greenland. In cases where Danish and Greenland interests might be so incompatible as to make it impossible for Danish negotiators to represent Greenland interests adequately, there is provision for representatives of Greenland to conduct direct negotiations. The Act establishes the key principle that natural resources in Greenland belong to her people. Exploitation will be conducted under agreements concluded between the Danish government and the *Hjemstyre*, which must be ratified by the *Landsting*.

The elections gave a clear majority to the *Siumut,* which formed the first Home Rule Cabinet, led by Mr Motzfeldt and with Mr Christiansen (Schools and Cultural affairs), Lars Emil Johansen (Trade and Industry), Moses Olsen (Social Affairs) and Mr Andreasen (Development) as its other members.

	Votes	%	Seats
Siumut	8,580	47.1	13
Atassuit	7,808	42.9	8
Sulissatut	1,042	5.6	0
Inuit Ataquatiquit	815	4.7	0

The development of political parties in Greenland is very recent. Until 1975 both *Folketing* and *Landsråd* elections were conducted in single-member constituencies, which favoured the election of local 'notables' and discouraged the development of organised parties. In addition to this change in the electoral law, the referendum campaign of 1972 on EEC membership had a considerable politicising and radicalising effect. Despite its own massive 'No' to the EEC, Greenland became part of the Community, which started debate about the island's constitutional status.[8]

The key political issues were Greenland's future political status and the closely-linked question of the model of economic and social development to be pursued. Danish policy had aimed at 'Danishisation'—the creation of a modern, capitalist economy on Greenland, which was profoundly changing the distribution of population and the nature of economic and social life.

Early attempts to import the Danish political system by the creation of parties similar both to the Social Democrats and Conservatives failed because such parties were unable to build up any popular support. *Siumut*,[9] established in 1975 after a long gestation, is the first and best-structured of the parties. It developed the so-called 'new politics' as a reaction to the debate surrounding the EEC referendum, and participated actively in the Commission on Home Rule. It accepts the Home Rule arrangements, but seeks the widest and most rapid autonomy. It favours an economic policy adapted to Greenland's needs, but essentially socialist in character, based on active co-operation between the *Hjemstyre* and local authorities, which will establish considerable public sector production and the co-operative sector. *Siumut* opposes Greenland's membership of the EEC, and in the short term seeks a special status for the island. It does not raise the position of the U.S. bases in Greenland as an issue of principle, but seeks negotiations with the Danish and American governments on their size and status, the rent to be paid and the relations between the American authorities and the Home Rule administration.

The other parties are either splinters from or reactions to *Siumut* —*Attasuit* was formed as a reaction to it. Its structures are as yet undeveloped. It supports Home Rule, the Danish model of development and EEC membership. Whereas *Siumut* is a party of the left, which corresponds ideologically to the left wing of the Social Democratic Party or SF, *Attasuit* is a moderate centre party.

Both *Sulissatut* and *Inuit Attaquatiquit* are splinters formed by former *Siumut* supporters. *Sulissatut* was formed in 1979 by trade unionists, who felt that *Siumut* was too much concerned with global, ideological issues and too little with bread-and-butter issues of concern to trade unions. *Inuit Attaquatiquit* is overtly Marxist-Leninist in its approach. It was formed in reaction to *Siumut* compromises on the issue of the ownership of natural resources in Greenland. It opposes Home Rule as inadequate, and is sceptical about the value of taking part in elections and parliamentary institutions. It totally rejects the Danish model of development.

REFERENCES

1. Miller, *op.cit.*, pp. 18 – 19.
2. Westergaard Andersen, *op.cit.*, p. 113.
3. *Karnovs Lovsammling*, 9th ed., p. 304.
4. *Keesings Contemporary* Archives 1978.
5. J. Viemose, *Danmarks Kolonipolitik i Grønland*, Copenhagen, 1977.
6. See O. Olesen, *Politisk og Administrative Forhold i Grønland*, Copenhagen: Gyldendal, 1975.
7. For details, see J. Miechelsen, 'Grønland : et Partisystem i Udvikling', *Politica*, 11th Year, No.3, 1979, pp. 39 – 75, especially p. 52.
8. Michelsen, *op.cit.*, pp. 52 – 3.
9. Michelsen, *op.cit.*, pp. 59 – 61.

V. POLITICS AND PARTIES

In Chapter 3, we looked at the organisation and functioning of the Danish state; we saw how the parliamentary system worked, and how Denmark has produced a particular form of 'co-operative parliamentarism' in which pragmatism, tolerance, willingness to negotiate and competence are key behavioural norms, supported widely even by those whose ideologies lead them to seek major social and political change. We shall turn in this chapter to look at the wider context of politics. We shall look at the national organisations, especially the 'social partners' (labour and employers' organisations) which play a major role in modern Danish politics; at the press and media, which do much to shape opinion and influence the political agenda; and at the political parties, which are a vital two-way transmission-belt between the electorate and political institutions.

1. *The Role of Organisations*

Naturally a very wide range of organisations is active in Danish public life. Our focus here will be on those which, because of their size, salience or activism, have attained an important role in the political process. We shall look at both the traditional and the newer populist organisations. Among the first, trade unions, employers' organisations, co-operatives, trade associations, are the most important. Among the second are such groups as the Women's Movement, the anti-nuclear power movement, and the 'Peoples' Movement against the EEC' which has operated both as a pressure group and, in the 1979 European Elections, as a political party.

Organisations operate at three different levels in Danish public life. First, they can have direct influence (formal or informal) on certain political parties. Here the clearest examples would be the organic relationship between the Social Democrats and the LO (trade unions) and the Co-operative Movement, and the less formal relationship between the Farmers' organisations and *Venstre*. Secondly, groups and organisations have an input into the decision-making process. Again, this may be formal, through Royal Commissions and evidence to parliamentary committees, or informal through their influence on public opinion. Thirdly, organisations are themselves directly involved in the development and administration of policy through direct representation, often with MFs, on bodies which are not merely consultative but have decision-making powers. Thus representatives of organisations sit on the Radio

Council, the state Land Law Reform Commission, the Labour Court, and the two sides of industry, which control the centralised national collective bargaining system and participate directly in the formulation of economic policy.

The role of such organisations has been growing continuously since 1914 or even earlier to the point where they play an institutionalised role in decision-making and represent a real force in Danish politics.[1] Their power is based largely on mass membership. Their technical knowledge of issues, which is vital in a modern state, and their ability to deliver not only opposition to the government but also support for it, has led governments to co-opt them into the decision-making process and accept their influence. The influence of organisations has developed to the point where political opinion is inclined to be in two minds about their role, frequently deploring their growing influence, which is seen as giving them too much power.[2] However, even the Conservatives, Radicals and the DR, which incline to this view, seem to regard the role of organisations in a modern industrial welfare state as both essential and basically positive. They consider that the political parties can and broadly do maintain their independence of organisations. However, the KF does consider that the links between LO and the Social Democrats raise problems.

It would require considerable space and go beyond the scope of this book to examine the topology, role and influence of interest groups in Denmark in any detail. We shall therefore limit ourselves to a general overview of the scene. It has been estimated that there are some 2,300 interest groups[3] in the country. The Labour movement is composed of about fifty-four unions, with eight umbrella organisations; forty organisations belong to the *Landes organisation i Danmark* (LO), the Danish central trade union organisation; the *Kooperative Faellesforbund* (Co-operative Federation) groups five organisations. White-collar workers and academic professions account for 215 organisations grouped under twenty-six umbrella bodies. The twelve bodies representing the different liberal professions belong to the *Liberale Erhevsråd* (Liberal Professions Council). The partner of LO on the employers' side, *Danmarks Arbejdsgiverforening* (DA), has 118 member-organisations; some twenty other employers' bodies do not belong. Agriculture and horticulture, fishing and forestry account for another seventy-seven organisations, of which sixty-five are concerned with agriculture. Most of the latter are members of the *Landsbrugsråd* (Agriculture Council), founded in 1919, but there is also the *Samvirkende Husmaendsforening* founded in 1910 (small farmers). The industrial and small business sectors involve some 223 local and national organisations. The main central organisations are *Industrirådet* (Industrial Council), founded in 1910, linking 2,300 firms and fifty-seven organisations, and *Handvaerksrådet* (Artisans Council), founded in 1879, linking 300 organisations with 40,000 members. There are some 164 trading organisations, mostly grouped under the *Grossersocietet* (Traders' Association). In the housing sector, there are two main central bodies: the *Lejernes Landes-organisation* (Tenants' Association) and the *Samvirkende Grundejerre* (Federation of Landlords), linking five bodies. The consumer movement has its central organisation, *Forbrugerrådet*, linking twenty-four member-organisations. Eight TV and radio users' organisations belong to the *Danske Lytternes og Fjernseernes Faellesforbund*, but two others, the more radical *Aktiv Lytter og Seer* and *Socialistiske Lytter og Seer forbund*, do not belong.[4] Seventeen organisations represent local government.

The most influential and indeed the most politically active organisations are the labour market organisations: the LO and DA. For almost a century, wage bargaining has been centralised between these bodies. The DA was formed in 1896, and the LO (then called *De Samvirkende Fagforbund* - DSF) in 1898, with 60,000 members;[5] it now has forty-four member-unions with a total of 953,000 members. This is twenty fewer unions than a decade ago. Of the labour force fifty-five per cent are unionised. The LO conference held every four years lays down the central policy guidelines. As in Britain, Danish unions are mainly craft unions. There are now two main industrial unions, which together account for 40 per cent of union membership: the *Metalarbejderforbundet* (Metal Workers) and the semi-skilled and unskilled workers' union (DASF). There is also, as in Britain, a developed system of shop stewards (*Tillidsmaend*) who are elected for two years. Since the early 1970s, DA and LO have adopted closely similar structures.[6] In 1899, after a bitter conflict, DSF and DA signed the *Septemberforlig*, which was a basic code of conduct for collective bargaining. This text was to remain in force until 1960. A second agreement was signed in 1969 after prolonged negotiations (and amended in 1973), and negotiations are now in process for a new Basic Agreement.[7] In 1980 the LO was arguing for a more decentralised system under national guidelines.

The more recent Basic Agreements have extended the matters covered by the Collective Agreements, but the basic system has remained unchanged. Agreements run for two years from 1 March and cover all aspects of wages and conditions of work. Since 1910, a new refinement has been added. An official independent government mediator meets the parties and considers the outstanding issues. If by 15 February the parties have not reached agreement, he may propose a draft agreement which is then voted on by the parties. However, given the vital importance of global wages policy to governments' macro-economic policy, and the serious impact of a national strike which could occur if no settlement were to be reached, governments have become active participants in the process. For instance, in response to LO demands they have—as in 1973—provided a non-wage element in a package deal with such as, for example, commitments on taxes and rents.[8] The LO policy seeks a 'solidarity wages policy' for the reduction of differentials, economic democracy and social advances, all of which require government action. The Social Democrats especially support co-operation between LO, DA and the government on such packages. Governments may also intervene (as in 1976, in advance of the 1979 round) by fixing wage norms. Finally, where agreement is not possible, parliament has (as in 1975 and 1977) imposed the mediators' proposal by law.[9]

There is considerable interaction between the Social Democratic party and the organisations of the labour movement. The LO is represented in the Party's national executive and vice-versa. The Party is represented on the executive of the *Arbejderbevaegelsens Erhervsråd* (Workers' Movement Joint Committee) composed of the LO and the Co-operative Movement.

The Labour movement through the *Arbejderbevaegelsens Erhervsråd*[10] and the employers' organisation, has direct represen-tation on a myriad of bodies which influence or administer policy. It is represented on the *Økonomisk Råd*, founded in 1962 to provide economic advice and analysis which often form the basis of 'package deals' proposed by the government. They are represented (with members of parliament) on bodies such as the Tariff Council, the Land Reform Committee which administers land reform laws, the Apprenticeship Council, the *Monopoltilsynet* (Monopolies Com-mission), and the Regional Policy Council. They are also regularly consulted on all legislation involving their interests.

Other economic interest groups such as the agricultural, trade, industrial and consumer organisations also have representation in the various advisory and administrative councils and committees which concern them. They are fully involved in the network of consultation on legislation and policy,[11] many are also involved in the self-policing arrangement for fair competition, restrictive practices and advertising standards. These organisations are consid-erably less influential than the labour market partners, but they can exercise considerable influence on technical legislation.

Groups such as the Peoples' Movement against the EEC or the *Oplysning om Atomkraft* (OOA—Atomic Energy Information

Organisation)[12] were organised in response to an expected referendum. The Peoples' Movement played a major role in the EEC referendum in 1972, and then continued to operate after the vote. It was, as we have seen, able to put the pro-Marketeers on the defensive. In 1974, the *Folketing* held its first major energy debate, and the government thereafter set up the *Energi Oplysnings Udvalg* (EOU) to organise a public information campaign in the perspective of a referendum. At the same time, the OOA was set up to oppose the generation of atomic energy in Denmark. It is a stronger organisation than the *Folkebevalgelsen*, as it is based on individual membership, has a stronger secretariat and had received some financial aid from the EOU as an information organisation. These organisations have worked on public opinion; they have resisted being co-opted into the decision-making process, and so have maintained their independence and credibility as opposition groups. In February 1980, the Prime Minister took the decision to put the matter off for the future.

Organisations play an important role in Danish co-operative democracy. They are part of a two-way process: they can influence government, but government can also influence the organisations, and can obtain their support. It is certainly a basic principle of Danish politics that as wide a consensus as possible of parties and organisations should be arrived at before decisions are taken. That, no doubt, is extremely positive; on the other hand, there is the danger that organisations will obtain too much influence or may lose their independence by becoming too closely enmeshed in the process of decision making.

2. *The Role of the Media*

Denmark has always been a country with many newspapers.[13] Initially, after the 1849 constitution, newspapers were Conservative; then *Venstre*, Social Democratic and Radical papers appeared.

A pattern developed which was to last down to the postwar period of papers being tied closely to parties. Each town would have three or four papers tied to one of the 'old' parties. As late as 1950, there were 100 newspapers in Denmark, and 80 per cent of Danes subscribed to at least one of them; daily press sales corresponded to 120 per cent of households. Less than 5 per cent of adults read no newspaper.[14]

Since then, the structure, sales and content of the press has changed greatly under the impact of rising costs, new technology, the arrival of television (in 1954), social change and a weakening political stability. Double readership was still 26 per cent in 1965, but has since declined. However, still only about 7 per cent of the adult population read no newspaper. Total sales per thousand of the population were 364 in 1955; 354 in 1966 and 365 in 1973.

As regards political affiliation, there were also major changes. Few towns would now have more than one paper, and as a result it would tend to become a 'community' paper rather than a 'party' paper. The Conservatives 'lost' seven or eight papers, the Radicals two papers and the Social Democrats all but their national paper, either through closures or through papers choosing independence. In 1965, *Venstre* had twenty-seven papers (30.0 per cent of circulation), the KF nine papers with 32.4 per cent of circulation, and the Social Democrats eleven papers with only 9.9 per cent of circulation. Independent papers (of which there were nine) had 11.2 per cent of circulation. The 'quality press' suffered a relatively more serious decline. Two Copenhagen tabloids, *BT* (so referred to in Denmark) and *Ekstra-Bladet*, came increasingly to dominate readership: 30–40 per cent of Copenhageners read no other paper. Their circulation rose to over 250,000, overtaking that of such established papers as *Berlingske Tidende* (established 1749) and *Politiken* (1884), which in 1965 had still held a considerable lead in circulation figures. The *BT* and *Ekstra-Bladet* are totally independent, iconoclastic, even muck-raking, and at times nihilistic and sensational with a low level of news or serious comment. The *Ekstra-Bladet*, for example, had much to do with creating the climate which launched the Progress Party, and gave its ideas some support. The table, showing changes in the political tendency of the press,[15]

COPIES SOLD PER 1,000 OF POPULATION

All Newspapers	1950	1965	1975
Conservative	123	121	—
Liberal	104	108	104
Radical	77	58	11
Social Democrat	47	35	17
People's Socialist	—	—	1
Communist	5	1.5	2
Independent (Right)	18	15	14.3
Independent	23	11	5
Independent (Left)	—	—	74
Tabloids only			
Conservative	17	35	—
Liberal	22	17	—
Ind. (Right)	—	—	47
Ind. (Non-aligned)	10	—	—
Ind. (Left)	—	—	47
Social Democrat	—	—	—

makes it clear that there is now much less diversity in newspaper reading. The changes have hurt the Social Democrats and Radicals most.

Radio, which began in the 1920s, did little to affect the dominant role of newspapers as the most important political medium.[16] With television, introduced in 1954, it was different. By 1960, more than half the population had access to TV. By 1973, there were 287 television licenses per 1,000 inhabitants, which meant that 75 per cent of households had television.[17] Surveys showed that by the elections of 1971, 42 per cent of voters regarded TV as their most important source of political information (radio 8 per cent and newspapers 31 per cent). At the end of the campaign, the dominance of TV had increased to 64 per cent.[18]

As we have seen, *Denmarks Radio* is a state monopoly for radio and television, run by a Radio Council(Board) with twenty-two members appointed by parliament and five nominated by viewers and listeners' associations.[19] DR is scrupulous in ensuring equal time in elections to *all* parties, of whatever size, that are participating, but at other times its 'uncommitted' BBC style has tended to prevent minority expression and has meant that in reality it has been an instrument of the four 'old' parties which dominated the Radio Council. These parties created a middle-of-the-road consensus. In the 1960s, the staff of DR attempted to develop a more radical, committed and challenging style of TV journalism. The success of this movement was very short-lived, since after 1974 the permissive centre-left coalition, which had existed in the Radio Council on many issues, was replaced by a more overt centre-right coalition under pressure from Erhard Jakobsen's CD and the FRP, which had turned the question of left-wing cultural influence in DR into a major vote-getting political issue.[20]

Television has now become the dominant political medium for most voters. Newspapers and meetings (fewer than 5 per cent of voters now attend meetings, but with some increase in 1973) are less important, both relatively and in absolute terms, than before. However, the image, especially in volatile elections such as that in 1973, is of TV and periodicals (as opposed to dailies) providing the basis for discussion which, contrary to expectations, seems to remain a vital part of political choice mechanisms. Changes in 1973 (made by close on 40 per cent of all voters) were on average greater among media-users—not only TV, but all media—especially those who moved towards small or new parties. There seems to be less propensity than in Britain for changers to be politically apathetic or ill-informed. Partisans use the media to confirm their vote, and non-partisans (floating voters) to change their vote. There is no doubt that the period of television politics and tabloid press has been conducive to a more 'dramatic' and personalised style of politics, with Glistrup and Jakobsen as evident examples. Good television performers—Baunsgaard (Radical), Aksel Larsen (SF) and Knud Jespersen (DKP)—helped their respective parties considerably.

3. *Voting Behaviour*

Voting behaviour, and in particular movements between the multiplicity of Danish parties, is a complex phenomenon; there we can make no pretence to rival the more specialised literature on the subject, but will try to sketch in the main parameters of the problem.[21]

There are long and short-term determinants of voting behaviour. Some parties have more voters motivated by long-term considerations: these are 'core voters'. The Social Democrats (33 per cent), Communists (28 per cent), Radicals (30 per cent), *Venstre* (31 per cent) and Conservatives (21 per cent) have an above-average proportion of votes motivated by long-term factors.

These parties—with the exception of the Radicals—are all class parties. Class perception is a major determinant of voting behaviour. In 1977, 66 per cent of workers voted for the Social Democrats and 11 per cent for the three parties of the far left (14 per cent in 1975). Among unskilled workers (77 per cent) and retired workers (83 per cent), the proportion of voting for the four socialist parties is even higher. Among union members, the proportion rose to 84 per cent (72 for the Social Democrats and 12 for the 'left wing'). Where a voter's father was working class, 82 per cent voted for the socialist parties, otherwise only 62 per cent. Income too, also a class-related factor, appears as an independent variable. Voters with an income (1977) of under 70,000 Kroner per annum showed 77 per cent for the left, but only 7 per cent for the 'far left', whereas among those with incomes over 100,000 Kroner per annum, only 55 per cent voted Social Democrat, but 13 per cent voted for the far-left. Those in rented accommodation are also likely to vote for the socialist parties (72 per cent) and 19 per cent left wing, but among owner-occupiers 58 per cent vote 'S' and 7 per cent left wing. In the capital, among workers 26 per cent voted for the left wing and 62 per cent for the Social Democrats, as against 7 and 62 per cent respectively in provincial towns and 5 and 57 per cent in the country.

Clearly, as Mr Worre puts it, 'It is a sort of class norm for workers to vote Social Democrat.' Other forms of voting behaviour among workers are a deviation. The left wing obtains most support typically among Copenhagen skilled workers in the age bracket between twenty and twenty-nine living in rented accommodation. The Progress Party gains its highest support among workers from owner-occupiers (16 per cent), in the country (17 per cent) and from specialised workers (20 per cent). The 'bourgeois' parties have support among non-unionised (33 per cent), unskilled (17 per cent) and older workers (18 per cent among workers over sixty-one).

Looking at the category of white-collar workers and officials, one finds that even here the Social Democrats are the dominant party, with 30 per cent of the vote, and the left wing has more than among workers (12 per cent). The 'bourgeois' parties have 40 per cent and FRP 9 per cent. The 'bourgeois' parties do best among those with a clear middle-class identification (46 per cent). The Progress Party has lost sharply among this category, falling from 18 per cent in 1973 to 9 per cent in 1977. The 'bourgeois' parties do well among those who are not unionised, among owner-occupiers (47 per cent; CD alone scores 13 per cent). The left wing (23 per cent) and the small 'bourgeois' parties (R, DR, KRF) do well with 18 per cent, and the Social Democrats with 55 per cent dominate among retired white-collar workers.

Among independent businessmen (tradespeople), the four socialist parties together scored 9.4 per cent in 1977. In 1975 there were radical swings, with the socialists scoring only 6 as against 20 per cent in 1973 and 24 per cent in 1971. *Venstre's* share rose from 15 per cent in 1973 to 40 per cent in 1975 and fell back to 9 per cent in 1977. The Progress Party had 23 per cent in 1977 (28 per cent in 1975) and Conservative support had fallen from 34 per cent in 1971 to a low of 12 per cent in 1975 and rose to 20 in 1977. CD too has significant support (11 per cent in 1977). The small centre parties' support has declined from 29 per cent in 1971 (most Radicals) to 13 per cent in 1977. This category is electorally extremely volatile. The smallest businessmen without employees behave rather differently from those with employees. Among one-man businesses, the four socialist parties obtained 28 per cent in 1977 as against 13 per cent among larger businessmen, whereas among those employing people 33 per cent voted for the Progress Party.

Support for Venstre among farmers is falling. It was a dominant 70 per cent in 1971, and is now 58 per cent, having been 54 per cent in 1973. The same is true of the Radicals, historically with support among small peasant-farmers (down from 15 to 8 per cent since 1971). KRF has 6 per cent (11 per cent in 1973) and FRP 14 per cent. All other parties (including Social Democrats) had a mere 14 per cent (as low as 6 per cent in 1975).

The 1970s saw sharp movements in voting behaviour, the Social Democrats suffering a serious reverse; in 1973 the 'bourgeois' parties obtained 45 per cent of the votes of the working class as against 39 per cent for the Social Democrats, but by 1977 S had regained 55 per cent of working-class votes, returning to the level of the 1960s. Turning now to the profiles of the different parties, the Social Democrats (84 per cent), *Venstre* (90 per cent), Radicals (77 per cent), Communists (71 per cent) have strongest 'core voting' profile. Women (52 per cent of the whole population) were a minority of the voters of V, FRP, DR and DKP. They were 77 per cent of KRF's voters, 55 per cent for S and 57 per cent for KF. The professional profile of the parties is shown in the table:

	Whole pop.	S	V	K	FRP	CD	RAD	KRF	DR	SF	DKP	VS
Unskilled workers	25	37	11	1	29	7	16	11	25	13	42	13
Skilled workers	12	19	5	3	6	12	2	4	7	21	16	7
Minor officials	27	27	18	13	22	30	27	26	37	33	27	30
Higher officials	12	9	8	23	8	28	12	21	17	13	7	27
Independent businessmen	10	5	7	30	20	17	16	13	9	3	2	7
Farmers	11	1	50	8	13	3	27	21	3	—	2	3
Students, etc.	3	2	1	2	2	3	—	3	2	17	4	13

(percentages)

The Social Democrats, Progress Party and Justice Party have the most evenly spaced electorate. *Venstre* (50 per cent farmers), DKP (42 per cent unskilled workers) and the Conservatives (30 per cent of independent businessmen) have the most 'skewed' profiles.

The Social Democrats have the most uneven educational profile: 78 per cent of their voters have only the most basic schooling, whereas for SF (31 per cent) and VS (29 per cent), a large proportion of their voters have had higher education. The figure for the whole population is 9 per cent. Of VS voters, 48 per cent have incomes in excess of 120,000 Kroner per annum (1977). Only CD (49 per cent) has a higher-income electorate (professors, teachers, media people). The DKP, VS and SF electorate are young (50 per cent in the 20-29 age bracket).

There are other variables that influence voting behaviour, e.g. ideological factors and responses to the parliamentary situation. These factors will appear in a different guise from one election to another, but the general pattern of reaction is similar. Voters will strengthen or weaken parties in relation to the perception of the coalition or alliance possibilities. An analysis of the 1977 election will produce conclusions of broader and more general interest; in this case there was reaction by the electors to the parliamentary situation. In the 1975–7 *Folketing*, there were two poles of attraction, S and V. There had been an S minority government, supported by a group of parties in what was called the *August forlig* (August pact). In the election, the Social Democrats made a net gain of 7 per cent. They lost 2.1 per cent (0.8 to CD; 0.5 to the three left-wing parties; 0.4 to FRP) and gained 2.4 per cent (1.9 net) from the far left; 1.7 per cent (1.3 net) from FRP; 2.0 per cent (1.9 net) from the Radicals; and 1.8 per cent (1.7 net) from *Venstre*. The other parties of the *August forlig* made a net gain of 2 per cent, but the flows were complicated; the Radicals and KRF lost in net terms. KRF made a net loss of 1.7 per cent (gained 0.7 per cent from other parties but lost 2.4 per cent to them). It had a net loss of 0.6 per cent to S and of 0.3 per cent to the Conservatives, as well as losses outside the *forlig* parties. The Radicals lost 1.9 per cent net to S and 0.8 per cent to CD, but nothing to the KF. CD gained votes outside (from FRP) and inside the *forlig*. The KF gained mainly outside the *forlig*—from *Venstre* 2.3 per cent and from FRP 0.3 per cent—but also from KRF inside it (0.7 per cent net).

The 'bourgeois' voters could adopt any of three positions. They could strengthen the *August forlig* by voting Social Democrat, which many Radical and KRF voters did. Secondly, they could strengthen the *forlig* and at the same time strengthen those 'bourgeois' parties (KF and CD) in the *forlig* which had shown the most toughness in negotiating with the Social Democrats: many 1975 *Venstre* voters no doubt chose this course in order to ensure, this time, the strong government which their 'wasted' *Venstre* vote of 1975 had not ensured, at least not directly. Thirdly, 'bourgeois' voters could try and create a clear 'bourgeois' alternative pole of attraction. These mostly stayed with *Venstre*, but some opted for the FRP (+ 2.7 per cent from 1975 *Venstre* voters). The votes of the four left-wing parties (S, SF, VS, DKP) could decide that the overwhelming need was to ensure the continuation of an S government and vote S, or they could attempt to strengthen the left-wing parties which most clearly opposed the 'bourgeois' alliances of the Social Democrats. Thus S exchanged voters with the left wing: S gained 2.4 and lost 0.5 per cent, leaving a net gain of 1.9 per cent. The DKP and SF lost support, but VS gained 1 per cent.

The election saw the continuation of a normalisation process after the seismic election of 1973, when no less than 40 per cent voted for a different party from 1971. Three of the 'old' parties stabilised their position—*Venstre*, the Conservatives and the Social Democrats. These three class parties continued to recover their positions. The overwhelming evidence is that voters opted for a stronger government. The *August forlig* constellation made a net gain of 9 per cent. The voters also opted for a government 'across the middle' in Danish politics, under Social Democratic leadership. Of all voters, 89 per cent sought a government under Social Democratic leadership. Even among *Venstre* (73 per cent) and FRP voters (63 per cent), this view was dominant. Among *Venstre* voters only 27 per cent wanted a 'bourgeois' coalition, which was *Venstre's* aim in 1975, and 66 per cent wanted a government 'across the middle'. Of all voters, 77 per cent wanted a broad coalition under Social Democratic leadership. Even among Social Democratic voters, only 48 per cent wanted a pure Social Democratic government, and a mere 9 per cent wanted co-operation with the left-wing parties.

Concentration on class factors and the right-left dimension, powerful as these are, is certainly inadequate to explain the success of new parties in the period after 1973.[22] Other, cross-cutting dimensions appear to be of more importance to some voters than the traditional right-left spectrum. The opinions of voters of the various parties on economic issues, equality and social rights tend to follow a clear left-right continuum DKP-VS-SF-S-R-V-K. The new arrivals on the political scene, such as FRP, KRF and CD, plus DR, can less easily be classified on the right-left dimension. On some issues, KRF and FRP appear on the far right and on others closer to the Social Democrats than to the other 'bourgeois' parties. Divisions on newer economic and political issues also fit the right-left continuum reasonably well, which shows that this cleavage pattern remains of major importance. However, it is noteworthy that several of the newer parties have a concentration of voter opinion which does not fit the right-left continuum. DR has 83 per cent of its voters opposed to EEC membership. FRP is as much a 'system-alienated' party as is the far left—more so in fact than SF (81 per cent of its voters believe that the present system fails to solve important problems, 59 per cent have no confidence in political leaders). The CD, KRF and FRP voters show above-average support for the view that undeserving people receive social benefits and that politicians are too ready to spend public money. It is surprising, however, to note that even 53 per cent of DKP voters hold these views, much more than in the 'new left'—the largely middle-class left-wing parties SF (29 per cent) and VS (15 per cent)—which illustrates that the Glistrup themes appeal strongly to the working class too. Moral and cultural issues divide KRF, FRP and CD voters from other 'bourgeois' voters. More KRF (89 per cent) and FRP (58 per cent) voters believe that the current moral trends give cause for concern than do V (51 per cent), RV (56 per cent) and even KF (60 per cent) voters. Issues such as opposition to 'progressive culture' on TV or in schools also strongly defines KRF, CD and, to a less extent, FRP voters, marking them off from other 'bourgeois' voters and, of course, from the left.

In general, there has been a discernable pattern of change in attitudes towards the political system since 1971, reaching a significant peak in 1973, with some recovery of confidence in the system intervening since then.[23] It is probably more valuable to see individual salient issues such as taxation bureaucracy and high levels of public expenditure, the EEC issue, and tolerance of deviant social and cultural behaviour, less as immediate and direct causes of changes in voting behaviour than as contributors to a climate of instability, dissatisfaction and alienation from the existing parties. As we have seen, most Danish voters are essentially pragmatic and motivated by material or practical considerations. Even Socialist and Social Democratic voters tend not to hold extreme views. If a. measure of party distance is taken on a scale between $+100$ equalling extreme sympathy and -100 equalling extreme antipathy, even voters of the left-wing parties only produce a score of -34 for *Venstre* and -29 for the small bourgeois parties, and the Social Democratic parties scores of -6 for the small bourgeois parties and -1 for *Venstre* as against -18 for the left. The bourgeois parties show scores of $+12$ and $+5$ (*Venstre*) for the Social Democrats. In 1971, 83 per cent of Social Democratic voters and even 76 per cent of SF voters agreed that savings should not be penalised by property taxes; and 72 per cent (S) and 57 per cent (SF) that there was too much government interference with private property. Only 67 per cent (S) accepted that high incomes should be more heavily taxed. In the 1971–3 period, the highly moderate and pragmatic Social Democratic voters were clearly vulnerable to the new parties in a period when the Social Democrats' ability to 'deliver the goods' was manifestly declining. Neither opposition to taxation nor the EEC issue (0.06 correlation between positions on taxation and anti-EEC position) is a good direct indicator of changes in voting behaviour. These issues, however, lowered the prestige of the 'old' parties and weakened party allegiance. If we look at low party identifiers with a low trust in government, 47 per cent of these switched to a minor or new party and only 39 per cent voted for the same party in 1973 as in 1971. Of party identifiers in 1971 with a high trust in government, 84 per cent supported the same party. Of low identifiers with a high trust in government 48 per cent voted for the same party, and only 32 per cent voted for new or minor parties.

In general, ideological as well as class parties have shown the highest degree of permanent voter commitment. Looking at shifts between 1975–7, S held 93 per cent of its 1975 voters in 1977, FRP

79 per cent, DKP 71 per cent, and VS 71 per cent. Bridging parties
such as RV and SF have a 'pipeline' function. They only held 41 and
48 per cent respectively of their votes between 1975 and 1977. Parties
tend to lose or gain support to and from parties perceived as nearest
to them in the ideological spectrum. SF lost support in 1977 both to S
and DKP; R lost to S and CD. S, KF and CD gained from ideological
neighbours but not from each other. These patterns are characteristic and can be seen in all Danish elections and in opinion polls
taken between elections.

4. *The Parties*

The political parties are central actors in the political process and we
have already come across them at every point of our analysis—in
government, in parliament, in voting behaviour. We shall now
attempt to look at them more systematically, in themselves rather
than for their role in the political process. We shall look at their
history, their structure and policies, and finally at the party system
which they form.

(a) *The Left*

Collectively called the Socialist parties, the left is now represented in
parliament by three parties, the Social Democrats (S), the Socialist
People's Party (SF) and the left Socialists (VS). The left now has
about 42 per cent of the vote. It has rarely obtained an overall
majority, although for two short periods, 1966–8 and 1971–3, S
and SF obtained a slender majority. In the late 1950s and early
1960s, either S and DKP or SF and S came very close to an overall
majority, but for political reasons this potential was ignored.
Earlier, S (with 42.1 per cent in 1960 and 46.1 per cent in 1935) and
the combined left (S and DKP in 1935 and in 1945) obtained a higher
percentage than now. As for the parties to the left of the Social
Democrats (SF, DKP, VS), these have never obtained more than
12.5 per cent, and now have 11.9 per cent.

The parties of the far-left, despite their continued collective
strength, have played no significant role in parliamentary politics
since 1973. They could no longer give the Social Democrats a
majority in what was in 1973, 1975, 1977 and 1979 clearly a 'bourgeois' *Folketing*. The Social Democrats ignored them, and their role
was limited to lending weight to the designation of a Social Democratic minority government after each election. The positive,
moderate elements in SF were, after Aksel Larsen's death, increasingly on the defensive. SF, DKP and VS were furthermore rarely in

agreement, and used much energy in mutual strife and recrimination. Attempts in the 1978–9 period to offer an 'alternative' or 'worker' majority to the Social Democrats to carry through a number of agreed issues, based on three parties of the far-left and DR (which proclaimed itself to be a 'workers' party'), which would have provided just the ninety votes representing a *Folketing* majority,[24] were not realistic. The 1979 election saw the parties of the far left with 11.9 per cent of the vote (+ 1.6 per cent),[25] but with only seventeen (– 2) seats due to the elimination of the DKP; it had no visible political strategy. However, their continued advance in recent opinion polls (especially SF) may bring about a reversion to the 1968–73 strategy, but that depends greatly on the attitude of the Social Democrats who, at least for the moment, do not appear to envisage that option seriously.

(b) The Social Democrats (S)

S was organised by Louis Pio in 1871 as a Danish section of the First International. After initial repression, the movement grew, largely through the trade unions which numbered over 100 by 1875. The first congress was held in 1876, with seventy-five delegates representing fifty-six organisations (forty-one unions and fifteen political associations) with 6,000 members. Like the British Labour Party, *Socialdemokratiet* began as an outgrowth of the trade union movement and was at first indistinguishable from it. However, at the first congress in 1876, it developed into a political party with organic links to the unions, and with its own organisation.[26] Here the *Gimle* programme (named after the place near Copenhagen where the first Congress was held) was adopted, and a party organisation was formed, under the chairmanship of Pio. The programme, closely modelled on the SPD 'Gotha' programme, showed clear Marxist influences in that it declared for wide common ownership, albeit by legal means. There were also calls for immediate reforms: full political democracy, the repeal of indirect taxes, regulation of working hours, and welfare measures. The subsequent programme of 1913 was more moderate in tone, and added demands for measures in support of small farmers. In its 1919 policy statement, the party adopted wide-ranging proposals for public ownership of insurance companies, the shipping industry and coal and food importing companies.

The 1945 manifesto adopted after the liberation, entitled 'The Future Denmark', was radical, in the belief that a decisive move to the left had occurred; nonetheless the party rejected overtures for a merger from DKP. This manifesto condemned monopoly capitalism and proposed wide government intervention and nationalisation. The programme was an electoral liability; votes were lost to the Communists and co-operation with the Radicals was made difficult. Soon, implicitly, it was in cold storage. The party's third programme, adopted in 1961, is rather general, and emphasises democratisation more than socialisation. It proposes a 'democratisation of society as a whole so that the possibilities of free choice, economically and culturally, are brought within the grasp of each individual'. It was supplemented in 1969 by a working programme entitled 'the New Society—Policies for the 1970s'. In this document emphasis was placed on industrial democracy and progressive co-ownership.

The 1973 congress called for a new programme to be prepared for the 1977 congress. The drafting committee set up by the national executive in September 1974 completed its work in the autumn of 1976 and the resulting programme was adopted in September 1977. This new programme declares the aim of democratic socialism to be 'the liberation of man, to ensure his security and give him the possibility of full development in society and responsible to society', and 'it builds on respect for the individual and equal opportunity for all'. It condemns both private and state capitalism equally and seeks to further equality, freedom and solidarity. The programme recognises the vast improvements in living standards and of freedom for the working class, but emphasises the steady concentration of economic power in few hands to which the party must respond. Here it places the main emphasis on economic democracy, the quality of life and of economic growth, and the economic context of Denmark's new relationship with the Third World and membership of the EEC.

The party has, as we have seen, suffered from an ageing membership and voter structure, and has had difficulties in obtaining support among the new voters and intellectuals. For all that, it comes nearest, among the Danish parties, to being a truly national party with a strong basis of support in almost every class (except farmers) and in every part of the country.[27] The ups and downs since 1973 have had relatively little effect on the balance of class and regional support. It is and remains overwhelmingly a 'workers' party', but has increasingly attracted white-collar workers and civil servants. It is strongest in Copenhagen and the provincial towns and weakest in the Jutland countryside; but it is in fact very evenly supported all over the country, support being within 5 per cent of its national average everywhere.

Early in its history, it became a parliamentary and evolutionary force for change, accepting the inevitable compromises entailed in governing as a minority party in a 'bourgeois' state. It soon became central to Danish politics, and so it was to remain. Currently, it straddles the centre strategically, the only large party in parliament, with potential allies (or opponents) to the left and right. Its main characteristic, especially since the assaults of the seismic election of 1973 and the world recession, has been its pragmatism in the defence of the achievements of the welfare state. It has not been an intensely ideological party, at least since the early days, but the programmatic work of the 1970s did seek to give the party a more coherent and attractive image in the face of new challenges, such as demands for more economic and political democracy, the ecological movement, greater consciousness of the Third World, and demands for a better quality of life.

The party gained representation in the *Folketing* for the first time in 1884 with two seats, which had increased to twelve by 1898. In 1909 it helped the Radical Party to office, thus inaugurating a political partnership which was to dominate Danish politics for the next fifty years. During the First World War, when the country's delicate neutrality policy required broad support, S first entered the government. After the 1924 election, it emerged as the largest party and Thorvald Stauning formed an S minority government which was unable to achieve major reform, but lasted two and a half years and proved the party's respectability. In 1929 Stauning was able to form a majority coalition with the Radicals, which was to last until the occupation, and succeeded in putting through major social reforms.

After the war, the party lost support to the Communists and had to go into opposition until 1947. From then until 1966 it governed first as a minority government, and later with the Radicals or with the Radicals and the Justice Party, except for a short three-year period of Liberal-Conservative government in 1950–3. In 1960 the DKP had been replaced on the far left by the SF under the popular Aksel Larsen, which obtained 6.1 per cent and eleven seats. This new party could less easily be contained in a ghetto as a political 'untouchable', and in 1966, for the first time, S and SF gained a Socialist majority, slender though it was. Aksel Larsen refused a formal coalition, which would have committed SF to supporting NATO and Danish EEC membership; however, the two parties did form a 'contact committee', and co-operated on domestic issues for fourteen months until the split in SF broke the majority. This led to a polarisation, throwing the Radical Party into the arms of the 'bourgeois' parties and leading to the creation of a VKR government under Hilmar Baunsgaard (R), which lost its majority after the 1971 election which saw Mr Krag return to power in an S minority government supported by SF. He resigned immediately after the EEC referendum and was replaced by a more left-wing former union leader Anker Jørgensen. A number of factors—the leftward movement in the Social Democratic Party, the growing revolt against high taxation, the bitter aftermath of the EEC referendum campaign—contributed to the dramatic 1973 election, provoked by Erhard Jacobsen quitting the Social Democrats. This colourful and energetic character left S as a protest against its leftward trend, and founded the Centre Democrats.

At this election all the previously represented parties lost ground, even SF. However, the result was worse for S, which fell back to 25.7 per cent, its lowest percentage since before 1914, and furthermore it now found two (after 1975, three) parties to the left of it. It lost power to the Liberals until the 1975 election, when it made a partial recovery to 29.9 per cent and again formed a precarious minority government which had to call an election in February 1977; this was because it could not obtain a long-term agreement on certain aspects of economic policy, which would have provided at least a minimum of political stability. The 1977 election saw stabilisation, but no dramatic return to the position of the 1960s.[28] The party had by 1977 largely recovered its pre-1973 strength and central position in Danish political life. It had borne the brunt of governing in an economic recession without suffering electoral 'wear and tear'. However, by mid-1978 it was running into tactical difficulties. Its range of partners for 'package deals' was diminishing, and the seriousness of the economic situation made greater long-term stability desirable.

At the same time, a credible 'bourgeois' grouping was emerging. In the teeth of violent opposition from LO and the party's left wing, Anker Jørgensen formed the S-V coalition. Its formation and fall, and the subsequent election, are occurrences from which the lessons to be drawn appear somewhat ambiguous. LO could not prevent the formation of the S-V coalition. Thomas Nielsen's '100 days' ultimatum given at the December 1978 congress had little visible impact, but no doubt LO opposition was a considerable element in the government's final collapse. On the electoral front, it is hard to tell whether the 1.3 per cent gain—totally unexpected—was a reward for forming or ending the S-V experience; such evidence as there is points to the former.

Membership of the party is individual and based on the local branches, of which there are 700. There are no affiliated organisations as such. However, there is cross-representation on the party executives, unions and co-operatives which go to make up the labour movement.[29] Each branch elects its representatives to branch and *Amt* organisations. The supreme policy-making body of the party, which elects officers and approves programmes and now a list of candidates for the European Parliament, is the congress held (in principle) every four years. Congresses were held in September 1974 and in 1977 ('continued' in December 1978 to complete its business which ran overtime, and to choose the candidates for the European elections). The congress has about 500 delegates from the local branches, and is much more highly organised than the conference of the British Labour Party. It can handle discussion of a detailed programme; it sets up working parties and considers amendments in detail. Each year a smaller *Landsmøde* (annual conference) is held in September. It receives a report from the party chairman and may pass recommendations to the national executive or general statements. The national executive is a large body composed of elected and *ex-officio* members. In addition to the party chairman (now Anker Jørgensen), vice-chairmen and general secretary elected by the congress, it currently embraces thirty-five of the *Amt* organisations on the basis of one representative per *Amt* and an extra representative for each 10,000 members and three representatives for Copenhagen; also the chairman of the *Folketing* group, three representatives for LO, three from DSU (youth organisation), and four from the co-operative organisation. It meets on average monthly (twelve meetings in 1973/4, but only seven in 1976/7). The inner leadership is the *Forretningsudvalg* (steering committee), composed of one representative each from the organisations (LO, co-operative, DSU) and the *Folketing* group, six *Amt* representatives chosen by the executive as a whole, and the chairman, vice-chairman and general secretary. It meets at least monthly (seventeen meetings in 1973/4, ten in 1976/7).[31]

The party membership has recently been falling. In 1903 it stood at 22,061; by the start of the Second World War, it had risen to 206,995, reaching a peak of 316,027 members in 1948. In 1974, it had fallen to 122,722, and reached a low point of 122,394 in 1976. It was on the rise again in 1977, reaching 123,140.[32] At the 1980 Congress there was severe criticism of the Party's organisation and membership loss, leading to the election of a second vice-chairman to supervise party organisation (now a woman).

The party's parliamentary candidates are chosen by 103 *opstillingskreds* (nomination district) organisations, and additional candidates may be put up by the *Amt* organisations.[33] Candidates must be re-selected annually by a meeting at which all party members may attend and vote. Existing candidates are automatically re-nominated, but only twenty-five party members may propose another candidate; in that case a vote must take place. Candidates are, as we have seen in Chapter 3, nominated '*sideordnet*', which means that the personal votes decide the order of election.

(c) The Communist Party (DKP)

The party was founded in 1919 from a number of splinter groups from S and other socialist societies.[34] It contested its first election in 1920 and first won representation in the *Folketing* in 1932 (two seats) and obtained modest representation through the 1930s. With its role in the Resistance, immediate post-war admiration for the Soviet Union and the general shift to the left, the election of 1945 saw an explosion with the party gaining 12.5 per cent of the vote and eighteen seats (out of the then total of 149).

With the onset of the Cold War and the cold-shoulder tactics of S, which refused to co-operate with the Communists, this ground could not be held and support was halved at the next election and by 1957 had fallen to 3.1 per cent and six seats.

Meanwhile, rumbling dissent and internal contradictions had set in, fuelled by the general secretary Aksel Larsen, who returned from the XX Congress of the Soviet Party to issue a denunciation of DKP's blind loyalty to Moscow. In his report he stated: 'The party should free itself from the tradition that we automatically support everything that comes from the Socialist countries.'[35] He was to continue in this manner, criticising the Soviet invasion of Hungary and supporting the Yugoslav position against the Soviet Union, as well as proposing a specific Danish road to socialism. In November 1958 the central committee expelled him from the party. He was to found the Socialist People's Party (SF), which led to the DKP losing all its seats in the *Folketing* in 1960. From then until the 1973 election, it was not represented in the *Folketing* and concentrated on maintaining party discipline, organising in factories, and campaigning on issues such as opposition to NATO and particularly opposition to Danish EEC membership, which could bring it support from outside the ranks of normal DKP voters. It was returned to the *Folketing* in 1973 and improved its position slightly both in 1975 and 1977. The political situation did not permit the far-left parties to play a major role in this period. Furthermore, the presence of three Marxist parties to the left of the Social Democrats had led to strong ideological conflict among them, which has tended to limit their individual and collective impact on politics as a whole. The main goal of the DKP, particularly in the February 1977 election, has been to attempt to bring the Social Democrats to co-operate with the parties of the left rather than with the centre-right. It claims an 8 per cent increase in members between the 1976 and 1980 congresses. In 1975, membership stood at about 7,000.[36] However, its political failure is evident by its elimination from the *Folketing* in 1979.

(d) The Socialist People's Party (SF)

After his break with DKP, Aksel Larsen founded SF as 'a real mass party. . .and not a steel-hard militant sect'. It was to be a party 'which builds on working people, but which is able to stimulate Danish politics and co-operate with all democratic and socialist forces'.[37] The main policies of the party, as set out in its 1963 programme and in subsequent policy statements, are anti-capitalist, emphasising public control and intervention in the economy, workers' participation in industry, and strong social services. In foreign policy, the party seeks closer ties with the Socialist states and the Third World. SF opposed NATO and Danish EEC membership.[38] At the time of the accession to EEC membership, the party was the only anti-EEC party in the *Folketing*. Since 1973, its members (Per Dich, Jens Maigaard, Gert Petersen and, since 1979, Mrs Boserup) have been active in the European Parliament and the *Folketing's* Market Relations Committee, following the line that the 1972 referendum gave a limited mandate only for entry to the Community as it then was, not for further institutional development.

The first congress was held in February 1959, and the party obtained eleven seats at its first election in 1960, thus becoming larger than the Radicals. Stability was maintained at the 1964 election. At the 1966 election, the party almost doubled its number of seats to twenty, a spectacular leap forward, which created with S the first 'labour' majority in the *Folketing*. For the next fourteen months the Social Democrats, in a reversal of their earlier cold-shoulder policy, co-operated closely with them and they even offered SF seats in the cabinet. A joint SF-S committee was formed (the so-called 'Red Cabinet') to determine the outline of the policy to be followed, except in foreign affairs, defence and EEC questions where the government co-operated with the 'bourgeois' parties. There was growing tension within SF over this moderate line, and the issue of an incomes policy, which arose in December 1967 after devaluation, was only an immediate pretext for six MPs to rebel against the 'Larsenist' line and defeat the government.[39] SF lost in the ensuing election and was reduced to fourteen seats. The 1971 election saw a return to S minority government after the bourgeois VKR coalition had been defeated. At the 1973 election, SF lost votes like all the established parties, in spite of its association with opposition to the EEC. Since 1973, it has found itself considerably squeezed between S on the one hand and DKP and VS on the other. In this situation, its support has been constantly eroded, and the 'generation shift' after the death of Aksel Larsen in 1971 has not been easy; there has been constant tension between the *Folketing* group and the mass party, culminating in a purge of five MPs before the 1977 election. Attacks on the S government incomes policy were counter-productive, and SF reached its lowest ebb at the 1977 election with seven seats and no evident political role.

The 1977–9 parliament was a turning-point for SF. The situation was more stable than in 1977 and the mood on the far left more pragmatic. SF saw its vote rise to 5.9 per cent, with a gain of four seats, thus regaining its pre-1973 strength. Post-1979 opinion polls show a further progress, but it was, during the talks on the 1980 'Easter package' of economic measures, still hamstrung by divergences between the parliamentary party, which wanted to reach an agreement, and the Executive.

(e) *The Left Socialists (VS)*

The VS was formed in December 1967 by the six SF rebels, led by Erik Sigsgaard.[40] Four of them secured election, but the small group was plagued by factionalism and political impotence, with two of its more talented and popular members, Hanne Reintoft and Pia Dam, leaving the group to sit as independents. As a result of this, the party lost its seats in 1971, and remained out in 1973 (1.5 per cent), but returned in 1975 with just 2.0 per cent and four seats, increasing to five in 1977 and six in 1979. The party is strongly anti-EEC and anti-NATO, but opposes state capitalism. Sceptical about parliamentary institutions, it believes in active work among trade unionists, women's rights groups, tenants associations, the anti-atomic energy movement, etc. It believes that such activity can heighten political consciousness and create a 'revolutionary situation' in which the institutions of capitalism will ineluctably and irreversibly melt away. As a parliamentary force, VS is relatively ineffective, but it has tabled interesting proposals on energy saving and alternative energy sources.

(f) *The Centre and Centre-Right*

These terms do not exist as such in Danish usage. All non-socialist parties are classified as 'bourgeois' parties. This designation referred historically to *Venstre* and the Conservatives, but since the polarisation of 1968 it came unequivocally to include the Radical Party. There is now a tendency to identify three groups of 'bourgeois' parties: the moderate parties (Radicals, Centre Democrats, Christian People's Party) or the traditional 'bourgeois' parties (V, K) or others (Progress Party, Independents 1953–66, Justice).

Except for the two very short periods of 1966–8 and 1971–3, the 'bourgeois' parties as a whole have always represented a majority in the *Folketing*. Taking the period before 1973, their high point was the early 1920s when *Venstre* and the Conservatives often came close to a majority, and in more recent times in 1968 when the VKR triangle obtained ninety-eight seats. Before 1973, the 'bourgeois' parties were essentially *Venstre* and the Conservatives. *Venstre* has shown an organic-decline from 34 per cent in 1920 to their present 13 per cent. In this light, the 1975 result must seem an aberration. The Conservatives were until 1968 always the smaller of the leading 'bourgeois' parties, their share of the vote—until 1973—remaining remarkably stable. The Radicals have been in an ambiguous position. Until 1968 they did not act as a 'bourgeois' party, but rather as a 'bridge' across the centre. In fact, they have only joined one 'bourgeois' coalition (1968–71), whereas they have very frequently supported S governments. It seems, too, that their period as a 'bourgeois' party is now over. The party seems to desire to revert to a bridging role.

Relations between the 'bourgeois' parties have often been difficult, which goes far to explain the fact that the theoretical 'bourgeois' parliamentary majority has rarely been fully exploited. At first there remained historical antagonisms between V and K; later, in the 1950s, each suspected the other of seeking to mount a takeover bid which torpedoed periodic moves for amalgamation. Even before the SV government, the urban *Venstre* supporters hankered after co-operation with the Social Democrats. Repeated attempts since 1973 to assemble a 'bourgeois' coalition (the so-called 'four-leaf clover') of V, K, KRF and CD have floundered on refusal to co-operate with FRP on its excessive conditions, and on *Venstre's* aggressive leadership under Hartling and its later defection to form the S-V government in 1978–9.

(g) The Liberals (Venstre - V)
The party came into being in the period after 1848 in the struggle for democratic parliamentary government. In 1872 the various Liberal factions joined in the United Left (*Venstre* means 'left') and issued the first modern party programme.[41] In the 1880s local branches were formed. However, the party was beset by factionalism, as it has been ever since. One section compromised with the right. In 1901, with the *systemskift* (system change, i.e. introduction of parliamentary government), the Liberals formed their first government. The party began as the Farmers' Party, but now subtitles itself 'Denmark's Liberal Party'. Its main support is to be found in rural areas such as northern and central Jutland, but the 1975 gains also resulted in an inflow of urban voters, largely from other 'bourgeois' parties. The party has traditionally sought balance and moderation. It supported and indeed fought for the parliamentary system, but in the 1930s and early 1940s it opposed too radical reforms of the

constitution. At first it opposed the abolition of the *Landsting* and only came to accept it when the principle of the abrogative referendum was accepted by the other parties. It believes in 'freedom under responsibility'. Economic freedom cannot be total, and social solidarity must be expressed through a system of social security, which, however, has in recent years become too extensive.

The party supports a limited incomes policy and limited forms of industrial democracy. It strongly supports tax reductions and savings in public expenditure, but as a government party in 1968–71 and 1973–5 it became acutely aware of the very real practical obstacles in the way of such a policy. As was seen in the most recent election campaign, V now gives absolute priority to measures for economic stabilisation. These are the main themes of the 1970 programme 'Towards the Year 2000', which also presents V as a forward-looking modern party, as well as resting on its traditions.[42] The aggressive tactics of its leader Poul Hartling in the period after 1973 have produced mixed results. His insistence on forming a government with a mere twenty-two seats and then surviving for a year before going to the country with a coherent economic programme enabled him almost to double V's representation from twenty-two to forty-two in 1975. However, this was a pyrrhic victory, since V lost power to S. His refusal to adopt a constructive attitude to the minority S government has been heavily sanctioned by the electorate, with V dropping back to twenty-one seats in 1977, less than in 1973 and indeed less than at any time in this century.

The organisation of V is similar to that of S but rather simpler. Congress is the supreme authority. It is made up largely of delegates from the local branches, with some *ex-officio* delegates. The national executive has between fifty and sixty members, of whom only three are chosen by the congress, the rest being *ex-officio* members. There was no central party organisation until 1929, and it remains weaker than in some other Danish parties.

The party has suffered at least three significant splits. The first was that of the Radicals in 1905 (smallholders, pacifists and urban intellectuals). The second was from the right. Led by a former leader and prime minister Knud Kristensen, the group quitted the party due to its opposition to the constitutional reform of 1953, to form the right-wing Independent Party, which was represented in the *Folketing* in 1960–6. Thirdly, in the early 1960s a group called Liberal Debate was formed to combat moves to the right and more specifically a fusion or close alliance with the Conservatives which had been mooted. This group was mainly centred in Copenhagen and broke away *en bloc* with two MPs (Westerby and Diderrichsen) to form the Liberal Centre in 1965.

(h) The Conservatives (KF)

The Conservative People's Party was formed in 1915 by the more progressive elements in the old right. KF is mainly an urban and suburban party, especially in Copenhagen.[44] The Conservatives have rarely been in government (1950–3 and 1968–71). Like *Venstre*, KF emphasises freedom and economic initiative and incentive, but it is not neo-Liberal. It supports the welfare state as necessary. KF has a strong nationalist tradition. It strongly supports NATO and the defence effort. It has been the most pro-EEC of all the Danish parties.[45]

Participation in the 1968–71 VKR government, in which Poul Møller was Minister of Finance (he introduced the PAYE tax system) and Knud Thestrup was Minister of Justice (he abolished censorship and obscenity laws), lost the party considerable support and led eventually to the débacle of the 1973 election. KF lost heavily to both the Christian People's Party (KRF) and the Progress Party (FRP). At the same time it lost representation in the European Parliament. Since then, the policy of the party's new chairman, Poul Schlüter—co-operation with the S minority government in a number of 'package deals'—has paid off, leading to the party's quite considerable gains in the February 1977 general election. The party already gained 0.3 per cent net from the Progress Party and 0.7 per cent net from KRF in that election, and these trends continued in the 1979 election and in subsequent opinion polls. The Conservatives are clearly regaining their dominant position in the 'bourgeois' group. In 1980, as at other periods in Danish history, the KF appears a more likely partner for S than does V.

The party executive has between sixty and sixty-five members and a representative assembly of 300-500 members. The supreme organ is the national council (900-1,100 members), representing largely the local party districts in proportion to Conservative votes at the last election. The *Folketing* group has a separate chairman, and it is the group which does most of the preparatory work on policy matters, subject to the final ratification of the national council.[46]

(i) The Radical Left (RV)

The RV is a centre-left party which broke away from *Venstre* in 1905 and rapidly gained influence on the political scene, forming its first government under Zahle as early as 1909. In 1913 RV began its co-operation with the Social Democrats, which was to dominate Danish political life for the next fifty years.[47] The party represented the urban left, intellectuals and smallholders, as well as pacifists. These various strains remain important in the party even today. In its heyday, RV obtained 21.1 per cent of the vote in 1918, but in

1929–68 its share never rose above 10 per cent. It reached 15 per cent in the landslide of 1968, when it gained many floating voters in the general polarisation of that election, a figure it virtually held in 1971. In successive elections in 1973, 1975 and 1977, its vote declined to a low of 3.6 per cent; in 1979 this had recovered to 5.4 per cent. However, Radical influence has always been greatly disproportionate in its moderate size, on account of its strategic position in the political spectrum, to the immediate right of the Social Democrats often in evenly-balanced parliaments. The main aim of RV is to promote co-operation on a broad basis, across the centre of Danish politics. The party has always acted as a bridge, moderating both Socialist and bourgeois blocs. Votes flow to and from the party from both left and right. The large gains in 1968 were a clear recognition of this bridging function. RV clearly said 'Yes' to a 'bourgeois' government, but also 'Yes, but. . .'.

Today the party is mostly a middle-class, white-collar party, but it retains elements of its original voter clientele, in that about 8 per cent of its electorate still come from small farmers; 54 per cent of its vote is in rural areas.

These origins are reflected in the party's policy concerns: measures to assist small farmers; initial opposition to NATO; opposition of a minority to EEC membership. In 1971, 21.3 per cent of the party's voters were in some degree hostile to NATO and in the same year 18.7 per cent were opposed to EEC membership. This rose to 57 per cent in 1977.

The structure and organisation of RV is similar to that of other 'old' parties. The national conference elects members of the executive and approves programmes. The executive follows the familiar pattern of a few representatives of the national conference and a majority of *ex-officio* members from the *Folketing* group, Radical Youth, the Radical press and the local and regional party organisations.[48]

In recent years RV has suffered from identity problems and resulting internal tensions. Was it a 'bourgeois' party? If so, should it, as in the 1968–71 period, commit itself to an alliance with the 'bourgeois' parties? Or was it a centre-left party, closer to the Social Democrats? Its unclear position and therefore its unreliability both to any potential 'bourgeois' bloc centred around *Venstre* and to the Social Democrats has cost the party support and now leaves it in serious difficulties, even if it has recovered from the low point of 1977. Tension between the more 'bourgeois' wing and the more 'radical' wing, reinforced in the 1979 *Folketing* group, continues and still prevents the party from developing a clearer profile.[49]

(j) The Centre Democrats (CD)

This party was formed just before the 1973 election by Erhard Jacobsen, then a Social Democrat MP and the well-known and popular mayor of Gladsaxe, a Copenhagen suburb. He left S and formed the new party in protest against the move to the left by Anker Jørgensen after 1972. He criticised the over-close identification of S with the trade unions and its alliance with SF, as well as the general increase in left-wing influence in cultural life and the media.

CD is avowedly a centre party, opposing ideological confrontation and bloc policies. It opposed growing left-wing influence, and in the European Parliament (after 1975) joined the Conservative group, but at the same time sought to prevent the formation of a minority 'bourgeois' government which would have been dependent on the Progress Party. It is loosely organised and decentralised, depending for its impact largely upon the charismatic personality of Erhard Jacobsen and a few other leaders. The party has recently suffered from internal problems over the treatment of its spokesman, René Brusvang, but this hides a more serious crisis of authority and identity for a centrist party with an ever more right-wing electorate.

CD unequivocally favours the mixed economy, but seeks to spread wealth and economic power more widely. It opposes special interests such as trade unions gaining what appears to be excessive influence in government. Enterprise and initiative should be rewarded, but the welfare state should not be dismantled. CD has strongly attacked left-wing and 'modernist' influence in state-subsidised culture and in radio and television. The 1973 election gave CD an excellent result, with fourteen seats, but in 1975 it only just retained its representation with a mere four seats, some of its votes going to *Venstre* and some perhaps back to the Social Democrats. In 1977 it gained seven seats, to reach eleven. This would seem to indicate that CD had become a relatively permanent feature of the political landscape, but in 1979 it fell back to 3.2 per cent and current opinion polls give it under 2 per cent.

(k) The Christian People's Party (KRF)

KRF was founded in April 1970 during the VKR 'bourgeois' coalition, largely as a protest against the legalisation of pornography and the easing of the abortion laws, measures proposed by the Conservative Justice Minister Thestrup, and supported by all five parties then represented in the *Folketing*. More widely, KRF was, as were other new-old parties such as the CD, Progress Party and the Justice Party, a protest against the failure of the 'bourgeois' coalition to pursue a 'bourgeois' policy and against 'moral permissiveness'. The first party programme, filling out the statement issued by the founders, was adopted in 1971.

The KRF is ecumenical, with representatives of both the high and low church wings of the Lutheran Church, the Catholics and the free churches in its leadership. The party sought to being a Christian moral *Weltanschauung* into politics. In the words of its programme, it supports 'the pillars of society: the home, church and school'. Many Danish church leaders did not react favourably to the formation of a specifically Christian party, with the clear implication that the other parties were not, could not be and even need not be Christian in outlook. KRF replied to this criticism by referring to the existence of Christian Democratic parties in many other European countries, and to the successful sister-party in Norway. At the same time, the party proposes to act as a core or catalyst to a Christian outlook in Danish politics, exercising in this way a pressure on the other parties.

KRF was soon to suffer from considerable internal dissensions on these and other issues, which probably contributed largely to its failure to gain representation in 1971. The central issue was the attitude to the 'bourgeois' VKR government then in power: should KRF support its continuation in office, or propose an alternative, to be formed by S, V and KRF? How 'purist' should the party be? These tensions and its defeat in 1971 provoked a leadership change, and in March 1973 Jens Møller became chairman. KRF profited, as did all the 'out' parties, from the public mood of disenchantment, at the 1973 election. Modest gains were made in 1975 but lost again in 1977. KRF has been a full participant in the numerous pacts made by both the Hartling and Jørgensen governments. In 1979, it fell back to 2.6 per cent.

The position of KRF can be summarised by the slogan 'To the right in cultural matters and to the left in social matters'. KRF is pro-NATO and pro-EEC, and supports increased aid to the Third World. More recently, the moral and cultural issues which were at the origins of the party have tended to recede into the background, and the party has operated more as a classic centre party.

(l) The Progress Party (FRP)
The Progress Party was a new experience in Danish politics. It burst on the scene and spread like a bush-fire.[52] Its message was simple, even simplistic, and its leadership was charismatic, chaotic, anarchic and iconoclastic. With no organisation but merely a leader, the tax lawyer Mogens Glistrup, who had already made himself famous and

tweaked the establishment by the nose in asserting that he had—
quite legally, by exploiting the idiocies of the system—paid no tax
for many years, it reached 25 per cent in the opinion polls and at its
first election in 1973 it reached 15.9 per cent of the vote and obtained
twenty-eight seats in the *Folketing*, becoming the second largest
party and the largest 'bourgeois' party. The party was formed at a
restaurant in the Tivoli Gardens on 22 August 1972.[53]

The party's name and records were purchased for about 800
Kroner from its former leader, who had been attempting to form a
pensioners' party. The FRP developed rapidly through the formation of local branches following mass meetings. Soon it had over
40,000 members and a newspaper, *Fremskridten*, founded in
October 1973. It was above all the speaking and publicity talents of
Mogens Glistrup which caught the public imagination and brought
in the support. By the summer of 1973, when an election was
looming, the FRP reached over 20 per cent in opinion polls. Its
appeal was avowedly populist; its main targets were high income tax,
government expenditure and bureaucratic interference in economic
life. At the 1973 election, the party obtained 15.9 per cent of the vote
and twenty-eight seats at its first attempt, thus becoming the second
largest party in the *Folketing*. At the 1975 election, after some
internal splits, it fell back to twenty-four seats, but in 1977 obtained
twenty-six seats. At the 1979 election, it fell back to 11 per cent and
twenty seats and the opinion polls now show its support hovering
around 10 per cent.

Party organisation, both inside and outside the *Folketing*,
remains loose. The party did not have a statute until 1974. Group
meetings are held in public, and party discipline only applies to the
most fundamental points in the party programme. On other issues
each MP and indeed each party member is free. The somewhat
anarchic manner in which the party was founded and developed, and
the uneven character of its vote over the whole country, brought a
somewhat unbalanced group into the *Folketing* in 1973. The attempt
of the far-left and the FRP to topple the Hartling government in
September 1974 was torpedoed by four dissident members of the
group. The style of the party is unique; it depends on the personality
of its leader. Mr Glistrup has a talent for political theatre. He has
coined phrases of his own, attacking 'paper-pushers' and 'desk
popes' (bureaucrats). Initially, FRP proposed as its defence policy
the replacement of the armed forces by an automatic reply system in
the ministry, saying 'We surrender' in Russian. Mr Glistrup has also
attacked state subsidies to the arts, all foreign aid, Nordic co-operation and even Danish diplomatic representation.

The basis of the party is its offensive against taxation and bureaucracy. It proposes to abolish income tax gradually over five years and to abolish all wealth and capital gains taxes. Such a programme would be made possible by massive and radical cuts in public spending and in the level of state activities. All state subsidies would be phased out, as would state intervention in economic activity. There would be major savings in military expenditure and in foreign policy activities. All foreign aid would be abolished. These savings would total 30 milliard Kroner. The sole area in which expenditure would actually be increased would be that of control of environmental pollution, where more severe standards would be applied. Its response to the recession and rising unemployment has been to propose freeing private initiative.

The party also emphasises the fight against bureaucracy. Social services would be reduced, restructured and decentralised. The number of members of the *Folketing* would be reduced to forty and the cabinet to eight. Local authorities would be given greater autonomy, provided that they accepted total financial responsibility. There would be numerous reductions in the staffing of the public services (by about 150,000 jobs). Pensions would be simplified by making them equal for all. In foreign policy, FRP is pro-EEC, but vigilant against excessive bureaucracy. A large current in FRP is opposed to NATO and desires large cuts in military expenditure.

The party soon faced the difficulties of all protest parties: how to translate votes into practical influence without losing those votes. FRP's electorate is volatile; it has few members, its voters being influenced mainly by short-term factors of economic and political dissatisfaction. With the DKP, it is the most strongly 'anti-system' party. More than other parties, its ups and downs have affected its geographical distribution: it has become predominantly rural, especially in Jutland. The party has become in course of time increasingly structured and disciplined; greater professionalism has replaced some of the early naïve crusading spirit, but the basic virulence of its political message and its uncompromising slogan-like policies and populist rhetoric have survived. It has asked the most questions and tabled the most bills (twenty-eight out of eighty-six private members' bills in the 1978–9 session)[54] and is the most obvious 'opposition' in the *Folketing*. There have been internal debates, but all attempts to moderate the party line have been quashed by Mr. Glistrup, most recently at the party's September 1979 conference. For a time, its support seemed to stabilise at about 14 per cent with gains and losses around that figure, but in 1979 its support fell decisively to 11 per cent and subsequent opinion polls have shown a progressive further fall to 9.1 per cent (March 1980).

Despite the party's size and its 'sterilisation' of up to 15 per cent of the parliamentary seats, it has never won acceptance as a valid partner from the other parties,[55] which have not been prepared to negotiate with it. For a short period, Hartling appeared willing to 'use' its votes, but this did not produce any positive result since he was not willing to deal with FRP on policy. The Social Democrats have mounted vigorous attacks on FRP in party brochures under such headings as 'If Glistrup got power. . .' and 'The truth about the Progress Party'.[56] At first, the other parties perceived FRP as a real threat and, although unwilling to deal with it, probably modulated their policies to deal with that threat, so securing FRP some indirect influence.[57] This threat is declining: Denmark is a 'co-operative democracy' where voters are, above all, pragmatists eager to see their vote 'work' in parliament. The quarantine tactics of the other parties have been extremely effective, and will force FRP to make some hard choices about its future. Can it gain acceptability and, if so, can it do so without losing even more support? The case of the Justice Party—another protest party in the 1950s—is there as a warning.

(m) *The Justice Party (DR)*

The Justice Party is unique in the world and a permanent survivor on the Danish political scene. It was founded in 1919 from a number of small movements which had adopted the economic theories of the American Henry George ('Poverty and Progress') and the theories on moral justice of Danish philosophers such as Severin Christensen and Aksel Dam.[59] It gained representation in the *Folketing* in 1926 and was thereafter continuously represented until 1960. It was in the late 1940s and early 1950s that DR reached its peak, with 8.2 per cent and twelve seats in 1950. It gained nine seats in 1953, fell back to six at the second election of that year, and rose to nine seats in 1957. It owed these results probably more to the incipient protest vote and to the personality of its leader Viggo Starcke. In 1957 it entered a coalition government with S and RV. This strange coalition, which some considered 'against nature', arose from the purely negative desire of the three parties to keep the Liberals and Conservatives out of power. The coalition was fairly successful, but it proved disastrous for DR, which lost all its seats in 1960. It was then to remain in the wilderness until 1973, to drop out again in 1975—no doubt considered to have supported Hartling too closely—and then to return in 1977, with 2.6 per cent in 1979.

The Justice Party claims to be the only non-Socialist party with a coherent ideology, and rejects the 'bourgeois' label.[60] Its two central planks derived from Henry George's work are a single tax (hence the name often used in English, 'the Single Tax Party'), replacing other taxes on labour or consumption on incremental land values, and total economic liberalism, since DR believes that only the total free play of market forces and free trade can achieve social justice. This leads to it taking positions similar to the Socialist parties on issues such as housing policy and land speculation, strongly opposing EEC membership, opposing compulsory military service, and tolerating new-left alternative life-styles in the name of total freedom, but to be nearer to FRP on taxation, public expenditure, state intervention in industry and opposition to bureaucracy.[61] It therefore has points in common with both left and right, and defies classification. Its bitter experience in government and in the 1973–5 period when it supported Hartling's package deals has led it to eschew bloc politics. It seeks a broad-based government. Characteristically, commenting on the Prime Minister's 1980 Easter package proposals, it argued that he should break down the package and find majorities here and there on the individual components.[62] In the period of the S-V government, it flirted with the idea of a broad left-wing majority with the Socialist parties. Surprisingly, in view of its earlier experience in bloc parties, it held its vote in 1979, indicating that 2.5–3.0 per cent is its hard-core support on which it can survive.

(n) The Folkebevaegelsen mod EF (FB)[63]

The *Folkebevaegelsen mod EF* is not a party in the normal sense. It has been a campaign organisation, as we have seen. It is included briefly here because it operated as a party in European elections and secured 20.9 per cent of the vote and four seats in the European Parliament. The FB is a broad umbrella organisation composed of both local committees such as '*Glostrup mod EF*' or '*FB i Aarhus*' and the anti-EEC parties which are directly represented in its executive (SF, VS, DKP, SF, *Dansk Samling, Nordisk Folkeparti*). The organs of the FB are the Congress, which chooses the Executive to include representatives of affiliated parties, individual members and local committees and from other parties chosen by congress.

The EEC issue is divisive in all parties. In 1979, 8 per cent of *Venstre's* voters were against the EEC and 9 per cent of SF's voters were favourable. Even in the VS (9 per cent favourable) and the Justice Party (10 per cent) there are pro-Marketeers. DKP alone appears practically monolithic (only 4 per cent for EEC membership), although in 1972 19 per cent of its voters voted 'Yes'. This situation favours a body like FB. Anti-EEC voters of pro-EEC parties (Social Democrats in particular) can support FB on the European issue and return to their basic national allegiance for *Folketing* elections. However, FB's mobilisation of the anti-EEC vote is not total. In the June 1979 European elections, 20 per cent of anti-EEC voters supported pro-EEC parties. Those were naturally 'bourgeois' voters.

There were difficulties inside FB on taking part in the European elections. A considerable proportion of the delegates from outside the political parties favoured a boycott. The FB's programme for the election was adopted in Odense on 28–29 October 1979.

Given the electoral system, it was obvious that FB should put up a list in association with lists from the four anti-EEC parties. Here the FB's role would be to obtain 'bourgeois' and Social Democrat anti-EEC voters who would not vote for other parties. This moderate and pragmatic strategy was undermined by the refusal of the DKP to follow the 'five-finger solution' (SF, VS, DKP, DR, FB lists) and its insistence on putting up only on the FB list. FB nearly split with SF, calling it a Communist front. The difficulty was forgotten by June 1979, and FB had a good campaign, forcing the pro-Marketeers and especially S totally on to the defensive. In the course of the campaign, FB gained from both S and the 'bourgeois' parties, as well as from the anti-EEC parties (these last gains were minor).

The FB is a broad church of necessity and avoids ideological divergences and positions. Of the four elected candidates, one is a Communist, one possibly a Communist, one a Social Democrat and one a Radical; one SF member was also elected. Four out of five anti-Marketeers are clearly on the left. Surveys of FB supporters show them to be on average young, with higher education, living in Copenhagen and holding new-left views; they oppose nuclear energy, support the 'small is beautiful' line, oppose NATO, and lack confidence in politicians.

FB electoral success raises serious questions for both pro- and anti-Marketeers, and must limit the room for manoeuvre of any Danish government in EEC matters. However, the Social Democrat FB voters easily returned to the fold in November 1979. FB's position in the European Parliament is uncomfortable, since it must be purely negative and must by self-denying ordinance avoid ideological stands. Will this line help to achieve FB's objective of withdrawal from the EEC? Indeed, is there not a paradox in a party which seeks to return decisions to the Danish *Folketing* campaigning only at the European level? Of course FB could not seriously campaign for the *Folketing* as a one-issue group. This seems to condemn it to impotence and to the role of a lightning conductor for anti-EEC sentiment, which can hardly further its long-term aims.

5. Party Interraction

The situation can be broadly divided into three periods, but each period exhibits many common features.

(*a*) Pre-1966
The *Folketing* was dominated by the four 'old parties'—S, R, V, K—which in the period 1920–66 never fell below 85 per cent of the vote. Smaller parties which appeared, such as DR, DKP, SF and U, were ignored and, to a considerable extent, were allowed to wither away from the indifference of the 'old parties' who did not wish to co-operate with them.

Danish democracy is co-operative; a party excluded from co-operation with others will achieve nothing. In this period, government was based on either the S-R or the V-K formula. These were perceived as the rival combinations around which calculation revolved. The 1957–60 'triangular' government was formed precisely to permit a basic S-R government and prevent a V-K one.

(*b*) 1966–1973
This was a short but interesting period, which saw a fundamental change and indeed polarisation in Danish politics. SF gained twenty seats in 1966 and forced its way upon the scene. There was now an S-SF majority, and SF could no longer be ignored. The Social Democrats, therefore, took SF as a serious partner. This provoked a reaction from the Radicals, who joined the 'bourgeois' VKR bloc, the latter emerging as an alternative government in 1968. When it in turn was defeated in 1971, it was replaced by a Social Democrat minority government relying on SF (1971–3). Denmark was moving towards, if not a two-party system, a two-bloc system on the classic right-left alignment.

(*c*) Post-1973
The 1973 election saw five new or 'new-old' parties returned, and all (even SF) existing parties lost ground. This shock has not completely ceased to reverberate through the system. All the new parties have proved more durable than past experience would have suggested. The continuing relative return to normality heralded by the 1975, 1977 and 1979 elections has not brought their former prominence back to the old parties. The 'system', if there is one, could be likened to that found in a number of multi-party chambers in periods of political instability—the French Fourth Republic, the Weimar Republic's *Reichstag* and the present Italian parliament before the

PCI proposed the 'historic compromise'. Here certain parties, often both of the far Right and Left, were not considered respectable—they were not part of the normal political process. This left political interaction concentrated in a narrow band of the political spectrum——usually the broad centre. Since 1973 neither the Progress Party nor the far-left (DKP and VS) has been considered part of the political mainstream.

Within the centre there have been two 'poles of attraction': the *Venstre* (1973 – 5) and S (1975 – 8). The issue has been, within a given centre bloc, which party would exercise leadership? Would government be centre-right or centre-left? In this process the votes of the far-left and even of the FRP have been counted as a *masse de manoeuvre* without there being any thought of giving those parties any equivalent influence. The search has been for stability through the various August and September pacts and, when such possibilities were wearing thin, through the S-V coalition. Since the breakdown of the S-V coalition, the Social Democrats, strengthened in the 1979 election, have found no difficulty in reverting to the balancing act of 1975 – 8. All these were efforts to achieve greater long-term coherence for economic policy in a fragmented *Folketing*. The voters, since 1975, have gradually assisted this process. Denmark is not Italy or Germany. Destabilisation was always only relative and, having reached a rapid peak, began to recede. Normalcy began to return. The FRP and the far-left's gains were contained. S regained strength and confidence. By 1977, KF was regaining strength as were the Radicals. The voters in 1977 and 1979 strongly rewarded moderation and co-operativeness and penalised irresponsibility. The contours of the political system and the old parties have shown their continuity and durability.

These dynamics are the essence of Danish co-operative democracy. Parties must cultivate a co-operative image; even at election time they must behave in a constructive manner which will minimise rather than maximise political distance from potential allies. Even the far-left and FRP must accept this basic truth. A party which cannot enter into package deals with others will have little or no influence on public affairs and in the longer term will lose the esteem of the public. Ideological purity and extreme isolation rarely pay, for no party can ever expect a majority on its own.

Parties must master the delicate art of inter-party negotiation; participating in package deals, accepting compromise, without losing essential party identity or abandoning key issues for which the party stands. The losses of *Venstre* and R and the gains of K and S in the 1977 election are but the most recent illustrations of the penalties of refusing reasonable co-operation and gains from promoting it.

REFERENCES

1. K.E. Miller, *Government and Politics in Denmark*, Boston, Mass.: Houghton, Mifflin, 1968, pp. 170–1.
2. P. Møller (ed.), *De Politiske Partier*, Copenhagen: Det Danske Forlag, 1974, pp. 163 and 166.
3. The data which follows is taken from J.A. Baksti and L. Nørby-Johansen, *Danske Organisationers Hvem, Hvad, Hvor*, Copenhagen: Politikens Forlag 1977.
4. A. Brink Lund, 'Danmarks Radio—et Magtobjekt i det Politiske System' in *Økonomi og Politik*, 50th Year, No. 3, 1976, p. 211–28.
5. For details, see B. Fog (ed.) *Danske Erherv*, Copenhagen: Forlaghiter 1975, p. 165–80.
6. A. Carew, *Democracy and Government in European Trade Unions*, London: Geo. Allen & Unwin, 1976, p. 45–50.
7. See Miller, *op.cit.*, p. 232–6, for details of the system of collective bargaining.
8. K.H. Cerny (ed.), *Scandinavia at the Polls*, Washington DC: AEI, 1977, chapter on 'Current problems of Scandinavian trade unionism', p. 283.
9. For details, see Socialdemokratiet, *Politisk og Organisatorisk Beretning til Kongressen*, 1977, p. 16.
10. Socialdemokratiet, *op.cit.*, p. 70.
11. Miller, *op.cit.*, pp. 229–31 and pp. 170–1.
12. For details on the *Folkebevaegelsen mod EF* and OOA, see Mouritzen, Brenholdt Larsen, Refslund Poulsen, *Borgerdeltagelse og Graesrodsbevalgelser*, Aarhus: Politica, 1978.
13. Miller, *op.cit.*, p. 123.
14. Figures from Miller, *op.cit.*, pp. 124–6 and Cerny (ed.), *op.cit.*, chapter 6, 'The Political Role of Mass Communication in Scandinavia', p. 184.
15. Cerny (ed.), *op.cit.*, p.204–5.
16. For a history of Danmarks Radio, see R. Skovmand, *DR50*, Copenhagen: Danmarks Radio, 1975.
17. Cerny (ed.), *op.cit.*, p. 186, table 6–1.
18. Cerny (ed.), *op.cit.*, p. 208.
19. For problems of structure and control, see R, Skovmand, *op.cit.*, and Law No. 421 of 15 June 1973.
20. A. Brink-Lund *op.cit.*, pp. 212 and 218–20.
21. The discussion in this section is based for the 1971 and 1973 elections on Cerny (ed.), *op.cit.*, chapter 1 (O. Borre, 'Recent Trends in Danish Voting Behaviour'). For the 1977 election and the table on p. 13, see T. Worre, 'Folketingsvalg 15 February 1977' in *Økonomi og Politik*, 52nd Year, No. 1, 1978, p. 18–47.
22. Worre, *op.cit.*, table 6 and p. 32, where he states, 'They do not represent a clear rejection of the traditional left-right dimension but take up a more radical stand-point on a range of additional ideological dimensions, to which they give more importance than left-right issues.'
23. For this analysis and figures, see Cerny (ed.), *op.cit.*, pp. 33–7.
24. For the Joint Statement of DR, SF, DKP and VS of 24 August 1978, see

Måneds Politisk Kalender, July-September 1978, p. 3.

25. For these and subsequent election results, see Appendix IV.
26. A.H. Thomas, 'Social Democracy in Denmark' in W.E. Patterson and A.H. Thomas (ed.), *Social Democratic Parties in Western Europe*, London: Croom Helm, 1977, p. 234−5.
27. For programme and policy, see P. Møller (ed.), *De Politiske Partier*, Copenhagen: Det Danske Forlag, 1974, and the 'Princip program' and 'Arbejds program' approved by the 1977 Congress.
28. Worre, *op.cit.*, Table 11 (p. 39) and p. 41.
29. Cerny (ed.), *op.cit.*, p. 12 and pp. 36−7.
30. For structure of the party organisation, see A.H. Thomas, *op.cit.*, p. 259−60; Miller, *op.cit.*, pp. 66−70. For the early history of the party organisation, see O. Bertolt and E. Christiansen, *En Bygning vi Rejser*, Copenhagen: Fremad, 1954, Vols. I and II.
31. For the composition and the working of the Hovedéstyrelsen, see *Love for Social Demokratiet* (Party Constitution), clauses 11 and 12, and *Socialdemokratiet, Politisk og Organisatorisk Beretning til Kongressen*, 1977, p. 36−7.
32. Membership figures are cited in A.H. Thomas, *op.cit.*, p. 270, and *Beretning*, p. 51.
33. *Love. . .* clauses 8a and b. For the impact on the 1969 reform which went over to *'sideordnet'* presentation of candidates, see *Beretning*, pp. 11−12.
34. Miller, *op.cit.*, pp. 86−7.
35. Quoted in A. Larsen, *De Levende vej*, Copenhagen: Eget Forlag, 1958, pp. 26−63, which gives an account of the crisis in DKP.
36. N. McInnes, *The Communist Parties of Western Europe*, Oxford University Press, 1975, p. 3.
37. A. Larsen, *Aksel Larsen seer tilbage*, Copenhagen Rodos, 1970.
38. P. Møller (ed.), *op.cit.*, passim. This work is arranged not by party but by policy area.
39. For an analysis of this conflict from the anti-Larsenist point of view, see E. Rigsgaard, *Aksel Larsen's 'Spil: SF'*, Copenhagen, Eriksens Forlag, 1968, and for a neutral view, Bille, *Kilder til belysning og forholdet mellem S og SF, 1959−77*, Copenhagen: Gyldendal, 1974, and E. Mader, *SF under det Rode Kabinet*, Odense Universitets Forlag, 1979.
40. See E. Rigsgaard, *op.cit.*, and for policies, see T. Krogh and M. Sørensen (ed.) *De Politiske Partier og deres Programer*, Copenhagen: Gyldendal, 1972, pp. 106−15.
41. J. Fitzmaurice, 'Denmark' in Henig (ed.), *Political Parties in the European Community*, London: Geo. Allen & Unwin, 1979, p. 36−7.
42. P. Møller (ed.), *op.cit.*, and 'P. Hartling' in Krogh and Sørensen (ed.), *op.cit.*, pp. 90−100.
43. Miller, *op.cit.*, diagram on p. 74 and pp. 73−7.
44. Fitzmaurice, *op.cit.*, p. 37−8.
45. P. Møller (ed.), *op.cit.*, and Knud Bro in Krog and Sørensen (ed.), *op.cit.*, p. 84−90. This is a pre-FRP statement for Bro was able to say, 'No taxes are not too high; I will not deny that they may even go higher' (p. 89).

46. Miller, *op.cit.*, pp. 79–82.
47. Fitzmaurice, *op.cit.*, p. 38.
48. Miller, *op.cit.*, p. 85.
49. Svend Skovmand to the author, 1980.
50. Fitzmaurice, *op.cit.*, p. 40, and P. Møller (ed.), *op.cit.*
51. For an account of the origins and policy of KRF, see P. Møller (ed.), *op.cit.*, chapter XII, pp. 223–40. Unlike the rest of the work, KRF, whose material arrived late, is not integrated but is placed as a separate chapter.
52. Fitzmaurice, *op.cit.*, pp. 41–3, and P. Møller (ed.), pp. 27–9.
53. Møller P., *op.cit.*, p. 27.
54. See an English-language publication of the Progress Party (1974): *How much does 60,000 Kr. per year tax-free cost?*
55. *Folketingets Aarbog 1978/79*, p. 15.
56. F.L. Hansen, 'Den Ulykkelige Trekant—eller FRP's Stilling i Dansk Politik' in *Økonomi og Politik*, 50th year, No. 1, 1978, pp. 50–7.
57. Socialdemokratiet, *op.cit.*, p. 12–14, for details of the anti-FRP campaign, and G. Rasmussen, *Det Småborgerlige oprør*, Copenhagen: Demos, 1977.
58. Cerny (ed.), *op.cit.*, pp. 36–37.
59. Fitzmaurice, *op.cit.*, p. 43.
60. Ib Christensen (party chairman) to the author, 1978.
61. Fitzmaurice, *op.cit.*, p. 43.
62. *Politiken*, 9 April 1980, p. 5.
63. Data on FB is taken from Mouritzen, Brenholdt-Larsen, Refslund Petersen, *op.cit.* (note 12), and from 'Europa-Valget' in *Økonomi og Politik*, 53rd year, No. 3.

VI. THE WELFARE STATE

We shall not deal here with the details of welfare state legislation and policy which are, as elsewhere, both complex and ever-changing. Our theme will be the principles behind the welfare state in Denmark, its origins and development, and, most important, its impact as a political issue, with ramifications for economic, fiscal, social and cultural policy.

1. *Development of the Welfare State*

In Denmark, as in most of Europe, welfare was in the hands of the Church and private charity, at least until the Reformation. In the eighteenth century, minimal public responsibility began to be recognised, and measures were taken to prevent local authorities merely expelling indigents from their own areas into those of other authorities. The first such ordinances were passed in 1708 and were improved in 1799.[1]

However, after the Napoleonic wars, economic and social laissez-faire, together with a limited 'ratepayer' democracy at the local level, had serious repercussions on attitudes to problems of social welfare. There was pressure to reduce public assistance to local government for relief of poverty. The poor and especially the unemployed were regarded as responsible for their own situation. As in Britain, the 1830s and 1840s in Denmark saw the progressive suppression of the socially more enlightened forms of 'outdoor relief' in favour of 'workhouse' institutional poor relief, which was cheaper, made for easier control, and was more humiliating for the recipients.[2] There were even, from 1824, controls on the marriage of welfare recipients.

This situation led to two parallel reactions, which eventually converged. The first approach was self-help, through *Syge Kasser* (sickness insurance) and other mutualist organisations, often operated by the trade unions, especially in the case of unemployment insurance. The second approach was to get the demands of workers for a more effective, just and humanitarian system of social welfare, backed by state aid, taken on board by the growing political parties, after the establishment of the constitution in 1849.[3]

New attitudes began to emerge, in particular through the distinction between 'deserving' poor, who were for example unemployed as a result of technical progress or recession, and 'indolent' poor. In 1863, a Commission was set up to look into the relationship between the state and the *Syge Kasser* and other self-help organi-

127

sations. Political pressure gradually brought about greater state involvement in welfare functions. The Slesvig-Holstein war and the subsequent constitutional battle prevented meaningful social reform for some three decades, but in 1891, a limited reform of the poor law was passed, which recognised certain categories of poor as 'deserving' and therefore not subject to the legal disabilities imposed on welfare recipients both by the 1849 constitution and earlier legislation, which could go as far as deprivation of the right to vote. These 'exempted' categories were sick, blind and handicapped people.

A law of 1892 introduced an important new principle:[4] for the first time, the state granted subsidies to the sickness insurance funds. In 1898, an accident insurance law was passed, establishing principles relating to insurance against accidents at work. For the first time, employers were required to subscribe to accident insurance, which was an important new compulsory principle. In 1907, a law provided for the first time for state subsidies to the trade union unemployment insurance funds, which had already existed for some time, and already represented one of the most comprehensive and impressive systems of unemployment assistance in Europe. The organisation and administration of the funds were still to remain in the hands of the trade unions. Already, therefore, by the early 1900s considerable progress had already been made in the direction of a comprehensive welfare system.[5]

Progress after the First World War was slow, and regressive measures were even taken, as the notions of national solidarity resulting from the crisis period rapidly yielded to a wave of laissez-faire and 'retrenchment'. The 1926–9 the VK coalition under Mygdal Madsen believed in the balanced budget and non-intervention in the field of social policy. Public expenditure on social welfare was reduced. The Social Democrats, in opposition, reacted with pledges to restore the cuts which had been made and to extend welfare policies.

In the Social-Radical coalition under Stauning, which held power uninterruptedly from 1929 till 1940, the Minister of Social Affairs was a former wartime civil servant, K.K. Steinecke, who had spent ten years codifying and tidying up the myriad laws on social welfare.[6] These codifications and improvements could not be introduced immediately since the coalition lacked a majority in the *Landsting* (Upper House) until 1935. A package deal was reached with *Venstre* in the '*Kanslergade forlig*' of 1933, after Venstre suffered serious election losses in the elections of that year. The package consisted of an approach to the economic crisis based on: 1, subsidies to agriculture; 2, the maintenance of public and private sector wages (cf.

the public sector wage cuts imposed in Britain by the so-called 'Hatchet Committee' of 1931); and 3, social reforms. At last Steinecke's reform package could be passed. Social legislation was codified into four laws, which with amendments were to remain the basic foundations of social policy for the next forty years.[7]

2. *The Current Situation*

It was in the mid-1960s, a fertile period of social and organisational reformism, that a new comprehensive reform of welfare legislation was set in train. This reform took almost as long to come to realisation as the earlier one. On 29 May 1964, the *Folketing* approved a Resolution calling for a Royal Commission on welfare services. The Commission started work in September 1964 and presented its First Report in 1969, and its Second (final) Report in 1972. A further Committee examined the organisation of certain special institutions such as those for mentally handicapped people.[8]

Legislation based on these reports was first tabled in 1970. The key item of legislation, Law No.333 of 19 June 1974 on Social Assistance, was introduced into the *Folketing* in at least three sessions. It came into force on 1 April 1976.[9] Subsequent legislation on family allowances, pensions, sickness insurance (Law No.94 of 4 March 1976) and special hospitals fitted other aspects of the welfare system to the new structure set-up by the *Bistandslov* (Social Security Act). Important reforms in the pension system have also been carried through. The basic pensionable age remains sixty-seven for men and sixty-two for women, but the possibility of early retirement has been greatly extended and the age reduced from sixty to fifty-five. Since 1964, there have been supplementary earnings-related pensions. Social pensions have become tax-free and important housing subsidies have been accorded to pensioners.

The main thrust of these social reforms was, as in the 1930s, a simplification and codification of a piecemeal and increasingly complex system. At the same time, it was intended to ensure a total decentralisation of the administration of social welfare. The social committee of each *Kommune* is now the basic unit to assist any person in need or difficulty (not only Danish citizens). He need only present his problem to the Social Committee of the *Kommune* where he resides; his sickness insurance is also administered via the *Kommune*'s social committee. Even if the social committee has to refer to certain specialised bodies such as specialised hospital facilities controlled by the *Amts Kommuner* (counties) or directly by the State, it remains the channel for counselling, assistance and administration of aid. This system involves therefore both a decentralisation and simplification of welfare administration.

At the same time, objective need rather than status—pensioner, unmarried mother, young person, unemployed, etc.—has become the determinant of aid. The possible forms of aid and counselling have been greatly widened and generalised.

There have also been changes in the system of health insurance. Early in the 1960s, free medical treatment by GPs was brought in for certain categories. The latest reform of health insurance—in 1978—provided for administration of the scheme by local authorities; the traditional system of two categories of insurance (Group I giving entitlement to free health care and Group II only providing a proportion of cost) was been maintained, but the income criterion for admission to the categories was abolished.[10]

Since the onset of the recession in 1974, important measures have been taken to deal with youth unemployment. Each local administration has provided 40 Kroner per head of its population for measures to combat youth unemployment and a scheme, including subsidies for the cost of the first nine months of a new job, costing 100,000 Kroner over the period 1977–80, has been introduced. The early retirement measures have also helped to reduce unemployment; this measure covered 43,000 people in 1979. There has also been an increase of employment in the public sector (40,000 additional jobs in 1979), which now represents some 30 per cent of total employment. However, in 1980 this increase must be much less.[11]

Certain aspects of housing policy—rents, security of tenure, taxation—have long been subjects of considerable political controversy in Denmark. Despite this, there has been a considerable increase in the proportion of houses in one way or another receiving a public subsidy, from 16.7 per cent in 1973 to 34.1 per cent in 1977. Housing subsidies to pensioners have been an important factor here. Nevertheless, since 1973 housing completions per year have dropped seriously from 55,566 in that year to 36,270 in 1977.[12]

3. *The Political Debate*

As we have seen, there was lively political debate about the value and extent of the welfare state in the nineteenth and early twentieth century. By the 1950s and 1960s, this controversy had died down and all political parties fell into a certain consensus about the welfare state. Whatever detailed criticisms might be levelled against particular items of policy from time to time, no party—except briefly the Independent Party[13] in the late 1950s and, to a certain extent, the Justice Party—contested the view that the welfare state 'was a good thing' and had 'come to stay'.

However, by the early 1970s, the 'Welfarist consensus' was coming under direct attack from many varied directions. The most frontal assault came from the Progress Party, which attacked the heavy cost of welfare and its effect on taxation, but also criticised the 'bureaucratic' and 'initiative-sapping' character of Danish welfare legislation. It has argued that the prevailing ethic among social workers and welfare administrators is anti-industry;[15] that welfare legislation should be made more basic and simpler with, for example, the same basic pension for everyone. The fact that by 1971 public expenditure represented 49.4 per cent of national income (20.4 per cent in transfer payments) and public employment approached 30 per cent of the labour force was grist to their mill.[14] The centre democrats argued that the spiralling welfare costs could not continue to disregard economic factors. The Justice Party could reiterate with renewed confidence that its '*Retsstats*' ideology is basically opposed to welfarism[16].

The attacks on the welfare state from the KRF were based less on its costs or on grounds of individualism than on a belief that the moral aspects of the welfare state were being neglected. The welfare state undermined family responsibility and excluded the Church, as well as fostering a purely materialist outlook in society.[17]

On the far left, too, the welfare state came increasingly under attack. Naturally the far left did not support the FRP line, but did not seem—'objectively', to use a favourite Marxist concept—all that far from it in the sense that they shared the general disillusionment with the high cost and ineffectiveness of the system. However, they went further, pointing to the continued existence of pockets of real poverty, and insisting that the redistribution of income towards lower income groups (5.5 per cent since 1949; 6.0 per cent since 1955 and 7.0 per cent since 1963)[18] was too slow and was inadequate. The welfare state 'was an empty phrase', in the words of a DKP policy statement.[19]

Those who have been the traditional upholders of the welfare state—especially the Social Democrats, the radicals and, to a lesser extent, *Venstre*—found themselves on the defensive. *Venstre*'s position became equivocal: 'There have been in recent years massive increases in the budget of the social sector; *Venstre* must raise the question: can this go on? We answer No.'[20] The radicals have taken up the position of the quality of welfare as against its quantity. The Conservative Party—which was able to argue in 1971 when asked if taxes were too high 'No, and I can not exclude that they will go even higher'[21] now considers that the welfare state is too 'collectivist'.

The Social Democrats, the pillars of the welfare state, were able to see that the existing welfare state has less appeal to the younger generation, which on the one hand takes it for granted, and on the other hand regards it as part of the 'materialist' culture of their elders and indeed almost symbolic of it. It no longer excites any political idealism. Furthermore, there could no longer be any question of extending its boundaries; it was now merely a matter of defending what had been attained: 'The Social Democrats are unconditional supporters of the welfare state . . . this does not mean that we must accept over-bureaucratisation or abuse, against which we must remain on permanent guard; . . . if our 1969 Programme is compared with our 1973 Programme, it will be seen that the latter demands much smaller increases in expenditure, since we are well aware that the coming years will not permit expensive reforms.'[22] The main thrust of the social policy proposals of the Party's most recent Programme (1977) is preventative social action and decentralisation of administration rather than costly new schemes or increased levels of benefits[23].

These ideas have been S's preoccupations in the long rounds of debate on political package deals and expenditure cuts. It has sought to defend the welfare state and resist the pressure from the Right[24] which has built up in recent years. In this it has not been unsuccessful, and here the worthwhile reforms of the mid 1970s stand as concrete evidence of that success.

Despite recent difficulties and controversies, the Danish welfare state has reached a high level of excellence and compares most favourably with the situation in any advanced industrial society. Denmark's GNP per head was fifth in the world and third in Europe (US$8,450 in 1977). There are kindergarten places for 36 per cent of children; maternity leave is fourteen weeks, while hospital care is free; holidays are twenty working days per year; unemployment and sickness benefits are 90 per cent of the wage up to DKr.225 per day.

As the Hudson Institute study *Denmark in Europe 1990* points out (1977), the controversies over the welfare state will continue. The study expects current trends to accentuate; more decentralisation and selectivity without major modifications in the universality or solidarity principle of financing the system.

REFERENCES

1. K. Phillip, *Staten og Fatigdom*, Copenhagen: Gjellerups Forlag, 1947, p.16 – 22.
2. Miller K.E., *Government and Politics in Denmark*, Boston, Mass.: Houghton, Mifflin, 1968, pp. 204 – 5.

3. Phillip, *op.cit.*, pp. 50–7.
4. Phillip, *op.cit.*, pp. 67–8.
5. Miller,*op.cit.*, pp. 205–6.
6. For the background, see Phillip, *op.cit.*, pp. 70–91.
7. See K.K. Steinecke, 'Lidt om Dansk Sociale Lovgivning' in N. Jorgensen (ed.), *Hvad er det at vaere Dansk?*, Copenhagen: Nordisk Forlag, 1953, pp. 54–63.
8. For the setting up and report of this committee, see explanatory footnote to the text of the Law in *Karnovs Lovsamling*, 8th ed., p. 351.
9. For the law and commentary, see *Karnovs Lovsamling*.
10. Socialdemokratiet, *Politisk og Organisatorisk Beretning til Kongressen*, 1977, pp. 17–18.
11. *ibid.*, pp. 14–15, and European Commission, *Report on the Social Situation in the Community*, 1978.
12. European Commission, *op.cit.*
13. See Arne Bertelsen (Independent Party MF) in 'Afsked med Folketing' in *Perspektiv*, February 1963, p. 23, where he stated: 'It is a matter of reducing us all to passive, initiativeless consumer slaves, resulting in an ever-larger administrative apparatus with an ever-larger number of party-loyal functionaries.' The FRP would agree.
14. *Perspektivplans redgørelsen*, 1973, pp. 395 and 415.
15. Møller P., *De Politiske Partier*, Copenhagen: Det Danske Forlag, 1974, p. 107–10.
16. Møller, *op.cit.*, p. 120.
17. *ibid.*, p. 230.
18. S.A. Hansen, *Økonomisk vaekst i Danmark*, Akademisk Forlag, 1974, p.185.
19. Møller, *op. cit.*, p. 118.
20. *ibid.*, p. 110.
21. Knud Bro (KF) in Krogh and Sorensen, *De Politiske Partier og deres Programmer*, Copenhagen: Gyldendal, 1972, p.89.
22. Møller, *op.cit.*, p. 106.
23. *Socialdemokratiets Princip program*, 1978.
24. Socialdemokratiet, *Beretning*, p. 12.

VII. FOREIGN POLICY

For a small country like Denmark—dependent on trade for her economic survival; without major raw materials, particularly in the energy field; with indefensible borders and sitting astride the mouth of a major strategic waterway—it is clear that foreign policy will be an issue of major importance. Denmark has been faced with hard choices in economic and security relations since 1945, which have at times posed difficulties of national identity for a country which has at least three areas of identification: the Atlantic area, the Scandinavian countries and continental Europe. The difficulty of these choices has often meant that the moment of decision has been postponed as late as possible, and that the final choice was made more by a process of elimination—the absence of viable alternatives—than out of evident preference. This has been the case both for NATO and EEC membership. This approach may prevent or limit internal political conflict, but has the disadvantage of reducing Danish credibility and indeed influence in organisations that she appears to have so reluctantly joined. Indeed, in the EEC it earned the sobriquet 'those foot-dragging Danes'.

Foreign policy has as a result often had a salience that it has not had in other countries. Since 1945, at least three foreign policy issues have had important 'backwash' effects into Danish politics: the Slesvig border issue, on which the *Venstre* government fell in 1947; NATO membership (1949); and EEC membership (1970–2). The extent to which foreign policy issues affect voters' behaviour should not be exaggerated, but they do affect the nature of political debate and relations between the parties. For at least 5 per cent of voters the EEC was important in determining their voting behaviour in 1971, but this had fallen to 0.4 per cent in 1973 and 0.2 per cent in 1975.[1] In the late 1940s, the KF and *Retsforbundet* floated the idea of an 'Atlantic Party Government' (S, V, KF),[2] and in 1966 the coalition talks between S and SF largely failed on foreign policy issues.[3] The survival of the Social Democratic minority government (1971–3) was at least partly facilitated by the 'tolerance' of the 'bourgeois' opposition until Danish membership of the EEC was achieved. A resulting characteristic of Danish foreign policy-making is its relatively democratic character. The *Folketing* is closely involved, especially in EEC policy-making.

1. *The Making of Foreign Policy*

The Foreign Minister is responsible for foreign policy, but the Prime

Minister plays a major role in foreign policy issues, both internally, in the *Folketing*, and in negotiations with foreign countries. Other ministers such as those for Defence, Trade, Finance and, in the EEC context, Agriculture are closely concerned in the formulation of foreign policy over which the Prime Minister and Foreign Minister exercise co-ordination, but, at least in Nordic and EEC affairs, they do not exercise a monopoly of initiatives or contacts with foreign states.

The Foreign Minister must obtain approval from the Cabinet for all legislative, budgetary and other major initiatives. Under the constitution, the monarch (in practice, the government) acts on behalf of the kingdom in external matters; however, in foreign affairs, the government is subject not only to the normal parliamentary control, but finds its freedom of action limited by specific constitutional limitations. Article 19 provides that the consent of the *Folketing* is required to conclude treaties the implementation of which would require legislation, or which are otherwise important. Its consent is also required to abrogate such treaties. Its consent is needed to commit Danish forces (even without a declaration of war), except in self-defence.

The 1953 constitution envisages the participation of Denmark in 'supra-national' institutions such as the European Community, but sought to exercise careful control over delegations of sovereignty. Article 20 imposes two limitations. First, it provides that sovereignty must be delegated only to a defined extent, and then only to international organisations set up for the promotion of co-operation and international law. Sovereignty can be delegated neither to an unlimited extent nor to other states. Secondly, such a delegation must be approved either by five-sixths of the members of the *Folketing* or in a referendum. This provision was applied for Danish entry into the EEC.[4]

The Foreign Ministry has grown rapidly since the Second World War. Before 1939, the total staff was under 400; today it is over 2,000. The Ministry is organised into two departments. The first department, External Affairs, is itself divided into divisions dealing with administration, development aid, political questions and United Nations affairs. The second department is responsible for external economic relations, and at various periods (1966–73) has been under the authority of a separate minister, while remaining administratively in the Ministry of Foreign Affairs. This department deals with a wide range of matters; its central function is EEC policy, but it also has the task of trade promotion in general.[5]

2. *Foreign Policy and Parliament*

The *Folketing* has experienced the same problems as other legislatures in controlling foreign policy, which governments often tend to see as an exclusive domain of the executive. However, it has found several original devices and procedures which at least give some comparative substance to democratic control over foreign policy-making in Denmark.

The government is subject to the ordinary procedures of control, such as no-confidence motions. Here one can point to two cases. In 1947, defeated in a vote on Slesvig policy,[6] the *Venstre* government resigned. In 1973, a critical opposition on both the substance and procedure of agriculture negotiations in the EEC Council was only fended off by the Social Democratic minority government compromising with SF. Twice a year there are general interpellations on general foreign policy, and since 1973 this has been the case with EEC policy. These debates may end with votes on motions seeking to bind the government.

The Foreign Ministry's budget (including the overseas development aid budget) requires parliamentary approval. Defence expenditure of course also requires parliamentary approval. This tends to be secured by the negotiation of four-year 'defence policy pacts' with a group of *Folketing* parties, in which the three 'Atlantic parties' will be the central core. Down to 1968 (when the VKR coalition was formed), the Radicals often voted against these pacts—as have the Communists and, after 1960, SF, although in the 1966–8 period SF voted for annual finance bills which included military spending. In particular, the increases in defence expenditure voted immediately after Danish membership of NATO (increased from 359 milliard Kroner in 1950 to 859 milliard in 1953) were opposed by DKP, RV and DR. In 1960, the Radicals participated in a 'defence policy pact' for the first time.

Treaties require ratification by the *Folketing*. This is achieved by means of a *Folketings besluting* (decision), which requires two readings and examination in committee. As early as 1923, the *Folketing* passed a law creating an advisory Foreign Affairs Committee to be consulted by the government on major issues. This Committee is now mentioned in the constitution, and a new law was passed in 1954 fixing its role. It has seventeen members, as do other committees, but it deliberates in secret, and produces no report to the *Folketing*, nor any minutes. It does not examine bills. The Committee must be consulted by the government on all foreign policy decisions 'of major importance'. However, it has often been felt that the secret nature of the discussions in the Committee makes it difficult to bind the government, and at the same time the lack of information among parliamentarians makes effective scrutiny of government actions very difficult. The Committee, with all its imperfections, has permitted the parties to be consulted and to influence the negotiating position of the government on many issues in foreign policy.

Since the 1972 reforms, the *Folketing* also has an External Policy Committee, which is a regular committee under the rules of procedure. It deals with appropriations and administrative issues in relation to foreign policy and development aid. It also handles the small number of bills tabled in this area. In the 1977/8 session, it considered no bills and two draft *Folketing* decisions.[8]

It is in the field of EEC policy that parliamentary control is at its most rigorous.[9] It is carried out in the Market Relations Committee (MRC), which, at one and the same time, is an ordinary committee which can report matters to the *Folketing* (e.g. procedural changes) and handle bills (there have only been two, both on direct elections to the European Parliament), and exercises a special control function closer to that of the Foreign Affairs Committee, but more rigorous and detailed.

There are certain prerequisites for the establishment of a successful system of national parliamentary control over Community policy-making. There must be a strong and active parliamentary system, with parliament playing a central role in government. There must be a strong tradition of parliamentary involvement in the foreign policy-making process. The Community, i.e. both membership and the policies to be pursued within it, must be a political issue. There must be an active core of MPs interested (from whatever point of view) in the Community. As we have seen, these preconditions exist to an especially highly developed degree in Denmark.

In the first ten years of the Community, national parliaments were not expected to play any major role in its life; certainly they had not done so during the life of the Coal and Steel Community founded in 1952. This was essentially because the founders of the Community expected the European Parliament to develop rapidly in step with the other institutions and with the increasing competences of the Community. Implicitly, a transfer of sovereignty, increasing over time, was accepted, but the issue of democratic control in the interim was not faced. The Danish case is particularly interesting because it is the most extreme reaction against such an approach; indeed, it is almost a complete reverse. It is an extreme case, almost a *cas limite*, in that not only does the *Folketing*, through its chosen agent the Market Relations Committee seek to be informed by the government, but it actually seeks to mandate Danish ministers before they attend meetings of the Council of Ministers.

Since 1961, with the first attempt at EEC entry until accession in 1973, the MRC acted as a forum for debate on the options in Market policy, for discussion of the terms of entry on the relative merits of EEC, EFTA and NORDEK (a scheme for Nordic economic co-operation which aborted owing to the defection of Finland). Here the supporters and opponents of entry attempted to buttress their case. In this way the MRC played an important role in the formulation of Market policy before entry.

In its report to the *Folketing* on the bill of entry, the Market Committee had emphasised that the Luxembourg agreement was part of the legal and political basis for Danish membership. The report further took note of the actual power relations among the Community institutions and, in discussing possible ways of exercising democratic control of decision-making, it concluded that control over the Council of Ministers would be essential. This controlling function, according to the report, would have to be performed by national parliaments.[10]

After January 1973, the role of the MRC was to change from that of a deliberative forum to being the main agent of the *Folketing* in controlling the government's Market policy. It was now to undertake the power of co-decision with the government in Market affairs. This was already clear in general terms from Article 6 of the Danish Accession Act, which refers to the Committee.[11]

However, it was the political crisis of February 1973 (arising over the acceptance by the Minister of Agriculture of a highly disadvantageous interim price arrangement for Danish export bacon) which led to the strengthening and formalising of the MRC's role. The fact that the minister had accepted the arrangement without parliamentary backing for the final compromise led to a motion of censure from the Liberal/Conservative opposition which threatened to bring down the minority Social Democrat government. Only a compromise with the Radical Liberals and, above all, with the anti-EEC Socialist People's Party prevented defeat. This compromise involved the passage of a resolution[12] ensuring stronger prior control of decisions right up to the last moment, even if new compromise proposals were made. The question of detailed procedural arrangements was referred to a sub-committee of the MRC, which reported on 29 March 1973.[13] This report provided for a further review of procedure within one year, which was embodied in a report of 14 June 1974.[14] Currently, consideration is being given to the matter of publicity for the work of the MRC; otherwise, these, with certain practical extensions, are the procedures now in force.

The MRC has seventeen full members and fourteen substitute

members, chosen in proportion to party representation in the *Folketing*, as are its other committees. Any party with more than ten members is automatically entitled to committee representation; other parties may enter into pacts for committee election, as was the case of the two anti-market parties (which are otherwise quite opposed), SF and the *Retsforbundet* (Justice Party), in the 1973–5 *Folketing* and since 1977. When full members are present, substitute members may participate in debate, but may not vote. Members are usually high-ranking party leaders and not 'backbenchers'. In the early 1970s, there were two former Prime Ministers, one former Foreign Minister, several other former ministers and party leaders or spokesmen on Market affairs. It was intended at first that Danish members of the European Parliament should be chosen from the MRC; this has never been the case, but now all EP members are either full or substitute members of the Committee. Membership of the Committee has also been extended to at least one Social Democrat opponent of membership of the Community. With Community affairs seeming to become more routine and less politicised, especially since the British referendum, some expected that the level of interest and party representation in the MRC would decline. Till now this has not happened. By custom, the chairmanship goes to the government party (Mr Dalsager in 1973 and Mr Christiansen 1973–5).

It is the corollary of strict parliamentary control (although other reasons may also be involved) that there should be strong co-ordination of Market policy inside the government machine.[15] There is a Cabinet EEC Committee—presided over by the Minister of Foreign Affairs, who (at the time of writing, though this conjunction is not invariable) is also Minister of External Economic Relations (EER)—with the Prime Minister as a member. On parallel lines, there is the Official EEC Committee on which all the obvious ministers and the Prime Minister's Cabinet and the Legal Department of the Justice Ministry are represented. Under this Committee, there are twenty-one groups with from two to nine members representing from two to five ministries. While the official committee is chaired by the senior civil servant in the EER Ministry, the groups have varied chairmanship from the competent ministries. All points on the agenda of the Council of COREPER (the Committee of Permanent Representatives in Brussels) are discussed by both these committees, at least as 'A' points, and the Foreign Ministry alone issues instructions to the Danish permanent representation in Brussels. The political co-operation machinery is co-ordinated by the Foreign Ministry, and summit conferences are prepared by both ministries. This tight system enables political co-ordination and control of Market policy. Thus political responsibility is clear, and the government itself must decide on consultation or non-consultation of the MRC from case to case.

Every fourteen days the MRC receives from the government a list of Commission proposals, with a standardised form for each one giving certain basic information such as the main aim of the proposal, its legal and financial implications, and the probable timetable for its adoption by the Council. A copy of each proposal goes to the Secretariat of the *Folketing*, the MRC Secretariat and the party Secretariats of each party.[16] The MRC also receives more general Community documents such as reports, draft Council resolutions and explanatory statements from the government to other *Folketing* committees. The government has responsibility for consulting the MRC, but the Committee can itself raise issues (SF raised the Directives on banking and insurance activities), although this is rare; in this, party secretariats are an element of vigilance. The government has an interest in avoiding a new crisis by ensuring adequate consultation. The MRC has also considered more general issues such as summit conferences and documents of a preliminary nature, such as the Commission's first document on regional policy.

The MRC meets at least once a week for two to three hours and may meet at any time, at short notice, even at night and in the recess. The Committee procedure is flexible and fairly informal. The points on the agenda of every Council meeting in the coming week are gone through. The documentation on each item, which may include opinions from other *Folketing* committees, is supplemented by a short oral presentation by the minister of the negotiating mandate which he proposes to take with him to the Council of Ministers. The Committee is a political committee; it meets with ministers and not with civil servants or experts. Competent departmental ministers such as the Minister of Agriculture and, for summit conferences, the Prime Minister attend; the ministers will reply to questions and comments made by members. As in the Foreign Affairs Committee, the minister or the chairman may declare information confidential (this has only been invoked twice), which precludes its public use, but not its discussion in party groups.[17]

No quorum is required in the Committee since, except in rare cases where the MRC acts as a normal committee examining a bill or on procedural matters, it does not hold ordinary votes. The chairman must sum up the discussion on each issue and declare whether or not there is a majority against a proposed mandate. There is no requirement for a positive vote; if there is no majority against the mandate, the minister may negotiate on that basis. If the MRC fails to adopt a position, then the minister is free to act as he thinks fit. The chairman does not count heads in deciding the opinion of the Committee; he takes account of the support represented on the floor of the House by the different party spokesmen. This 'negative clearing procedure' gives the government a certain amount of room for manoeuvre.

The MRC does not make written reports or adopt resolutions (though its secretariat does draw up a summary record for internal use), nor does it report to the *Folketing*. It speaks with the full political (if not legal) authority of the *Folketing*; the minister is politically obliged to follow the MRC's opinion. Such a 'delegation' is quite in line with the traditions of the *Folketing*, especially in the Foreign Affairs Committee and the Finance Committee. Members of the MRC normally consult their groups; however, they are, as we have seen, usually party leaders who can, in urgent cases, commit their parties. By custom, parties in any case accept commitments made by their representatives in committees.

The mandate is, of course, not arrived at on a 'take it or leave it' basis, but can be negotiated with the Committee. It is inclined to be fairly general, but may in some cases go into some detail: setting a range of agricultural prices; imposing conditions on the free movement of doctors; guaranteeing that the European Parliament will use its right of global rejection of the budget responsibly; setting conditions on the conduct of direct elections to the European Parliament or the maximum size of the Regional Fund. In fact, attitudes have frequently been dictated to a large extent by a pro- or anti-Market attitude, which has ensured a solid pro-Market majority on most issues in the MRC.

Certain practical arrangements have been made to provide for an abbreviated procedure in urgent cases, as was explained by Mr Baunsgaard in an article in *Politiken* in March 1974.[18] Discussing the 1974 price review, he made it clear that where protracted negotiation or a rapid evolution in such negotiation makes a rapid judgement necessary, the political parties in the MRC have appointed a contact man (either for each issue or as a general contact man). The ministry calls this group of the parties' contact men together and it may approve the new mandate proposed by the minister (not necessarily the Foreign Minister). Failure to agree on a new mandate, or rather failure to approve the government's position, will lead to the full MRC being called into session.[19]

The MRC can call for an opinion from other specialised committees, and this possibility is increasingly utilised, e.g. in such matters as tax harmonisation and water pollution.

Special problems arise in connection with the MRC's relations with other *Folketing* committees in the foreign relations field.[20] The

Udenrigsnaevnet (Foreign Affairs Committee—FAC) was established by the constitution (Article 19) and its detailed working was laid down by a law of 1954. It must be consulted by the government on major foreign policy issues and can, like the MRC, receive confidential information from the government. At times, also like the MRC, it has 'mandated' the government on specific issues such as votes in the United Nations. In general, consultation with the FAC ensures the government parliamentary backing for its foreign policy initiatives. Also like the MRC, this committee has a semi-autonomous status and does not consider legislation. It is not competent for Market policy, but of course certain aspects of Market policy and of political co-operation do impinge on general foreign policy, and the FAC is interested in the general foreign policy context of Market policy, such as relations with the United States or the Security Conference on Security and Co-operation in Europe (CSCE) and East-West problems. This delineation of competence, discussions in party groups and joint membership, as well as occasional joint meetings, ensure co-ordination and consistency. Some issues which arise in different international fora: for example the issue of whether the EEC should have Observer Status in the United Nations concerned both EEC and UN policy, so involving both committees.

The *Udenrigspolitisk Udvalg* (External Policy Committee) is an ordinary committee of the *Folketing*, which examines bills in the field of foreign affairs and overseas development and scrutinises budgetary and administrative matters relating to foreign affairs and overseas aid. This committee may give the MRC an opinion, but its competence is quite different. It should be pointed out that the MRC alone retains the right to approve the ministers' mandate under the various resolutions of the *Folketing*.

As we have seen earlier in this chapter, other more traditional devices of parliamentary control and information can also be applied in the field of Market policy. In recent years there has been a marked increase in the number of questions on EEC policy.[21] The main device, however, is the interpellation. It may be of two kinds: specific, such as that on the UN Observer status issue, or general. Such general debates are held two or three times a year and may be as general as 'What information can the minister give on Market affairs?' Here the minister can give a general account of the development of the Communities and of government policy. The spokesmen of the political parties can make general policy statements. Rival pro- and anti-Market resolutions or amendments may be tabled; the voting on these gives an impression of the political climate and as such must be taken seriously by the government. The debates up to now (apart from those on specific issues) have followed a basic pattern: affirmation by the pro-Market parties of membership under strong parliamentary control and a restatement of their belief in the pragmatic development of the Community, against the reiteration of opposition to membership and to further supranational extension of the Community from the anti-Market elements (variously, SF, the Justice Party, the Communists, the left Socialists and individual members of the Radical, Social Democrat and Progress Parties). Both sides have repeatedly emphasised the narrowness of the 'social contract' on the basis of which membership was accepted. The debates showed that a core of anti-marketeers continued to exist. In the May 1973 debate, thirty-eight members opposed the pro-Market resolution. In December 1975, twenty-nine members voted against direct elections and ten abstained. This vote was not, of course, synonymous with opposition to the EEC as such. However, internal dissension in the Social Democratic Party has declined. The Progress Party of Mogens Glistrup is broadly a pro-Market party, but in the 1974 debate its spokesman declared that while he was not against membership, he was a 'sceptic' and insisted, as the Party has subsequently done, on the requirement of a new referendum if the supranational element in the Community is to be extended.[22] At the same time, there has been some development in the position of the SF, especially since the British referendum; total withdrawal from the EEC is no longer its policy, but rather what it calls 'constructive opposition'.[23]

Certainly the MRC has become 'a very important part of the whole decision-making process in relation to our Market policy'.[24] It is without doubt the most effective example of national parliamentary control in any member-state, but it is not without limitations and problems. Some early problems of a more or less technical nature—e.g. the flow of information, re-examination of amended proposals and the role of other committees—have largely been solved. The issues of greater public awareness of, and publicity for, the MRC's work are now the subject of reflection. On the whole, public hearings are not considered a good idea, but greater press briefing may be adopted. There are some who fear that the Committee will become increasingly bureaucratised and technocratic as political interest in the EEC as an issue wanes. However, at present the Committee remains political. At the same time it is feared that as the issue of EEC membership becomes less controversial, and if a clear majority were to take office for a longer period than the S-V coalition, party representation in the MRC would decline in calibre, with more 'backbenchers' and fewer leaders. At the moment, neither problem looms large.

There are difficulties in mandating ministers in fluid international

negotiating situations. Even if the *Folketing* does not feel the traditional reticence in intervening in foreign affairs that is found in
some parliaments, difficulties do arise in that much of the Community policy advances through complex package deals and compromises. Considerable information and knowledge of the overall
policy context is often needed to make intelligent intervention in the
process possible, to an extent that is perhaps beyond the capacity of a
parliamentary committee in the more difficult cases. At best, a committee can impose constraints on the government; it cannot develop
a positive, alternative strategy in Market policy. In such circumstances there have been demands for even tighter control and a more
coherent approach.

Anti-Marketeers wish to maintain the Committee as a bulwark
against what they consider to be new encroachments on Danish
sovereignty. Thus, in the May 1973 debate Jens Maigaard (SF) and
Gert Petersen (SF) argued for more written statements from
ministers, particularly on recurrent matters such as agricultural
prices, and written reports of MRC meetings. They also argued that
the government should set out a more coherent overall EEC
strategy.[25] For anti-Marketeers, greater control is justified precisely
because, once taken, Council decisions are binding and represent a
fait accompli, which of course does not, for all that, mean that
attempts to exercise controls should be abandoned, but only that one
should be aware of the difficulties. Such considerations led Ib Christensen (Justice Party) to suggest that the MRC should have a
quorum and that the mandate should be approved by a positive
majority.[26] Other parties (SF, DKP, FRP) have also suggested that
the rules should be tightened up. SF has proposed that written
reports of meetings should be made up and that more material
should be made available to members. The FRP has sought to have
more information systematically made available on the economic
consequences for the proposed mandate.[27] These different proposals
have not been accepted by the majority of the MRC.

Other proposals have not concerned procedure, but have sought
to increase the reach of the procedure to cover the European Council
meetings and political co-operation (foreign policy co-operation
between the EEC member-states). Mr. Glistrup has sought to
simplify the control of foreign policy by proposing the suppression
of the Foreign Policy Committee and passing all foreign policy
matters to the MRC. Mr. Maigaard simply proposed that political
co-operation should be subject to the same degree of control as ordinary EEC matters.[28] The other parties, representing the majority,
have considered, of successive annual reviews of the procedure, that
no change was needed and rejected the proposals from the minority.

However, the MRC has agreed that the European Council meetings should fall under the procedure.[29]

The majority seems to consider that the MRC has, so to speak, reached routine cruising speed. The difficult days of controversy over membership and its effects are past. The MRC has proved its worth, and on the whole the standard of its membership has been maintained—two new party leaders, Mr Glistrup (FRP) and Gert Petersen (SF) have become members. The majority seem to feel that the system is as tight as it can be without excessively tying Danish ministers in the Council, where other member-states do not apply (or even appear to understand) such a system. Indeed, the Danish reservations on some issues have aroused hostility from other member-states and the Commission. Recently, the problem seems less to the fore. It follows that a delicate balance must be maintained between the requirements of parliamentary control and correct functioning of the Community institutions.

For the moment, the present system seems to be right; direct elections have made no difference to the system. All Danish parties consider that, in the first instance, parliamentary control is a national matter, to which a directly elected parliament can be a useful adjunct.

3. *Danish Foreign Policy, 1864–1945*

After 1864, the critical question was what foreign policy lessons Denmark would draw from her disastrous defeat at the hand of Prussia and Austria.[30] She resisted the temptation to ally herself with France during the Franco-Russian War in 1870. Had she done so, no doubt she would again have been heavily defeated by Prussia. The key issue in the period down to 1914 was that of defence policy. Denmark sought to remain neutral in major international conflicts and to defend that neutrality. A battle developed inside *Venstre*, the governing party at the time, between I.C. Christensen and Mr Neergaard. Christensen wanted a defence system limited to Copenhagen, which in reality meant a neutrality leaning towards Germany. Neergaard wanted a more evenhanded neutrality. These issues were not resolved before 1914, when the Radical government under Zahle, with Erik Scavenius as Foreign Minister, safeguarded Danish neutrality by accepting, with British agreement, the mining of the Storbaelt (the sound between Fyn and Sjaelland) to close entry to the Baltic.

With the collapse of both German and Russian power in the Nordic area after 1918, and the reunification of North Slesvig with Denmark after 1920, there were real prospects that Danish neutrality

could continue without being threatened. Even the KF and V agreed
to reduce military expenditure in 1922. The Social Democrats and
Radicals voted against these reductions as being insufficient.

After 1933, the situation became progressively more dangerous.
With some equivocation, the Social Democrats moved towards
favouring rearmament, but in reality without outside aid (and
neither Britain nor Sweden offered any pledges of support)
Denmark was indefensible. Her policy was based on neutrality and
'non-provocation', supporting the illusory collective security
approach of the League of Nations, but not to the point of effective
action. Denmark abstained in the League on a motion to condemn
German military violations of the Versailles Treaty. She had also to
take account of the dangers posed by German minority in Slesvig. In
1938, Jens Møller, a Nazi, was elected leader of the minority, and
although the latter only increased its vote from 15.5 per cent in 1935
to 15.9 in 1939, the danger that a 'minority problem' might be
fomented with direct German intervention was ever present. When
Germany offered the three Nordic states a non-aggression pact in
1939, Denmark alone accepted. She had certainly not obtained satis-
faction or any pledge of support in the intermittent negotiations with
the other Scandinavian states on a military alliance in the period
1933–7, and as a result, her margin for manoeuvre was extremely
limited.

During the occupation itself, Danish foreign policy was in a
dualistic position and found expression through a variety of
channels. Down to 29 August 1943 when the legal government
refused to submit to further German pressure, the main concern of
that government had been to limit German interference in Danish
affairs—at the price, where necessary, of serious concessions. This
meant signing the Anti-Comintern Pact and accepting the recruit-
ment of *Frikorps Danmark* to join the 'crusade against bolshevism'
on the Eastern front and internal measures against the Communists
and other resisters. The Resistance movement, later under the
leadership of the *Frihedsrådet*, always pursued another line: it was
concerned not with German but with Allied reactions. It was concerned to ensure that Denmark was accorded Allied status and
United Nations membership in 1945. To this end, the Danish ambassadors in Washington (Henrik Kauffman) and London (Count
Reventlow) pursued an independent line, approving the occupation
of Greenland by the United States and Iceland and the Faeroes by
Britain. It also sought to co-operate with the British Special Operations Executive (S.O.E.) and sent a representative to Moscow.

4. *Security Policy after 1945*

Many in Denmark were now under no illusion about neutrality, broad collective security or the country's capacity to defend itself, but she continued to place her faith in the maintenance of the wartime alliance, through the United Nations, for as long as possible. However, her defence capacity was zero, and it had to be rebuilt. A 100,000 strong *Hjemmevaernet* (militia) was set up in 1946 (already DKP, RV and DR voted against this foreshadowing their later attitude on security policy questions). Already at that time an argument in favour was the need to improve Denmark's credibility in any future defence pact negotiations. But as late as 1948, Prime Minister Hedtoft was expressing himself against the Danish membership of any military bloc.[31]

Events moved swiftly: there was the strange 'Easter Crisis' in 1948 when there were strong (unfounded) rumours of Soviet military intervention in Denmark and possibly other Scandinavian countries; there was the coup in Prague in 1948 which eliminated the last democracy behind the Iron Curtain. There followed a complex interlude of initiatives and counter-initiatives among the Nordic countries. Sweden was basically sceptical towards a Nordic defence union, largely for foreign policy reasons, but feared (and sought to contain) Norwegian leanings towards an American alliance. Denmark favoured a Nordic defence alliance, with or without links to a wider Western alliance or aid from it. The Swedes proposed talks that were held in Karlstad, and continued in Akershus (Oslo) in January 1949. An alliance could not be formed; Denmark still proposed a joint Danish-Swedish alliance as an alternative, but Sweden was opposed to such an entity which would not be independent of the Atlantic alliance, which was already in the making. So it was that, left with no alternative, Denmark signed the NATO Treaty in Washington on 4 April 1949. The Treaty was ratified by the three 'NATO parties': *Socialdemokratiet, Venstre*, KF. It was opposed by the Communists and Radicals, who also proposed a referendum, and most of the Justice Party members.

Denmark became a 'low-profile'[32] member of NATO, keeping her military and foreign policy commitments at a strict minimum. For example, she is refusing to implement the 3 per cent increase in real expenditure agreed within the Alliance in 1978. She has always sought, since the darkest days of the Cold War, to give NATO a dual objective: to protect the security of its members, and to promote détente. She was thus an early supporter, from 1966, of the idea of a conference on security and co-operation in Europe; she was also an early supporter of the 'two Germanies' line. Initially she opposed the admission of Greece and Turkey to NATO; in her view, these new members greatly increased the risk of the alliance being drawn into war. She only gave way when she found herself isolated on the issue. Denmark was also reluctant to see Germany admitted to NATO, and only accepted when American pressure became overwhelming and impossible to resist. She has consistently rejected the installation of nuclear weapons or foreign bases on her soil. With the admission of Germany to NATO, the problem of joint commands in the Baltic area took on new overtones. Careful balancing ensured that in fact three out of four senior command posts were at any one time held by Danes. By this time, 63 per cent of the population accepted the arrangements as necessary, and an SF motion opposing these command arrangements in the *Folketing* only attracted one Radical vote in addition to the nine SF votes. The 1969 date for the renewal of the alliance came and went quietly; the VKR government did set up a committee to look at the issue—a sop to the Radicals' traditional susceptibilities on the issue—but conveniently the committee reported well after 1969. However, the recent refusal to accept theatre nuclear weapons and opposition to the NATO decision taken in Brussels in December 1979 to proceed with the production of these weapons indicated continuing ambiguity on the attitude to be adopted towards Western defence. At the same time, Denmark has been the most prudent of all NATO allies on the Soviet invasion of Afghanistan, an attitude attributable to her traditional attachment to détente.[33]

There is little doubt that the development of policy has been in tune with public opinion polls, showing support for NATO running at 40 per cent in 1949 and 41 per cent in 1966. Support was always above the number who opposed it. There was a marked growth in 'don't knows' in the 1960s. Peaks in support for NATO membership corresponded to crisis periods: 1956 (Hungary); 1961 (Berlin); 1968 (Czechoslovakia). On the other hand, if one looks at the falling support for neutrality in 1949, demonstrated in the accompanying table, based on opinion poll findings, the pattern is equally telling.[34]

Voters of:	For neutrality(%)			For NATO(%)		
	10 Feb.	2 Mar.	29 Mar.	10 Feb.	2 Mar.	29 Mar.
S	40	25	25	32	47	52
RV	60	54	61	17	25	19
K	20	13	9	62	76	78
V	25	14	7	58	68	72
DR	51	37	38	38	48	48
DKP	90	94	100	3	2	0

These figures show a clear general fall in support for neutrality and a rise in support for NATO, but they also show a clear polarisation, with opposition to NATO also growing in the Communist Party and the Radical Party, which of course voted against membership. The Justice Party electorate is plainly divided and indecisive, with a narrow margin (51 per cent) for neutrality turning into a plurality (48 per cent) for NATO membership, but with the largest pro-neutrality minority among 'pro-NATO' electorates. This can explain the fact that the parliamentary group split in the vote.

5. *European Integration*[35]

Denmark joined the non-supranational European institutions of the early 1950s: the Council of Europe, OECD and the European Payments Union. These organisations were limited in scope and did not affect fundamental trade or political orientations. It was the movement towards integration in the early 1950s which found concrete expression in the establishment first of the Coal and Steel Committee, and then of Euratom and the EEC, which faced Denmark with hard choices. In 1957, she stayed out because two of her three major trading partners (Britain and Scandinavia) remained outside the EEC. As a response, the European Free Trade Association (EFTA) was formed in early 1960. It was formed essentially of Britain, the Scandinavian countries, Austria, Switzerland and Portugal. It had no wider political implications, and no supranational institutions. Its aims were modest, being limited to industrial free trade. Bridge building between EFTA and the EEC was unavailing, and in July 1961 Britain applied for EEC membership. Were Britain to join the EEC, EFTA would be reduced to a rump with little economic interest to Denmark; furthermore, two-thirds of Denmark's agricultural market would be inside the protective wall of the EEC's common external tariff and eventually inside the wall of the Common Agricultural Policy.

So Denmark also applied for membership. This step was approved by the *Folketing* by 152 votes to eleven (SF), but the resolution linked Danish and British membership, which led the government to reject the French offer of unilateral membership after General de Gaulle's veto on British entry in January 1963; however, in the next year the Conservatives and Liberal parties sought to make this linkage less absolute and hoped for the adoption of a new *Folketing* resolution. The Social Democrats, supported by the Radicals, refused. SF sought a totally different policy based on a Nordic customs union. With the British 15 per cent import surcharge in 1964—a clear breach of EFTA rules—confidence in EFTA suffered a severe blow.

Denmark sought to increase EFTA's role in agriculture and entered into discrete talks with France in an effort to reduce the effects of the division of Europe into two trading blocs. The new British application of 1967 was immediately followed by a second Danish application, approved in the *Folketing* by 150 votes to twenty (SF). In fact, this new application had no real chance of success. With the resignation of de Gaulle in April 1969, a new flexibility entered French policy; the veto on Britain was raised at the Hague Summit of late 1969, and formal negotiations opened at the end of June 1970.

As the issues at stake became more precise and clear, and as a real decision came nearer, the national consensus became more and more battered. Within political parties and organisations, divisions became apparent. The Social Democrats proposed, and the 'bourgeois' VKR coalition accepted, that the issue of membership should be decided by a referendum, even if the provisions of Article 20 did not require it. This was supposed to remove the issue from the 1971 election campaign—which in the event was only partially achieved. Divisions within the parties became ever more evident. Even those parties which took a clear and unequivocal stand on the EEC had appreciable minorities within their electorates which opposed the line of the leadership (up to 15 per cent for the SF and KF, less for *Venstre*). For the other parties, divisions showed up increasingly in the successive votes in the *Folketing*, which at the same time showed (see Table) that the hurdle of a five-sixths majority of the membership of the *Folketing* required by Article 20 of the constitution could not be achieved.[36]

After the signature of the Treaty of Accession in January and before the final *Folketing* vote on 8 September and the referendum on 2 October 1972, the debate became increasingly bitter. It was led by the pro-EEC parties such as the Social Democrats, *Venstre* and the Conservatives and the EF (EEC) Committee funded largely by industry, and on the other side the small anti-EEC parties in and outside the *Folketing*: SF (the only party then represented in the *Folketing*), DKP, VS, DR and *Dansk samling*, linked in the hastily formed and ill-financed Peoples' Movement against the EEC.

Both sides even now remember the campaign[37] as having been a hard one, each still accusing the other of demagogy, exaggeration, under-hand motives, 'violation of truth' and cynical use of advertising techniques. For the Peoples' Movement there was also the fact that the pro-Marketeers' financial resources seemed to enable them to 'buy' the referendum. Such disillusioned sentiments did much to persuade the essentially *ad hoc* Peoples' Movement to continue after the referendum as a focus for latent opposition to the EEC and eventually to fight the European elections.

Date of vote	Voting for Membership	Voting against Membership	Abstentions	Absent
11 Nov. 1967	152 (S + RV + KF + V)	11 (SF)	1 (Faeroes)	8
11 Nov. 1970	119 (S + RV + KF + V)	13 (SF & Others)	0	47
18 May 1971	132 (S + RV + KF + V)	12 (SF & Others)	2 (1 Faeroes + 1 RV)	33
16 Dec. 1971	141 (S + RV + KF + V)	32 (SF + 11S + 4RV)	2 (1 Greenland + 1 RS)	4
8 Sept. 1972	141 (S + RV + KF + V)	34 (17 SF + 12 S + 4 RV + 1 Faeroes)	2 (Greenland)	2

The basic case of the pro-Marketeers was economic. Some saw it in terms of opportunity for agriculture and industry; others, more reluctant, saw it essentially in the negative terms of the absence of any viable economic alternative. The pro-Marketeers also argued that it was dangerous for Denmark to remain aloof from the growing power of the Community. They underplayed the political and foreign policy aspects, arguing that the Community was not going to become a 'political union' and that Denmark could defend her interests and singularity inside the EEC, retaining the right of veto over important decisions.

The anti-Marketeers emphasised the political aspects: the irrevocable nature of membership, and the dangers of being gradually forced to accept a European foreign policy and a European defence policy, which would bind Denmark and break her Nordic links. The dangers of integration in a unit dominated by what were seen as socially and politically more reactionary partners were underlined. The possibility of a progressive abandonment of sovereignty was a major anti-Market theme. The economic arguments were less important for the anti-Marketeers, especially in the agriculture field, where it was hard for them to deny the benefits. They simply denounced what they regarded as the excessive optimism of the pro-marketeers. Much of their argumentation was nationalistic, not to say chauvinistic: appeals to national sentiment and to national independence. The comment of one leading anti-Marketeer after it became known that there was a 'yes' majority shows the general tone. He called 2 October (the day of the referendum) 'a new 9th of April'. The 9th of April 1940 was the date of the Nazi occupation.

Denmark voted overwhelmingly for membership. The turnout was 90.19 per cent and 64 per cent voted 'yes'. However, the 36 per cent who voted 'no' was considerably in excess of the 13.8 per cent of the voters who had supported the four anti-Market parties at the 1971 elections. Many of them were Social Democratic voters, perhaps up to 500,000. Although Denmark voted to join the EEC, it was not an act of unmitigated enthusiasm; nor did it represent a blank cheque. There was an implied 'contract'. Support for entry was essentially contingent on obtaining economic benefits and on the proviso that there would be no substantial change in the powers of the institutions and that the veto right in the council would be maintained. The tactics of the anti-EEC parties in the *Folketing*[38] and the People's Movement after 1973 were constantly to recall these conditions attached to the 'Yes' of October 1972, to point out violations of them and to insist on strong internal parliamentary control. Their line was that any change in these conditions required another referendum. This position retained some credibility until the British referendum in June 1975, because it is clear that British membership was both an economic and a political precondition for Danish membership. Since that time, SF initially gave the impression of moving towards a more flexible line, but internal upheavals in the party, as well as the issue of direct elections, prevented the development of this approach. Ironically, direct elections—which the Peoples' Movement had strongly opposed—gave it a second wind, not least because during the campaign it was able to put the pro-Market parties and especially the Social Democrats on the defensive, in what was to become almost a plebiscite on EEC membership.

The approach of the pro-Market parties was often a good deal less clear in its direction. All parties opposed 'federalism' and institutional experiment, as was exemplified in the negative reaction of the Danish government to the Tindemans' Report (1976) on European union, and in the initial opposition to direct elections, except on conditions which would have greatly limited their impact in Denmark: the compulsory dual mandate and the holding of elections on the same day as *Folketing* elections. This position was reluctantly abandoned since it lacked majority backing in the *Folketing*.

The Danish government and the pro-Market parties (with varying emphasis) have underlined the economic benefits that have accrued to Denmark, or at least the protection from the hostile economic forces outside the Community. They declared themselves to be in favour of all forms of closer pragmatic co-operation in the EEC, especially in the energy field, in monetary policy, in economic co-ordination and in employment policy. It is significant that Denmark joined the European Monetary System (EMS) at its inception in 1979, because it represented effective co-operation in an area of vital interest to Denmark. Denmark initially placed great importance on being close to Britain in EEC questions (e.g. on institutional issues), and British membership was of course a *sine qua non* of Danish membership. However, in more recent years, divergences of interest on issues such as fisheries policy, the budgetary contribution, the level of prices under the Common Agricultural Policy, and the EMS have led to a less close identification with Britain.

The issue of Danish membership of the Community is kept alive by the Peoples' Movement against the EEC. It argues for Danish withdrawal and points to recent opinion polls giving over 50 per cent of the votes against membership, and to the results of the European elections, where its list obtained four seats and one other anti-Marketeer (SF) was elected. Paradoxically, however, the Market seems to have few direct consequences in domestic politics. The European elections which were so disastrous for the Social Democrats (21.9 per cent and three seats) were followed within four months by their gaining four seats in the *Folketing* elections; the excellent result for the anti-Marketeers was followed by a reduction of their number in the *Folketing*. At all events, the issue remains there in the background and can revive at anytime, but there would seem to be immense difficulties in the way of those who would seek withdrawal. However, it is undeniable that they exert a certain restraint on market policy.[39]

6. *Nordic Co-operation*

Nordic co-operation is one of the central pillars of Danish foreign policy,[40] even if the results have not always been as great as hoped for. Denmark's instinct has often been to pursue the Nordic option first and to look at other options only when it fails, but even then trying to keep the door open to her Nordic partners. The balance between Nordic and other commitments is one of the problems of Danish foreign policy-making.

Nordic co-operation has a long history in many fields,[41] being as often as not initially the product of private and semi-private initiatives. Regular conferences of lawyers, judges and officials began in the 1870s. In 1880, identical legislation on bills of exchange was adopted in Denmark and Sweden. Most judgements have been made mutually enforceable. Since 1946, a Nordic committee on legislative co-operation works to promote legislative unity on matters such as patents, company law and taxation, criminal procedure and citizenship law. Co-operation in social policy began in 1907, and conferences now cover all areas of the welfare state. Sixteen reciprocity agreements were consolidated into one general convention in 1955, and a labour market convention (1954) created a single Scandinavian labour market. Postal co-operation began in 1869, and in 1946 a Nordic postal association was set up. Railway administration began to co-operate in 1874. The Nordic area is also, since 1952, a single passport area, and Nordic citizens may travel within Scandinavia (Denmark, Norway and Sweden) without a passport. Nordic citizens can, after a short period of residence, vote in local and regional elections in Nordic countries other than their native country. Thus, for example, Nordic citizens can vote in *Kommune* and *Amtskommune* elections and stand for election.

As early as 1863, the first Scandinavian Economic Conference was held among businessmen, economists and politicians, and later conferences produced monetary agreements. Plans for an economic union have appeared from time to time, but have not achieved results. However, a Joint Scandinavian Committee for Economic Co-operation was set up in 1948.

Co-operation in the field of security and foreign policy has, as we have seen, produced less concrete results. However, even in the 1930s Nordic Foreign Ministers met to attempt to reach a common line on issues facing the region. The Nordic Foreign Ministers now meet twice a year to discuss international issues. They co-operate closely in the U.N. and other international organisations, often jointly supporting candidates for office, taking joint positions and voting the same way.

As early as 1938, the Danish Foreign Minister proposed giving these essentially informal and unstructured relations a more institutionalised setting through the creation of a 'Nordic Council'. This proposal was not followed up before the war. After the failure of the Nordic defence negotiations after the war, the Danes re-launched the idea at the 1951 meeting of the Nordic Interparliamenty Union. In parallel, other initiatives in the field of parliamentary co-operation were taking place. In January 1951 initiatives were taken in the Swedish, Danish and Norwegian parliaments for the creation of a Nordic Committee for Traffic Freedom. This Committee worked from 1951 till 1956, and succeeded in removing many minor restrictions on inter-Nordic movement and promoted a passport union. It was replaced by a smaller permanent body under the Nordic Council, set up in 1952. Again, on Danish initiative, a conference of government experts, Ministers and seventeen legislators from the Nordic parliaments was held in Copenhagen on 8–9 May 1950 to consider divergences over the implementation of the work of an expert committee on a new uniform citizenship law. A similar meeting (outside the Nordic Council) was held in Stockholm in 1960 on the proposal for a uniform copyright law.

Denmark had always felt that Nordic co-operation, although essentially pragmatic, should be given a more permanent and coherent framework. She now revived her 1938 proposal for the establishment of a Nordic Council. The proposal was followed by involved negotiations. The Danes wanted a strong central secretariat and parliamentary organs; the Norwegians were sensitive to any apparent 'supra-national' element, however minor; while the Swedes were in an intermediate position. In the final text, initial proposals for ministerial voting participation and a central secretariat were eliminated. Even so, the Norwegian bourgeois parties voted against the statute. Again, in order to avoid any impression of 'supra-nationality' the statute of the Nordic Council is not an international treaty. It has simply been adopted in parallel by each member-state. Indeed, only in Denmark did this adoption even take the form of a law.

The Nordic Council consists of sixty-nine[42] representatives of the five parliaments of Denmark, Norway, Sweden, Finland and Iceland. The four larger countries each send sixteen members, and Iceland sends five. The members are selected by the national parliaments for such terms and by such procedures as they choose; however the Council statute does provide that different political opinions shall be represented. Usually, the delegations have been selected proportionally to the composition of the national parliaments, but smaller parties have mostly not been able to obtain represetation. The Danish delegation chosen for the 1978 session included representatives of S, V, K, CD, FRP, DR, DKP; sometimes smaller parties obtain an alternate member. In the 1978 meeting, Mr Steen Folke(VS) attended in place of Mr Ib Nørlund (DKP) whose alternate he was. Historically, Social Democrats have usually held just under a majority of the sixty-nine seats, and there has been a small 'bourgeois' majority, with a few representatives of the far left

(SF and the Finnish SKDL).

The organs of the Council are the five national working committees (a steering committee for each delegation), which together form the joint working committee. The leaders of the national working committees are by tradition their countries' representatives in the Praesidium. The national working committees are responsible for nominating members of committees. The joint committee, the national committees and the Praesidium are to consult to prepare the work of the Council. The Praesidium receives proposals, refers them to the committees and may undertake preliminary studies on them; it also calls committee meetings between sessions, supervises the secretariats and follows up the recommendations of the Council. There is no central secretariat. Each national delegation has a secretariat, and the secretariat of the host-country services the annual session. The committee originally set up *ad hoc* or interim committees, but since 1955 permanent standing committees have been set up. There are now five committees: legal affairs; cultural affairs; social affairs and environment; transport; economic affairs. The economic affairs committee has twenty-two members, the cultural affairs committee has seventeen members and the other committees have thirteen members each. Since 1964, the committees have been authorised to meet outside the annual sessions.

The Council holds an annual session in one of the national capitals (18–22 February 1978 in Oslo) lasting about five days. The Council is 'an organ for consultation between the parliaments of Denmark, Finland, Iceland, Norway and Sweden, as well as the governments of these countries, in matters involving joint action by one or all of the countries'. It receives proposals from the elected members and governments; it also discusses reports from governments on the action taken to follow up recommendations of the Council, and it discusses the reports from the governments on Nordic co-operation. The Praesidium asks the governments to submit reports on particular topics under this rubric. A general debate is organised in each session, usually on economic co-operation or on the general state of Nordic co-operation. Proposals are considered on first reading which has in the course of time become a mere formality, and are then referred to the committee. The committee may propose postponement or rejection of the proposal. It reports the matter to the full session with any minority report. The Praesidium may also receive amendatory proposals from members and governments.

In practise, very few proposals come from governments, in spite of repeated requests that they should be more active.[43] In the first ten years of the Council, governments were responsible for only twenty-one of the 215 proposals introduced, and only four contained a draft recommendation. Four were sponsored by more than one government jointly. The elected members introduced 194 proposals in the same period. In 1953, eight proposals were tabled. In 1978,[44] thirty members' proposals were tabled and four came from the Nordic Council of Ministers. Fifteen recommendations were issued in 1978. Cross-national political activity is small; in the first ten years, only twelve proposals were sponsored by members of the same political tendency, but of different nationality. However, over two-thirds of the proposals have sponsors of at least two nationalities.

It is clear that Nordic co-operation has simply grown on an *ad hoc*, pragmatic basis through private initiative and governmental and parliamentary co-operation, always avoiding the difficult issues of supra-nationality and 'high politics', as evidenced by the failure to reach agreement either on a Nordic economic union in the 1960s, or on a defence union in the 1940s.

However, in the 1960s the need was felt to give more co-ordination and direction to Nordic co-operation. The Helsinki Agreement of 1962 is a codification of existing practices, which are thus placed in a coherent legal and binding framework.[45] It lays down regulations for co-operation in the fields of legal, cultural, social, economic and transport policies, and exhorts mutual co-operation in international fora (the U.N., etc.). It provides for continued inter-governmental co-operation and includes the Nordic Council (which remains unchanged) within the procedures for co-operation. In 1971, a Nordic Ministerial Council was set up to co-ordinate inter-governmental co-operation. It meets with the different departmental ministers required present. The Ministerial Council takes its decisions by unanimous vote, but abstention does not block a decision. The Council of Ministers may make proposals to the Nordic Council.[46]

7. *Global policy*

Denmark was a founder-member of the United Nations and, like other Scandinavian nations, has been active in the General Assembly and in the specialised agencies and bodies.[47] She has sent forces to participate in U.N. peace-keeping operations in the Congo (300 men), Cyprus (1,000 men) and Gaza. She was an early supporter of U.N. membership for the People's Republic of China (after 1953), and an early proponent of the 'two Germanys' solution to German U.N. membership, which eventually prevailed in 1972. She has been strongly opposed to right-wing dictatorships, condemning Francoist Spain in the years after 1945, and actively participating in the campaign to investigate violations of human rights by the dictatorial military regime in Greece in 1967–74.

Denmark has tended to adopt positions—in close co-operation with the other Nordic countries—leaning towards the Third World. She has no recent colonial past, and has been a long-standing member of the U.N. Committee on Colonisation, although until 1953 the latter did report on Greenland. Here she has steered a middle way, supporting the movement towards self-determination in an ordered way. Thus, she has sought to distinguish between the position of, on the one hand, Britain, which sought to co-operate with the U.N., and, on the other hand, Portugal (before 1974), South Africa and, in the earlier period, France. Denmark was a sponsor, with other Nordic countries, of an early resolution (1963) condemning South African Apartheid, which was not passed, and voted for a Third World resolution in 1965, condemning that institution as a threat to peace. Here the opposition parties criticised the initiatives of the government. She has continued on this level, giving support to liberation movements in Southern Africa, though this matter has been the subject of domestic controversy, leading to motions in the *Folketing* from the Progress Party, which initiated a debate on the subject in 1978. In the debate on an interpellation on EEC co-operation on 12 January 1978, Mr Junior, FRP spokesman, sought 'an end to the hyprocritical witch-hunt against South Africa'.[48]

Denmark has attained the goal of setting aside 0.7 per cent of her GNP for official development aid, and in 1962 created a special agency (DANIDA) for co-operation. She has been specially active in Thailand and Tanzania. With the exception of the FRP, which strongly opposes foreign aid, support for the government's development policy has been almost unanimous.

Even when there has been a minority government, support for the main profiles of Danish foreign policy has been very broad: NATO membership, EEC membership, active Nordic co-operation, support for a fairer international order, and an active development policy. Each specific policy has or had its opponents, as we have noted; however, a core of parties in the *Folketing*—S, V and KF— has supported all these policies. It is noteworthy that the foreign policy of the SV government showed no change from earlier policy. The Foreign Minister Mr Christophersen (V), writing in *Fremtiden*, argued for 'more economic justice in the world' and stated that the foreign policy should be based 'not merely on interests, but on ideas and values as well'.[49] He supported the thrust of earlier African policy.

However, conflict has arisen at times between Nordic co-ordination and political co-operation in the EEC. Opponents of the EEC have argued in general terms that a European foreign policy is cutting Denmark off from her Nordic partners. The Left has gone further and argued that 'EEC co-operation has taken Danish foreign policy in a more reactionary direction. [. . .] Take the resolution calling for an end to all military and nuclear co-operation with South Africa. The other Nordic countries voted for it, but Denmark could not.' The government has seen these problems, but has regarded them as surmountable in the interests of the weight conferred by an EEC common line.

REFERENCES

1. K.H. Cerny (ed.) *Scandinavia at the Polls*, Washington DC: AEI, 1977, pp. 22–9.
2. T. Kaarsted, *Dansk Politik i 1960 'erne*, Copenhagen: Gyldendal 1969, pp. 54–66.
3. H. Westergaard Andersen, *Dansk politik i går og i dag*, Copenhagen: Fremad, 1976, p. 142.
4. *Redegørelse for statsretslige problemer i forbindelse med en Dansk tiltraedelse af EF*, Copenhagen: Foreign Ministry, 1972, pp. 3–21 and 48–57.
5. N. Amstrup, *Dansk udenrigspolitik*, Copenhagen: Gyldendal 1975, chapter I.
6. Westergaard Andersen, *op.cit.*, pp. 114–20.
7. J. Fitzmaurice, 'National Parliaments and European Policy-Making: the case of Denmark', *Parliamentary Affairs*, vol. XXIX, No. 3, 1976, pp. 281–93, esp. p. 286.
8. *Folketingsaarbog 1977/78*, p. 16.
9. J. Fitzmaurice, *op.cit.*, for an account of the work of the MRC.
10. Report of the Market Relations Committee of 29 March 1973.
11. Article 6 reads: 'The government shall report to the *Folketing* on developments in the European Communities. The government shall notify a committee of the *Folketing* of proposals for Council decisions which will become directly applicable in Denmark or whose implementation requires action by the *Folketing*.'
12. The resolution reads: 'The *Folketing* calls upon the government to inform all its members on current EEC affairs with a view to their being taken up in the MRC and other permanent committees and, in future negotiations and Council decisions of importance, to inform the MRC of the mandate given by the government to the negotiator in order thereby to ensure parliamentary backing for the mandate and, in the event that the negotiations render a new mandate necessary, to submit this also to the MRC, and proceeds to the next item on its agenda.'
13. Report of the MRC of 29 March 1973.
14. Report of the MRC of 14 June 1974.
15. Sasse, *op.cit.*, pp. 69–74.
16. Report of the MRC of 14 June 1974, Document 579, Art. 1a.

17. Per Dich (SF) in evidence to the House of Lords Select Committee, appendix 3, pp. 228 ff.
18. Hilmar Baunsgaard (former Prime Minister), *Politiken*, 25 March 1974.
19. The Hartling *Venstre* Government (1973 – 5) agreed informally to take no steps in Market policy without the approval of the Social Democrats.
20. A. Christiansen, 'Folketingets Inflydelse på Landets Udenrigspolitik', *Fremtiden*, no. 5, 1974.
21. In the period August-15 September 1975, eight questions were asked by members of three parties.
22. See *Folketingetstidende*, 15 – 17 May 1973, cols. 6263 – 93 and 6362 – 6497, and 30 January 1974, cols. 1332 – 1542.
23. Interview in *Europa*, September 1975.
24. Per Dich to the House of Lords Select Committee.
25. *Folketingetstidende*, 17 May 1973, cols. 6396 – 6407 and 6452 – 7.
26. See appendices 2, 3, 4 to the Report of 14 June 1974, where the demands of the Justice Party are examined.
27. See Minority Report in Report of the MRC of 3 June 1977, *Folketingetstidende*, 1976 – 7, col. 582.
28. See Report from the MRC of 28 May 1976, *Folketingetstidende*, annexe B, cols. 2107 – 8.
29. Majority conclusions of Reports of 28 May 1976 and 3 June 1977.
30. For summary of foreign policy problems after 1864, see K.E. Miller, *Government and Politics in Denmark*, Boston: Houghton, Mifflin, 1966, pp. 34 – 49, and Westergaard Andersen, *op.cit.*, pp. 48 – 52 and 76 – 95; 125 – 34 and 147 – 50.
31. For the debate about NATO membership, see Westergaard Andersen, *op.cit.*, p. 125 – 34 and 147 – 50.
32. N. Amstrup, *Dansk Udenrigspolitik*, Copenhagen: Gyldendal, 1975, p. 29.
33. Westergaard Andersen, *op.cit.*, pp. 184 – 6.
34. N. Petersen, *Folket og Udenrigspolitik*, Copenhagen: Gyldendal, 1975.
35. For a good general summary of the issues and the debate, see N. Petersen and J. Elklit, 'Denmark enters the EEC', *Scandinavian Political Studies*, Vol. 8, 1973, p. 193 – 213 and Westergaard Andersen, *op.cit.*, p. 178 – 206, on which the following is based.
36. N. Amstrup, *op.cit.*, p. 75.
37. See articles by J.O. Krag and S. Skovmand (R), an anti-Marketeer in 'Der Var engang en Folke afstemming', *Forlaget Samtid* (1979), pp. 5 – 8 and 9 – 12.
38. See *Folketingetstidende*, 1 Feb. 1973, statement by Mr Maigaard (SF) at cols. 3306 – 11 and *Folketingetstidende*, 30 Jan. 1974: Mr Maigaard, esp. cols. 1376 – 7; Mr Nørlund (DKP), cols. 1390 – 5; Mr Christensen (DR), cols. 1397 – 1405. More recently, for example, see debate on Interpellation on EEC co-operation on 12 January 1978, *Folketingetstidende*, cols 4376 – 4518.
39. For a discussion of the direct election campaign, see pp. 176 – 8 and 223 – 31 and 'Europa/Valget' in *Økonomi og Politik*, 53rd year, No. 3 (1979), pp. 259 – 85.

40. Foreign Minister Christophersen (V) in *Fremtiden* (1979), No. 1, pp. 4–10: '*Status over Dansk Udenrigspolitisk*'.
41. S.V. Andersen, *The Nordic Council: a study of Scandinavian integration*, Seattle: University of Washington Press, 1967, pp. 9–14, 15–25.
42. Andersen, *op.cit.*, pp. 26-55, and Appendix for the text of the Statute of the Council in English.
43. Andersen, *op.cit.*, pp. 61–2 and 63–5.
44. *Folketingsaarbog* 1977/78, p. 64.
45. Andersen, *op.cit.*, pp. 122–4.
46. Westergaard Andersen, *op.cit.*, p. 205.
47. M. Sørensen and N. Haagerup, *Denmark and the United Nations*, New York: Manhattan Publishing Company, 1956.
48. *Folketingetstidende*, 12 Jan. 1978, col. 4401.
49. Christophersen in *Fremtiden*, No. 1, 1979.

VIII. IN CONCLUSION

Drawing together the threads of our analysis, how does three-quarters of a century of democratic politics in Denmark appear from the vantage-point of 1980, and what developments can be expected in the future?

The salient and perhaps most interesting feature of Danish politics over the last half century since the party system solidified, if not the most dramatic one, has been its stability and continuity. Taking the longer view, whatever may have been its ups and downs, Danish political life has to a remarkable degree tended to find its own level, to flow in the well-tried channels of pragmatism. The very complexity of the system and its all-embracing flexibity has canalised, contained and absorbed successive pressures for radical change. Demands which were not formulated in terms of discrete and limited changes to the system have ebbed out in the labyrinths of the system. On the other hand, reformist forces which have formulated their demands in these terms have been remarkably successful in achieving their aims of creating a modern, compassionate welfare state, which enjoys one of the highest standards of living in the world. This has been the dominant Social Democratic ideology, to which all mainstream political forces in Denmark have eventually come to subscribe, implicitly if not explicitly.

Together with this consensus, a clear institutional stability developed. Since the basic pattern of Danish politics was laid down after the First World War, it has shown extraordinary resilience and ability to absorb major shock-waves without fundamental damage to the system. The introduction of proportional representation in 1915 did not create, but rather ensured, the maturation of the nascent four-party system, which was to survive in essence down to 1973 and which in modified form still shows considerable vitality today. By the early 1920s Denmark had a four-party system. The Social Democrats had already become the dominant force in Danish politics, which they remain to this day. In or out of power, they were —and are—the pivotal force which can not be ignored. They had abandoned their early Marxist positions in favour of a Scandinavian, pragmatic reformism, which entailed accepting the parliamentary road and participating in the system even without the power fundamentally to change it. This reformism involved accepting, and thereby reinforcing, the basic norms of the Danish parliamentary system. These are : readiness to co-operate with other parties; verbal and ideological moderation; the formulation of limited, practical policy aims; the practice of responsible and participatory opposition; and the acceptance of the primacy of the parliamentary leadership within the party. That the Social Democrats accepted these norms did much to anchor them into Danish political culture, not least because they have been in government for forty-five out of the sixty years since 1920 and forty-one out of the fifty years since 1930, with two periods of fifteen continuous years in power. They have never enjoyed a majority on their own, however. They have been associated with all the great decisions, but have also associated others with them. This is true of the great social reforms of the 1930s, the new constitution, the decision to join NATO and the EEC, and Home Rule for Greenland. Danish democracy was thus co-operative, constructive and pragmatic.

A four-party pattern was established. Except in 1945, these four 'old parties' (S-R-V-K) always obtained at least 90 per cent of the vote and often even more. Whatever their differences, these old parties regarded the system with a proprietary air; it was their system and each regarded the others as responsible partners in that system and sought to exclude new parties from influence, thus usually ensuring that they would wither on the vine. Within this group, there were two poles—*Venstre* and the Social Democrats—and two possible coalitions V-K or S-R. Added permutations were Social Democrat or 'bourgeois' minority governments. The S-R-DR Coalition of 1957–60 was in reality a basic SR coalition.

By the mid-1960s some cracks were showing in the facade. With the realisation of most of its central aims, the Social Democratic ideology had entered a mature, sluggish and at times self-satisfied phase. It had become entrenched in the system in which it had invested so much and was forced to defend it against the pincer movements which assailed it from both the political flanks. With its driving force burnt out, with the onset of recession and the critique from both right and left, the consensus around the old pragmatic certainties of welfarism has begun to be seriously called into question. At the same time, no alternative view has yet imposed itself, and as the elections of 1975, 1977 and 1979 showed, it is too soon to write off the Social Democrats, who remain a remarkably resilient and successful electoral force.

To these unresolved ideological questionings was added an institutional questioning, which threatened the stability of the system. The four-party system, which had easily resisted the short-lived strength of the Communists on the left and the Independents and the Justice Party on the right, was now breaking down. A new, if fragile, pattern of right-left polarisation was emerging. After the 1966 election there were two finely balanced blocs : the S-SF bloc and the 'bourgeois' VKR bloc. Danish politics was entering a new phase, which might have seen a profound transformation of the party system and the emergence of greater ideological cleavages.

The 1973 election brought a dramatic end to this new trend, as new political forces, with new priorities, thrust their way into the political arena. The paradox, however, is that in many ways 1980 is more like 1956 than 1966. The cataclysm of 1973 seems almost more like a temporary aberration than a decisive shift. Of course the new forces are there, with FRP, KRF and CD on the right and in the centre; the left is fragmented. The *Folketing* is certainly less manageable, but on the whole their impact is less than might have been expected. The 'old parties' have shown great resilience and ability to impose their rules of the game. The left is sterilised and ineffective. The new parties have either accepted the rules of the game (KRP, CD) or remained without influence (FRP). The Social Democrats are still the pivotal political force, centre-stage and seeking allies in the centre. The only difference is that the choice is wider and the bargaining more complex. *Venstre* has again become the alternative pole around which a 'bourgeois' coalition might form. CD and KRF have accepted the leadership of *Venstre* in the 'bourgeois' camp, but since the 1979 election, KF increasingly contests that leadership. The Radicals are moving back to their bridging position and took no part in the talks about a so-called 'Four-Leaf Clover Coalition' (V, K, CD, KRF). Not unnaturally, in a ten or eleven-party *Folketing* the day-to-day pattern seems more complex and the waters more muddy, with new permutations arising (the SV coalition), but the overall situation can be clearly discerned, and the underlying system would not have been alien to the 1950s or even the 1930s. This pattern appears to have considerable life in it yet.

There is also considerable continuity concerning the central issues which have dominated Danish politics over this period. These can be summarised as prosperity and identity. Denmark is a rich country, as we have seen—in the vanguard of the industrialised west. Prosperity, except in the depression period, has rarely been an issue in absolute terms, but rather in terms of maintaining and increasing the national standard of living in the face of external economic pressures, so as to be able to ensure an adequate distribution of real income increases to all classes of society and adequate increases in social expenditure. Relative success in these goals has underpinned the consensus politics, as we have seen, and cemented the stability of the system. Without sharp conflicts over the politics of distribution, it has been possible to minimise ideological conflict. The maintainance of growth in real incomes, however minimal, and the maintenance of the welfare state in the period since 1973 have played an important part in re-stabilising the system. This has been a constant concern of the Social Democratic Party. This level of performance —at the expense of an ever-increasing burden of external indebted- ness—will be increasingly difficult to maintain; and indeed the Danish people face severe falls in real income in the coming years, and rising unemployment. How severe an impact such a loss of economic performance will now have on the political system, as distinct from the 1973–5 period, is hard to predict, but economic performance will remain a key indicator of political developments.

The issue of identity is more complex. It has been a divisive politi- cal issue, cutting across established party lines and creating unorthodox cleavages, despite the best efforts of the dominant 'old parties' to minimise the amount of conflict with its potential destabi- lising effect on the system.

In fact the issue of identity has lain behind the choice of foreign policy orientation over economic and security needs. As with other issues, the choices have been evaluated pragmatically. If, on an ideal scale of values, Danes would have given their priority to indepen- dence, Nordic solutions, pan-European co-operation, Atlantic co- operation and European co-operation (in the EEC sense), in that order, realism has predominated over the ideal. In an inter- dependent world, practical politics would not permit Denmark's foreign policy to reflect these preferences. She has—after much apparent hesitation, and more by a process of elimination than by any sense of commitment—adopted a foreign policy based on her least favourite options, but seeking also to reflect her other concerns. Such a policy seeks to avoid absolute commitments; to keep options open as long as possible; and to limit freedom of action within one field for co-operation as little as possible. NATO and EEC membership have been accepted as necessities, in the absence of any viable alternatives, but other concerns such as détente (of which Denmark was an early exponent), Nordic co-operation and a pro- Third World stance have been maintained and at times have seemed to dominate foreign policy-making, creating an impression of vagueness, indecision and lack of clear commitment. Such an approach may of course have its attractions for a small nation at the cross-roads of Europe, between East and West, North and South, but it may create considerable annoyance in her more powerful allies and neighbours. Denmark has gained the reputation of being an unreliable and uncommitted partner both in NATO and the EEC. Her spokesmen argue that Denmark has always fulfilled the letter of her obligations. That may even be true, but her attitude has remained unconvincing. In the present becalmed EEC, with Britain at least equally negative, this may not matter a great deal, but if the

Community were to develop a new élan, Denmark's stance would soon bring her under fire. In NATO, moreover, the term 'Denmarkisation' has been coined to designate her unco-operative attitude.

Arguably, such 'soft' positions, the avoidance of conflict over foreign policy, the creation of a minimum consensus among the 'old parties' and a willingness to leave contentious issues on one side in the interests of consensus, has contributed to the maintainance of the stability of the political system. This consensus reflex was so strong that it even survived in the 1966–73 period of strong left-right polarisation on domestic issues. The debate about EEC membership threatened this low-profile approach. It split two of the Old Parties (S and R). The opponents of membership were not prepared to accept the traditional consensus-seeking approach. Indeed, the decision to hold a referendum precisely to avoid sharp conflict in the *Folketing* and in the 1971 election merely displaced the problem and aggravated it. Anti-Marketeers saw in this low-profile approach a conspiracy of silence, a protective reflex of the system. On the contrary, it was in their interest to deepen the conflict and give it a broader, ideological anti-system dimension—which they did, even though it is arguable that in terms of the narrow issue of EEC membership, this was a tactical error. The issue, in any case cut deep and contributed to the cataclysm of 1973. The scars remain and the wounds could re-open.

Prediction is of course extremely hazardous, but as the 1980s open, Danish politics would seem to be in calmer waters than could have been expected in the light of the economic and political difficulties of the 1970s. The system seems to have retained its resilience and flexibility. Confidence in the system and in the 'old parties' which make it work has recovered from the low point of the early 1970s. Indeed, the 'new parties' seem to have as great if not greater difficulties than the 'old parties'. That calm may be deceptive, dependent as it is on the absence of strong external pressures which could destabilise the system. The re-opening of the issue of British membership of the EEC, a sharp increase in East-West tension in the Baltic region or a considerable and prolonged deepening of the world recession, if they were to occur simultaneously or in close proximity, could overload the system to the point where a breakdown and restructuring would become inevitable. In the absence of such over-riding pressures, continued stability must appear more likely.

APPENDIXES

A. GOVERNMENTS SINCE 1929

Period of Office	Prime Minister		Parliamentary Basis
1929 – 40	T. Stauning (S)	II	S-R
1940 – 2	T. Stauning (S)	III	S-R-V-K
1942 (May-Nov.)	V. Buhl (S)	I	S-R-V-K
1942 – 5[1]	E. Scavenius (R)		S-R-V-K
1945 (May-Oct.)	V. Buhl (S)	II	S-R-V-K
			Resistance
1945 – 7	K. Kristensen (V)		V
1947 – 50	H. Hedtoft (S)	I	S-(R)*
1950 – 3	E. Eriksen (V)		VK
1953 – 5	H. Hedtoft (S)	II	S
1955 – 7	H.C. Hansen (S)	I	S
1957 – 60	H.C. Hansen (S)	II	S-R-DR
1960 (Feb-Nov.)	V. Kampmann (S)	I	S-R-DR
1960 – 2	V. Kampmann (S)	II	S-R
1962 – 4	J.O. Krag (S)	I	S-R
1964 – 6	J.O. Krag (S)	II	S-(R)*
1966 – 8	J.O. Krag (S)	III	S-(SF)*
1968 – 71	H. Baunsgaard (R)		V-K-R
1971 – 2	J.O. Krag (S)	IV	S-(SF)*
1972 – 3	A. Jørgensen (S)	I	S-(SF)*
1973 – 5	P. Hartling (V)		V
1975 – 8	A. Jørgensen (S)	II	S
1978 – 9	A. Jørgensen (S)	III	S-V
1979	A. Jørgensen (S)	IV	S

*Indicates support party.
1. Resigned on 29 August 1942 and was not formally replaced till May 1945.

B. ELECTION RESULTS SINCE 1968

	1968 %	1968 Seats	1971 %	1971 Seats	1973 %	1973 Seats	1975 %	1975 Seats	1977 %	1977 Seats	1979 %	1979 Seats
Social Democrats	34.2	62	37.3	70	25.6	46	29.9	54	37.0	65	38.3	68
Radicals	15.0	27	14.4	27	11.2	20	7.9	13	3.6	6	5.4	10
Conservatives	20.4	37	16.7	31	9.1	16	5.5	10	8.5	15	12.5	22
Justice Party	0.7	0	1.7	0	2.8	5	1.8	0	3.3	6	2.6	5
Socialist People's Party	6.1	11	9.1	17	6.1	11	4.9	9	3.9	7	5.9	11
Communists	1.0	0	1.4	0	3.6	6	4.2	7	3.7	7	1.9	0
Liberal Centre	1.3	0	–	–	–	–	–	–	–	–	–	–
Centre Democrats	–	–	–	–	7.8	14	2.1	4	6.4	11	3.2	6
Pensioners' Party	–	–	–	–	–	–	–	–	1.2	0	–	–
Christian People's Party	–	–	1.9	0	4.0	7	5.3	9	3.4	6	2.6	5
Venstre	18.6	34	15.6	30	12.2	22	23.3	42	12.0	21	12.5	22
Independent Party	0.5	0	–	–	–	–	–	–	–	–	–	–
Left Socialists	2.0	4	1.6	0	1.5	0	2.0	4	2.7	5	3.7	6
Progress Party	–	–	–	–	15.9	28	13.6	24	14.6	26	11.0	20

INDEX